D1069348

Of Valmiki, reputed author of *The Ramayana*, nothing is known, but the poem was written in its present form by a single hand in third or fourth century B.C. *The Mahabharata* is a compilation by various unknown hands of the same period.

The
Ramayana
and
Mahabharata

CONDENSED INTO ENGLISH VERSE

Translated by
Romesh C. Dutt

DOVER PUBLICATIONS, INC.
Mineola, New York

Bibliographical Note

This Dover edition, first published in 2002, is an unabridged republication of the 1955 edition of the work first published by J. M. Dent & Sons Ltd., London, 1910.

Library of Congress Cataloging-in-Publication Data

Dutt, Romesh Chunder, 1848-1909.
  The Ramayana and Mahabharata condensed into English verse / translated by Romesh C. Dutt.
       p. cm.
  Originally published: London : J. M. Dent & Sons Ltd. 1910.
  ISBN 0-486-42506-1 (pbk.)
    1. Mahåbhårata—Paraphrases, English. 2. Vålmåki. Råmåyaòa. I. Valmiki.
Ramayana. II. Mahabharata. III. Title.

BL1138.25.D38 R36 2002
294.5'92204521—dc21

                                                              2002029915

TO

THE RIGHT HON. PROFESSOR F. MAX MÜLLER

WHO HAS DEVOTED HIS LIFETIME TO THE ELUCIDATION OF

THE LEARNING, LITERATURE, AND RELIGION OF

ANCIENT INDIA

AND HAS RECOGNISED AND VINDICATED WHAT IS

TRUE AND GREAT AND ENNOBLING IN

MODERN INDIA

THIS TRANSLATION OF THE RAMAYANA

IS DEDICATED AS A

SINCERE TOKEN OF THE ESTEEM AND REGARD OF MY

COUNTRYMEN

A NOTE ON
THE LATE ROMESH C. DUTT

ROMESH CHUNDER DUTT, to whom English readers are indebted for the condensed metrical version of the ancient Indian epics given in this volume, was one of the most distinguished sons of modern India. He came of a Hindu family standing high among the Kayasths, second of the great castes in Bengal, was born in 1848, and grew to manhood amid influences of deep spiritual disturbance. In those days an Indian youth who had felt the call of the West encountered the sternest opposition from both his own family and the community, if he avowed his ambition of making the voyage to Europe. Romesh Dutt, having passed through the Presidency College, Calcutta, took his fate into his own hands. Accompanied by two friends, both of whom afterwards rose to eminence in Bengal, he secretly took ship, came to London, entered for the Indian Civil Service, and took third place in the open examination of 1869. He was the first of his race to attain the rank of divisional commissioner, and long before his retirement in 1897, at the end of twenty-five years' service, had made a high reputation as an administrator. He sat for a time in the Bengal Legislative Council, and, in recognition of his official work, received the Companionship of the Indian Empire. He died on November 30, 1909, at Baroda, the capital of the important Native State which he had served with brilliant success as revenue minister and dewan.

The influences which determined his literary activity were primarily European. As a student in Calcutta he had made acquaintance with the English classics, and later, while at University College, had read the poets insatiably. Nevertheless his first successes were achieved in his mother tongue. He wrote in Bengali poems and plays, historical and social novels, and aroused a storm of protest within the orthodox community of his province by publishing a Bengali translation of the *Rig Veda*. In English, of which he had complete mastery, his first considerable essay was a history of Civilisation in Ancient India, which, though not a work of original research, fulfilled a useful purpose in its day. When freedom from Government service gave him the opportunity he set himself to writing the *Economic History of India* and *India in the Victorian Age*, the two together forming his chief contribution to the subject which he, more than any other Indian of his time, had made his own. In these books, as in others of kindred theme and purpose, there is much criticism of British administration, strongly felt if temperately expressed. Apart from this, its more controversial side, the work of Romesh Dutt is valuable mainly in that it has helped to reveal to his own people no less than to ours, the spiritual riches of ancient India.

S. K. RATCLIFFE.

SELECT BIBLIOGRAPHY

The following is a list of the various editions of *The Ramayana*:

The Ramayana, edited by S. Gorcssio (with Italian translation). 10 vols. 1843–58, 1859–60 (Calcutta), 1888 (Bombay).

English translations: by Kirtee Bass. 5 vols. Serampore, 1802. *The Ramayuna of Valmeeki, in the original Sungscrit, with a Prose Translation and Explanatory Notes.* W. Carey and J. Marshman. 1806–10.

An English translation for *Nirvachanothara Ramayanum* (i.e. the *Uttara Ramayana* attributed to Vúlmíki, with Commentary). Madras, 1880.

Free English translation by R. T. H. Griffith. 5 vols. 1870–5.

Translation into English Prose. Edited by Manmatha Nath Dutt. 1889, 1892–4.

Condensed into English Verse by Romesh Dutt. 1899 (Temple Classics), 1900.

Two later renderings are those of R. T. H. Griffith, 1915, and of Hari Prasad Shastri, in progress (began publication 1952).

Works on:

Sir M. Williams: *Indian Epic Poetry, with full Analysis of the Ramayana and Mahabharata*, 1863.

J. T. Wheeler: *History of India*. 1867, etc.

J. C. Oman: *Struggles of the Dawn, the Stories of the Great Indian Epics, Ramayana*, etc. 1893. *The Great Indian Epics*, etc. 1894, 1899 (Bohn).

The following is a list of the various editions of *The Maha-Bharata*:

Complete edition, Calcutta, 1834–9, 4 vols.; Bombay, 1863; re-edited, with commentary by Nitakantha Govinda, 1890.

Translations into English Prose, by Protap Chandra Roy, 1883; (Sanscrit text of Maharshi Vyas, with complete English and Hindi translations, 1902, etc.).

Virtue's Triumph; or, The Mahá-Bharata. By Rai Bahadur, P. Anunda Charlu. 1894.

Prose literal translation, by Manmatha Nath Dutt. 1895.

Condensed into English verse by Romesh Dutt (Temple Classics). 1898. The same, with Introduction by W. Max-Müller. 1899.

(Many English translations of portions of the whole epic have been published.)

Works on:

H. H. Wilson: *Essays on the Religion of the Hindoos.* 1862.
Sir M. Williams: *Indian Epic Poetry,* etc. 1863.
J. T. Wheeler: *The Vedic Period and the Mahabharata.* 1867.
Buehler and Kirste: *Indian Studies, Contributions to the History of the Mahabharata.* 1892.
J. C. Oman (see above).
E. W. Hopkins: *The Great Epic of India.* 1901.
V. Fausboll: *Indian Mythology, according to the Mahabharata in Outline* (Oriental Religions Series, Luzac, vol. i.). 1903.
Rāgānāma Ramkrishna Bhāguvata, an attempt to analyse *The Mahabharata* from the higher Brahminical standpoint. 1905.
Chintāmani Vināyaka Vaidys: *The Mahabharata: a Criticism.* 1905. *Epic India; or, India as described in the Mahabharata and Ramayana.* 1907.

Later works in English include the following on *The Ramayana*: Mrs Annie Besant: *Sri Rama Chandra, the Ideal King,* 1901; Chintāmani Vinayaka Vaidya: *The Riddle of the Ramayana,* 1906; D. A. Narasimhani: *Valniki and his Epic,* 1923; E. W. Hopkins: *The Period of the Sutras,* etc., 1922; M. V. Kibe: *Ravana's Lanka in Central India,* 1928; S. Aiya Durai Aiyar: *Ramayana as an Illustration of Yoga-Sastra,* 1937; I. S. Peter: *Beowulf and the Ramayana,* 1938; M. Vencatesa Aiyangar: *The Poetry of Valniki,* 1940. And on *The Mahabharata:* an Analysis and Index by E. P. Rice, 1934; and Ethnical Study by G. S. Held, 1935; also M. Venkataratnam: *The Historical Element in the Mahabharata,* 1937, and Iravate Karve: *Kinship Terms and Family Organization as found in the Mahabharata,* 1944.

CONTENTS

RAMAYANA

MAHA-BHARATA

BOOK PAGE

V. PATIVRATA-MAHATMYA (WOMAN'S LOVE) . . . 215

VI. GO-HARANA (CATTLE-LIFTING) 231

VII. UDYOGA (THE COUNCIL OF WAR) 243

VIII. BHISHMA-BADHA (FALL OF BHISHMA) . . . 255

IX. DRONA-BADHA (FALL OF DRONA) 272

X. KARNA-BADHA (FALL OF KARNA) 288

XI. SRADDHA (FUNERAL RITES) 302

XII. ASWA-MEDHA (SACRIFICE OF THE HORSE) . . 312

CONCLUSION 321

TRANSLATOR'S EPILOGUE 323

GLOSSARY 334

The
Ramayana
and
Mahabharata

THE EPIC OF RAMA,
PRINCE OF INDIA

BOOK I
SITA-SWAYAMVARA
(*The Bridal of Sita*)

THE Epic relates to the ancient traditions of two powerful races, the Kosalas and the Videhas, who lived in Northern India between the twelfth and tenth centuries before Christ. The names Kosala and Videha in the singular number indicate the kingdoms,—Oudh and North Behar,—and in the plural number they mean the ancient races which inhabited those two countries.

According to the Epic, Dasa-ratha king of the Kosalas had four sons, the eldest of whom was Rama the hero of the poem. And Janak king of the Videhas had a daughter named Sita, who was miraculously born of a field furrow, and who is the heroine of the Epic.

Janak ordained a severe test for the hand of his daughter, and many a prince and warrior came and went away disappointed. Rama succeeded, and won Sita. The story of Rama's winning his bride, and of the marriage of his three brothers with the sister and cousins of Sita, forms the subject of this Book.

The portions translated in this Book form Section vi., Sections lxvii. to lxix., Section lxxiii., and Section lxxvii. of Book i. of the original text.

1

AYODHYA, THE RIGHTEOUS CITY

Rich in royal worth and valour, rich in holy Vedic lore,
Dasa-ratha ruled his empire in the happy days of yore,

Loved of men in fair Ayodhya, sprung of ancient Solar Race,
Royal *rishi* in his duty, saintly *rishi* in his grace,

Great as INDRA in his prowess, bounteous as KUVERA kind,
Dauntless deeds subdued his foemen, lofty faith subdued his mind !

Like the ancient monarch Manu, father of the human race,·
Dasa-ratha ruled his people with a father's loving grace,

Truth and Justice swayed each action and each baser motive quelled
People's Love and Monarch's Duty every thought and deed impelled,

And his town like INDRA's city,—tower and dome and turret brave—
Rose in proud and peerless beauty on Sarayu's limpid wave !

Peaceful lived the righteous people, rich in wealth in merit high,
Envy dwelt not in their bosoms and their accents shaped no lie,

Fathers with their happy households owned their cattle, corn, and
    gold,
Galling penury and famine in Ayodhya had no hold,

Neighbours lived in mutual kindness helpful with their ample wealth,
None who begged the wasted refuse, none who lived by fraud and
    stealth !

And they wore the gem and earring, wreath and fragrant sandal paste,
And their arms were decked with bracelets, and their necks with
    nishkas graced,

Cheat and braggart and deceiver lived not in the ancient town,
Proud despiser of the lowly wore not insults in their frown,

Poorer fed not on the richer, hireling friend upon the great,
None with low and lying accents did upon the proud man wait !

Men to plighted vows were faithful, faithful was each loving wife,
Impure thought and wandering fancy stained not holy wedded life,

Robed in gold and graceful garments, fair in form and fair in face,
Winsome were Ayodhya's daughters, rich in wit and woman's grace !

Twice-born men were free from passion, lust of gold and impure greed,
Faithful to their Rites and Scriptures, truthful in their word and deed,

Altar blazed in every mansion, from each home was bounty given,
Stooped no man to fulsome falsehood, questioned none the will of
    Heaven.

Kshatras bowed to holy Brahmans, Vaisyas to the Kshatras bowed
Toiling Sudras lived by labour, of their honest duty proud,

To the Gods and to the Fathers, to each guest in virtue trained,
Rites were done with true devotion as by holy writ ordained.

Pure each caste in due observance, stainless was each ancient rite,
And the nation thrived and prospered by its old and matchless might,

And each man in truth abiding lived a long and peaceful life,
With his sons and with his grandsons, with his loved and honoured
    wife.

Thus was ruled the ancient city by her monarch true and bold,
As the earth was ruled by Manu in the misty days of old,

Troops who never turned in battle, fierce as fire and strong and brave,
Guarded well her lofty ramparts as the lions guard the cave.

Steeds like INDRA's in their swiftness came from far Kamboja's land,
From Vanaya and Vahlika and from Sindhu's rock-bound strand,

Elephants of mighty stature from the Vindhya mountains came,
Or from deep and darksome forests round Himalay's peaks of fame,

Matchless in their mighty prowess, peerless in their wondrous speed,
Nobler than the noble tuskers sprung from high celestial breed.

Thus Ayodhya, " virgin city,"—faithful to her haughty name,—
Ruled by righteous Dasa-ratha won a world-embracing fame,

Strong-barred gates and lofty arches, tower and dome and turret high
Decked the vast and peopled city fair as mansions of the sky.

Queens of proud and peerless beauty born of houses rich in fame,
Loved of royal Dasa-ratha to his happy mansion came,

Queen Kausalya blessed with virtue true and righteous Rama bore.
Queen Kaikeyi young and beauteous bore him Bharat rich in lore,

Queen Simitra bore the bright twins, Lakshman and Satrughna bold,
Four brave princes served their father in the happy days of old !

II

MITHILA, AND THE BREAKING OF THE BOW

Janak monarch of Videha spake his message near and far,—
He shall win my peerless Sita who shall bend my bow of war,—

Suitors came from farthest regions, warlike princes known to fame,
Vainly strove to wield the weapon, left Videha in their shame.

Viswa-mitra royal *rishi*, Rama true and Lakshman bold,
Came to fair Mithila's city from Ayodhya famed of old,

Spake in pride the royal *rishi :* " Monarch of Videha's throne,
Grant, the wondrous bow of RUDRA be to princely Rama shown."

Janak spake his royal mandate to his lords and warriors bold :
" Bring ye forth the bow of RUDRA decked in garlands and in gold,"

And his peers and proud retainers waiting on the monarch's call,
Brought the great and goodly weapon from the city's inner hall.

Stalwart men of ample stature pulled the mighty iron car
In which rested all-inviolate Janak's dreaded bow of war,

And where midst assembled monarchs sat Videha's godlike king,
With a mighty toil and effort did the eight-wheeled chariot bring.

" This the weapon of Videha," proudly thus the peers begun,
" Be it shewn to royal Rama, Dasa-ratha's righteous son,"

" This the bow," then spake the monarch to the *risha* famed of old,
To the true and righteous Rama and to Lakshman young and bold.

" This the weapon of my fathers prized by kings from age to age,
Mighty chiefs and sturdy warriors could not bend it, noble sage !

Gods before the bow of RUDRA have in righteous terror quailed,
Rakshas fierce and stout *Asuras* have in futile effort failed,

Mortal man will struggle vainly RUDRA's wondrous bow to bend,
Vainly strive to string the weapon and the shining dart to send,

Holy saint and royal *rishi*, here is Janak's ancient bow,
Shew it to Ayodhya's princes, speak to them my kingly vow ! "

Viswa-mitra humbly listened to the words the monarch said,
To the brave and righteous Rama, Janak's mighty bow displayed,

Rama lifted high the cover of the pond'rous iron car,
Gazed with conscious pride and prowess on the mighty bow of war.

" Let me," humbly spake the hero, " on this bow my fingers place,
Let me lift and bend the weapon, help me with your loving grace."

" Be it so," the *rishi* answered, " be it so," the monarch said,
Rama lifted high the weapon on his stalwart arms displayed,

Wond'ring gazed the kings assembled as the son of Raghu's race
Proudly raised the bow of RUDRA with a warrior's stately grace,

Proudly strung the bow of RUDRA which the kings had tried in vain,
Drew the cord with force resistless till the weapon snapped in twain

Like the thunder's pealing accent rose the loud terrific clang,
And the firm earth shook and trembled and the hills in echoes rang,

And the chiefs and gathered monarchs fell and fainted in their fear,
And the men of many nations shook the dreadful sound to hear !

Pale and white the startled monarchs slowly from their terror woke,
And with royal grace and greetings Janak to the *rishi* spoke :

" Now my ancient eyes have witnessed wond'rous deed by Rama
    done,
Deed surpassing thought or fancy wrought by Dasa-ratha's son,

And the proud and peerless princess, Sita glory of my house,
Sheds on me an added lustre as she weds a godlike spouse,

True shall be my plighted promise, Sita dearer than my life,
Won by worth and wond'rous valour shall be Rama's faithful wife !

Grant us leave, O royal *rishi*, grant us blessings kind and fair,
Envoys mounted on my chariot to Ayodhya shall repair,

They shall speak to Rama's father glorious feat by Rama done,
They shall speak to Dasa-ratha, Sita is by valour won,

They shall say the noble princes safely live within our walls,
They shall ask him by his presence to adorn our palace halls ! "

Pleased at heart the sage assented, envoys by the monarch sent,
To Ayodhya's distant city with the royal message went.

III

The Embassy to Ayodhya

Three nights halting in their journey with their steeds fatigued and
    spent,
Envoys from Mithila's monarch to Ayodhya's city went,

And by royal mandate bidden stepped within the palace hall,
Where the ancient Dasa-ratha sat with peers and courtiers all,

And with greetings and obeisance spake their message calm and bold,
Softly fell their gentle accents as their happy tale they told.

" Greetings to thee, mighty monarch, greetings to each priest and
    peer,
Wishes for thy health and safety from Videha's king we bear,

Janak monarch of Videha for thy happy life hath prayed,
And by Viswa-mitra's bidding words of gladsome message said:

' Known on earth my plighted promise, spoke by heralds near and
    far,—
He shall win my peerless Sita who shall bend my bow of war,—

Monarchs came and princely suitors, chiefs and warriors known to
    fame,
Baffled in their fruitless effort left Mithila in their shame,

Rama came with gallant Lakshman by their proud preceptor led,
Bent and broke the mighty weapon, he the beauteous bride shall wed!

Rama strained the weapon stoutly till it snapped and broke in twain,
In the concourse of the monarchs, in the throng of arméd men,

Rama wins the peerless princess by the righteous will of Heaven,
I redeem my plighted promise—be thy kind permission given !

Monarch of Kosala's country ! with each lord and peer and priest,
Welcome to Mithila's city, welcome to Videha's feast,

Joy thee in thy Rama's triumph, joy thee with a father's pride,
Let each prince of proud Kosala win a fair Videha-bride ! '

These by Viswa-mitra's bidding are the words our monarch said,
This by Sata-nanda's counsel is the quest that he hath made."

Joyful was Kosala's monarch, spake to chieftains in the hall,
Vama-deva and Vasishtha and to priests and Brahmans all :

" Priests and peers ! in far Mithila, so these friendly envoys tell,
Righteous Rama, gallant Lakshman, in the royal palace dwell,

And our brother of Videha prizes Rama's warlike pride,
To each prince of proud Kosala yields a fair Videha-bride,

If it please ye, priests and chieftains, speed we to Mithila fair,
World-renowned is Janak's virtue, Heaven-inspired his learning
    rare ! "

Spake each peer and holy Brahman : " Dasa-ratha's will be done ! "
Spake the king unto the envoys : " Part we with the rising sun ! "

Honoured with a regal honour, welcomed to a rich repast,
Gifted envoys from Mithila day and night in gladness passed !

IV

MEETING OF JANAK AND DASA-RATHA

On Ayodhya's tower and turret now the golden morning woke,
Dasa-ratha girt by courtiers thus to wise Sumantra spoke :

" Bid the keepers of my treasure with their waggons lead the way,
Ride in front with royal riches, gold and gems in bright array,

Bid my warriors skilled in duty lead the four-fold ranks of war,
Elephants and noble chargers, serried foot and battle-car,

Bid my faithful chariot-driver harness quick each car of state,
With the fleetest of my coursers, and upon my orders wait.

Vama-deva and Vasishtha versed in *Veda's* ancient lore,
Kasyapa and good Jabali sprung from holy saints of yore,

Markandeya in his glory, Katyayana in his pride,
Let each priest and proud preceptor with Kosala's monarch ride,

Harness to my royal chariot strong and stately steeds of war,
For the envoys speed my journey and the way is long and far."

With each priest and proud retainer Dasa-ratha led the way,
Glittering ranks of forces followed in their four-fold dread array,

Four days on the way they journeyed till they reached Videha's land,
Janak with a courteous welcome came to greet the royal band.

Joyously Videha's monarch greeted every priest and peer,
Greeted ancient Dasa-ratha in his accents soft and clear :

" Hast thou come, my royal brother, on my house to yield thy grace,
Hast thou made a peaceful journey, pride of Raghu's royal race ?

Welcome ! for Mithila's people seek my royal guest to greet,
Welcome ! for thy sons of valour long their loving sire to meet,

Welcome to the priest Vasishtha versed in *Veda's* ancient lore,
Welcome every righteous *rishi* sprung from holy saints of yore !

And my evil fates are vanquished and my race is sanctified,
With the warlike race of Raghu thus in loving bonds allied,

Sacrifice and rites auspicious we ordain with rising sun,
Ere the evening's darkness closes, happy nuptials shall be done ! "

Thus in kind and courteous accents Janak spake his purpose high,
And his royal love responding, Dasa-ratha made reply :

" Gift betokens giver's bounty,—so our ancient sages sing,—
And thy righteous fame and virtue grace thy gift, Videha's king !

World-renowned is Janak's bounty, Heaven-inspired his holy grace,
And we take his boon and blessing as an honour to our race ! "

Royal grace and kingly greeting marked the ancient monarch's word,
Janak with a grateful pleasure Dasa-ratha's answer heard,

And the Brahmans and preceptors joyously the midnight spent,
And in converse pure and pleasant and in sacred sweet content.

Righteous Rama, gallant Lakshman piously their father greet,
Duly make their deep obeisance, humbly touch his royal feet,

And the night is filled with gladness for the king revered and old,
Honoured by the saintly Janak, greeted by his children bold,

On Mithila's tower and turret stars their silent vigils keep,
When each sacred rite completed, Janak seeks his nightly sleep.

V

THE PREPARATION

All his four heroic princes now with Dasa-ratha stayed
In Mithila's ancient city, and their father's will obeyed,

Thither came the bold Yudhajit prince of proud Kaikeya's line,
On the day that Dasa-ratha made his gifts of gold and kine,

And he met the ancient monarch, for his health and safety prayed,
Made his bow and due obeisance and in gentle accents said :

" List, O king ! my royal father, monarch of Kaikeya's race,
Sends his kindly love and greetings with his blessings and his grace,

And he asks if Dasa-ratha prospers in his wonted health,
If his friends and fond relations live in happiness and wealth.

Queen Kaikeyi is my sister, and to see her son I came,
Bharat prince of peerless virtue, worthy of his father's fame,

Aye, to see that youth of valour, by my royal father sent,
To Ayodhya's ancient city with an anxious heart I went,

In the city of Mithila,—thus did all thy subjects say,—
With his sons and with his kinsmen Dasa-ratha makes his stay,

Hence in haste I journeyed hither, travelling late and early dawn,
For to do thee due obeisance and to greet my sister's son ! "

Spake the young and proud Kaikeya, dear and duly-greeted guest,
Dasa-ratha on his brother choicest gifts and honours pressed.

Brightly dawned the happy morning, and Kosala's king of fame
With his sons and wise Vasishtha to the sacred *yajna* came,

Rama and his gallant brothers decked in gem and jewel bright,
In th' auspicious hour of morning did the blest *Kautuka* rite,

And beside their royal father piously the princes stood,
And to fair Videha's monarch spake Vasishtha wise and good :

" Dasa-ratha waits expectant with each proud and princely son,
Waits upon the bounteous giver, for each holy rite is done,

'Twixt the giver and the taker sacred word is sacred deed,
Seal with gift thy plighted promise, let the nuptial rites proceed ! "

Thus the righteous-souled Vasishtha to Videha's monarch prayed,
Janak versed in holy *Vedas* thus in courteous accents said :

" Wherefore waits the king expectant ? Free to him this royal dome,
Since my kingdom is his empire and my palace is his home,

And the maidens, flame-resplendent, done each fond *Kautuka* rite,
Beaming in their bridal beauty tread the sacrificial site !

I beside the lighted altar wait upon thy sacred hest,
And auspicious is the moment, sage Vasishtha knows the rest,

Let the peerless Dasa-ratha, proud Kosala's king of might,
With his sons and honoured sages enter on the holy site,

Let the righteous sage Vasishtha, sprung from Vedic saints of old,
Celebrate the happy wedding ; be the sacred *mantras* told ! "

VI

THE WEDDING

Sage Vasishtha skilled in duty placed Videha's honoured king,
Viswa-mitra, Sata-nanda, all within the sacred ring,

And he raised the holy altar as the ancient writs ordain,
Decked and graced with scented garlands grateful unto gods and men,

And he set the golden ladles, vases pierced by artists skilled,
Holy censers fresh and fragrant, cups with sacred honey filled,

Sanka bowls and shining salvers, *arghya* plates for honoured guest,
Parchéd rice arranged in dishes, corn unhusked that filled the rest,

And with careful hand Vasishtha grass around the altar flung,
Offered gift to lighted AGNI and the sacred *mantra* sung !

Softly came the sweet-eyed Sita,—bridal blush upon her brow,—
Rama in his manly beauty came to take the sacred vow,

Janak placed his beauteous daughter facing Dasa-ratha's son,
Spake with father's fond emotion and the holy rite was done :

" *This is Sita child of Janak, dearer unto him than life,*
Henceforth sharer of thy virtue, be she, prince, thy faithful wife,

Of thy weal and woe partaker, be she thine in every land,
Cherish her in joy and sorrow, clasp her hand within thy hand,

As the shadow to the substance, to her lord is faithful wife,
And my Sita best of women follows thee in death or life ! "

Tears bedew his ancient bosom, gods and men his wishes share,
And he sprinkles holy water on the blest and wedded pair.

Next he turned to Sita's sister, Urmila of beauty rare,
And to Lakshman young and valiant spake in accents soft and fair :

" *Lakshman, dauntless in thy duty, loved of men and Gods above,*
Take my dear devoted daughter, Urmila of stainless love,

Lakshman, fearless in thy virtue, take thy true and faithful wife,
Clasp her hand within thy fingers, be she thine in death or life ! "

To his brother's child Mandavi, Janak turned with father's love,
Yielded her to righteous Bharat, prayed for blessings from above :

" *Bharat, take the fair Mandavi, be she thine in death or life,*
Clasp her hand within thy fingers as thy true and faithful wife ! "

Last of all was Sruta-kriti, fair in form and fair in face,
And her gentle name was honoured for her acts of righteous grace,

" *Take her by the hand, Satrughna, be she thine in death or life,*
As the shadow to the substance, to her lord is faithful wife ! "

Then the princes held the maidens, hand embraced in loving hand,
And Vasishtha spake the *mantra*, holiest priest in all the land,

And as ancient rite ordaineth, and as sacred laws require,
Stepped each bride and princely bridegroom round the altar's lighted
fire,

Round Videha's ancient monarch, round the holy *rishis* all,
Lightly stepped the gentle maidens, proudly stepped the princes tall !

And a rain of flowers descended from the sky serene and fair,
And a soft celestial music filled the fresh and fragrant air,

Bright *Gandharvas* skilled in music waked the sweet celestial song,
Fair *Apsaras* in their beauty on the greensward tripped along !

As the flowery rain descended and the music rose in pride,
Thrice around the lighted altar every bridegroom led his bride,

And the nuptial rites were ended, princes took their brides away,
Janak followed with his courtiers, and the town was proud and gay !

VII

RETURN TO AYODHYA

With his wedded sons and daughters and his guard in bright array,
To the famed and fair Ayodhya, Dasa-ratha held his way,

And they reached the ancient city decked with banners bright and
brave,
And the voice of drum and trumpet hailed the home-returning brave,

Fragrant blossoms strewed the pathway, song of welcome filled the
air,
Joyous men and merry women issued forth in garments fair,

And they lifted up their faces and they waved their hands on high,
And they raised the voice of welcome as their righteous king drew
nigh.

Greeted by his loving subjects, welcomed by his priests of fame,
Dasa-ratha with the princes to his happy city came,

With the brides and stately princes in the town he held his way,
Entered slow his lofty palace bright as peak of Himalay.

Queen Kausalya blessed with virtue, Queen Kaikeyi in her pride,
Queen Sumitra sweetly loving, greeted every happy bride,

Soft-eyed Sita noble-destined, Urmila of spotless fame,
Mandavi and Sruta-kirti to their loving mothers came.

Decked in silk and queenly garments they performed each pious rite,
Brought their blessings on the household, bowed to Gods of holy
      might,

Bowed to all the honoured elders, blest the children with their love,
And with soft and sweet endearment by their loving consorts moved.

Happy were the wedded princes peerless in their warlike might,
And they dwelt in stately mansions like KUVERA'S mansions bright.

Loving wife and troops of kinsmen, wealth and glory on them wait,
Filial love and fond affection sanctify their happy fate.

Once when on the palace chambers bright the golden morning woke,
To his son the gentle Bharat, thus the ancient monarch spoke :

" Know, my son, the prince Kaikeya, Yudajit of warlike fame,
Queen Kaikeyi's honoured brother, from his distant regions came,

He hath come to take thee, Bharat, to Kaikeya's monarch bold,
Go and stay with them a season, greet thy grandsire loved of old."

Bharat heard with filial duty and he hastened to obey,
Took with him the young Satrughna in his grandsire's home to stay,

And from Rama and from Lakshman parted they with many a tear,
From their young and gentle consorts, from their parents ever dear,

And Kaikeya with the princes, with his guards and troopers gay,
To his father's western regions gladsome held his onward way.

Rama with a pious duty,—favoured by the Gods above,—
Tended still his ancient father with a never-faltering love,

In his father's sacred mandate still his noblest Duty saw,
In the weal of subject nations recognised his foremost Law !

And he pleased his happy mother with a fond and filial care,
And his elders and his kinsmen with devotion soft and fair,

Brahmans blessed the righteous Rama for his faith in gods above,
People in the town and hamlet blessed him with their loyal love !

With a woman's whole affection fond and trusting Sita loved,
And within her faithful bosom loving Rama lived and moved,

And he loved her, for their parents chose her as his faithful wife,
Loved her for her peerless beauty, for her true and trustful life,

Loved and dwelt within her bosom though he wore a form apart,
Rama in a sweet communion lived in Sita's loving heart !

Days of joy and months of gladness o'er the gentle Sita flew,
As she like the QUEEN OF BEAUTY brighter in her graces grew,

And as VISHNU with his consort dwells in skies, alone, apart,
Rama in a sweet communion lived in Sita's loving heart !

BOOK II

VANA-GAMANA-ADESA

(*The Banishment*)

THE events narrated in this Book occupy scarcely two days. The description of Rama's princely virtues and the rejoicings at his proposed coronation, with which the Book begins, contrast with much dramatic force and effect with the dark intrigues which follow, and which end in his cruel banishment for fourteen years.

The portions translated in this Book form Sections i., ii., vi., and vii., portions of Sections x. to xiii., and the whole of Section xviii. of Book ii. of the original text.

I

THE COUNCIL CONVENED

Thus the young and brave Satrughna, Bharat ever true and bold,
Went to warlike western regions where Kaikeyas lived of old,

Where the ancient Aswa-pati ruled his kingdom broad and fair,
Hailed the sons of Dasa-ratha with a grandsire's loving care.

Tended with a fond affection, guarded with a gentle sway,
Still the princes of their father dreamt and thought by night and day,

And their father in Ayodhya, great of heart and stout of hand,
Thought of Bharat and Satrughna living in Kaikeya's land.

For his great and gallant princes were to him his life and light,
Were a part of Dasa-ratha like his hands and arms of might,

But of all his righteous children righteous Rama won his heart,
As SWAYAMBHU of all creatures, was his dearest, holiest part,

For his Rama strong and stately was his eldest and his best,
Void of every baser passion and with every virtue blest !

Soft in speech, sedate and peaceful, seeking still the holy path,
Calm in conscious worth and valour, taunt nor cavil waked his wrath,

In the field of war excelling, boldest warrior midst the bold,
In the palace chambers musing on the tales by elders told,

Faithful to the wise and learned, truthful in his deed and word,
Rama dearly loved his people and his people loved their lord !

To the Brahmans pure and holy Rama due obeisance made,
To the poor and to the helpless deeper love and honour paid,

Spirit of his race and nation was to high-souled Rama given,
Thoughts that widen human glory, deeds that ope the gates of heaven

Not intent on idle cavil Rama spake with purpose high,
And the God of speech might envy when he spake or made reply,

In the learning of the *Vedas* highest meed and glory won,
In the skill of arms the father scarcely matched the gallant son !

Taught by sages and by elders in the manners of his race,
Rama grew in social virtues and each soft endearing grace,

Taught by inborn pride and wisdom patient purpose to conceal,
Deep determined was his effort, dauntless was his silent will !

Peerless in his skill and valour steed and elephant to tame,
Dauntless leader of his forces, matchless in his warlike fame,

Higher thought and nobler duty did the righteous Rama move,
By his toil and by his virtues still he sought his people's love !

Dasa-ratha marked his Rama with each kingly virtue blest,
And from lifelong royal duties now he sought repose and rest :

" Shall I see my son anointed, seated on Kosala's throne,
In the evening of my lifetime ere my days on earth be done,

Shall I place my ancient empire in the youthful Rama's care,
Seek for me a higher duty and prepare for life more fair ? "

Pondering thus within his bosom counsel from his courtiers sought,
And to crown his Rama, Regent, was his purpose and his thought,

For strange signs and diverse tokens now appeared on earth and sky,
And his failing strength and vigour spoke his end approaching nigh,

And he witnessed Rama's virtues filling all the world with love,
As the full-moon's radiant lustre fills the earth from skies above !

Dear to him appeared his purpose, Rama to his people dear,
Private wish and public duty made his path serene and clear,

Dasa-ratha called his Council, summoned chiefs from town and plain,
Welcomed too from distant regions monarchs and the kings of men,

Mansions meet for prince and chieftain to his guests the monarch gave,
Gracious as the Lord of Creatures held the gathering rich and brave !

Nathless to Kosala's Council nor Videha's monarch came,
Nor the warlike chief Kaikeya, Aswa-pati king of fame,

To those kings and near relations, ancient Dasa-ratha meant,
Message of the proud anointment with his greetings would be sent.

Brightly dawned the day of gathering ; in the lofty Council Hall
Stately chiefs and ancient burghers came and mustered one and all,

And each prince and peer was seated on his cushion rich and high,
And on monarch Dasa-ratha eager turned his anxious eye,

Girt by crownéd kings and chieftains, burghers from the town and
  plain,
Dasa-ratha shone like INDRA girt by heaven's immortal train !

II

THE PEOPLE CONSULTED

With the voice of pealing thunder Dasa-ratha spake to all,
To the princes and the burghers gathered in Ayodhya's hall :

" Known to all, the race of Raghu rules this empire broad and fair,
And hath ever loved and cherished subjects with a father's care.

In my fathers' footsteps treading I have sought the ancient path,
Nursed my people as my children, free from passion, pride and wrath,

Underneath this white umbrella, seated on this royal throne,
I have toiled to win their welfare and my task is almost done !

Years have passed of fruitful labour, years of work by fortune blest,
And the evening of my lifetime needs, my friends, the evening's rest,

Years have passed in watchful effort, Law and Duty to uphold,
Effort needing strength and prowess—and my feeble limbs are old !

Peers and burghers, let your monarch, now his lifelong labour done,
For the weal of loving subjects on his empire seat his son,

INDRA-like in peerless valour, *rishi*-like in holy lore,
Rama follows Dasa-ratha, but in virtues stands before !

Throned in Pushya's constellation shines the moon with fuller light,
Throned to rule his father's empire Rama wins a loftier might,

He will be your gracious monarch favoured well by FORTUNE'S QUEEN,
By his virtue and his valour lord of earth he might have been !

Speak your thoughts and from this bosom lift a load of toil and care,
On the proud throne of my fathers let me place a peerless heir,

Speak your thought, my chiefs and people, if this purpose please you
   well,
Or if wiser, better counsel in your wisdom ye can tell,

Speak your thoughts without compulsion, though this plan to me be
   dear,
If some middle course were wiser, if some other way were clear ! "

Gathered chieftains hailed the mandate with applauses long and loud,
As the peafowls hail the thunder of the dark and laden cloud,

And the gathered subjects echoed loud and long the welcome sound,
Till the voices of the people shook the sky and solid ground !

Brahmans versed in laws of duty, chieftains in their warlike pride,
Countless men from town and hamlet heard the mandate far and wide,

And they met in consultation, joyously with one accord,
Freely and in measured accents, gave their answer to their lord :

" Years of toil and watchful labour weigh upon thee, king of men,
Young in years is righteous Rama, Heir and Regent let him reign,

We would see the princely Rama, Heir and Regent duly made,
Riding on the royal tusker in the white umbrella's shade ! "

Searching still their secret purpose, seeking still their thought to know,
Spake again the ancient monarch in his measured words and slow :

" I would know your inner feelings, loyal thoughts and whispers kind,
For a doubt within me lingers and a shadow clouds my mind,

True to Law and true to Duty while I rule this kingdom fair,
Wherefore would you see my Rama seated as the Regent Heir ? "

" We would see him Heir and Regent, Dasa-ratha, ancient lord,
For his heart is blessed with valour, virtue marks his deed and word,

Lives not man in all the wide earth who excels the stainless youth,
In his loyalty to Duty, in his love of righteous Truth,

Truth impels his thought and action, Truth inspires his soul with
grace,
And his virtue fills the wide earth and exalts his ancient race !

Bright Immortals know his valour ; with his brother Lakshman bold
He hath never failed to conquer hostile town or castled hold,

And returning from his battles, from the duties of the war,
Riding on his royal tusker or his all-resistless car,

As a father to his children to his loving men he came,
Blessed our homes and maids and matrons till our infants lisped his
name,

For our humble woes and troubles Rama hath the ready tear,
To our humble tales of suffering Rama lends his willing ear !

Happy is the royal father who hath such a righteous son,
For in town and mart and hamlet every heart hath Rama won,

Burghers and the toiling tillers tales of Rama's kindness say,
Man and infant, maid and matron, morn and eve for Rama pray,

To the Gods and bright Immortals we our inmost wishes send,
May the good and godlike Rama on his father's throne ascend,

Great in gifts and great in glory, Rama doth our homage own,
We would see the princely Rama seated on his father's throne ! "

III

THE CITY DECORATED

With his consort pious Rama, pure in deed and pure in thought,
After evening's due ablutions NARAYANA'S chamber sought,

Prayed unto the Lord of Creatures, NARAYANA Ancient Sire,
Placed his offering on his forehead, poured it on the lighted fire,

Piously partook the remnant, sought for NARAYANA'S aid,
As he kept his fast and vigils on the grass of *kusa* spread.

With her lord the saintly Sita silent passed the sacred night,
Contemplating World's Preserver, Lord of Heaven's ethereal height

And within the sacred chamber on the grass of *kusa* lay,
Till the crimson streaks of morning ushered in the festive day,

Till the royal bards and minstrels chanted forth the morning call,
Pealing through the holy chamber, echoing through the royal hall.

Past the night of sacred vigils, in his silken robes arrayed,
Message of the proud anointment Rama to the Brahmans said,

And the Brahmans spake to burghers that the festive day was come,
Till the mart and crowded pathway rang with note of pipe and drum,

And the townsmen heard rejoicing of the vigils of the night,
Kept by Rama and by Sita for the day's auspicious rite.

Rama shall be Heir and Regent, Rama shall be crowned to-day,—
Rapid flew the gladdening message with the morning's gladsome ray,

And the people of the city, maid and matron, man and boy,
Decorated fair Ayodhya in their wild tumultuous joy !

On the temple's lofty steeple high as cloud above the air,
On the crossing of the pathways, in the garden green and fair,

On the merchant's ample warehouse, on the shop with stores dis-
        played,
On the mansion of the noble by the cunning artist made,

On the gay and bright pavilion, on the high and shady trees,
Banners rose and glittering streamers, flags that fluttered in the
        breeze !

Actors gay and nimble dancers, singers skilled in lightsome song,
With their antics and their music pleased the gay and gathered
        throng,

And the people met in conclaves, spake of Rama, Regent Heir,
And the children by the roadside lisped of Rama brave and fair !

Women wove the scented garland, merry maids the censer lit,
Men with broom and sprinkled water swept the spacious mart and
        street,

Rows of trees and posts they planted hung with lamps for coming
        night,
That the midnight dark might rival splendour of the noonday light !

Troops of men and merry children laboured with a loving care,
Woman's skill and woman's fancy made the city passing fair,

So that good and kindly Rama might his people's toil approve,
So that sweet and soft-eyed Sita might accept her people's love !

Groups of joyous townsmen gathered in the square or lofty hall,
Praised the monarch Dasa-ratha, regent Rama young and tall :

" Great and good is Dasa-ratha born of Raghu's royal race,
In the fulness of his lifetime on his son he grants his grace,

And we hail the rite auspicious for our prince of peerless might,
He will guard us by his valour, he will save our cherished right,

Dear unto his loving brothers in his father's palace hall,
As is Rama to his brothers dear is Rama to us all,

Long live ancient Dasa-ratha king of Raghu's royal race,
We shall see his son anointed by his father's righteous grace ! "

Thus of Rama's consecration spake the burghers one and all,
And the men from distant hamlets poured within the city wall,

From the confines of the empire, north and south and west and east,
Came to see the consecration and to share the royal feast !

And the rolling tide of nations raised their voices loud and high,
Like the tide of sounding ocean when the full moon lights the sky,

And Ayodhya thronged by people from the hamlet, mart and lea,
Was tumultuous like the ocean thronged by creatures of the sea !

IV

INTRIGUE

In the inner palace chamber stood the proud and peerless queen,
With a mother's joy Kaikeyi gaily watched the festive scene,

But with deep and deadly hatred Manthara, her nurse and maid,
Marked the city bright with banners, and in scornful accents said .

" Take thy presents back, Kaikeyi, for they ill befit the day,
And when clouds of sorrow darken, ill beseems thee to be gay,

And thy folly moves my laughter though an anguish wakes my sigh.
For a gladness stirs thy bosom when thy greatest woe is nigh !

Who that hath a woman's wisdom, who that is a prudent wife,
Smiles in joy when prouder rival triumphs in the race of life,

How can hapless Queen Kaikeyi greet this deed of darkness done,
When the favoured Queen Kausalya wins the empire for her son ?

Know the truth, O witless woman ! Bharat is unmatched in fame,
Rama, deep and darkly jealous, dreads thy Bharat's rival claim,

Younger Lakshman with devotion doth on eldest Rama wait,
Young Satrughna with affection follows Bharat's lofty fate,

Rama dreads no rising danger from the twins, the youngest-born,
But thy Bharat's claims and virtues fill his jealous heart with scorn !

Trust me, queen, thy Bharat's merits are too well and widely known,
And he stands too near and closely by a rival brother's throne,

Rama hath a wolf-like wisdom and a fang to reach the foe,
And I tremble for thy Bharat, Heaven avert untimely woe !

Happy is the Queen Kausalya, they will soon anoint her son,
When on Pushya's constellation gaily rides to-morrow's moon,

Happy is the Queen Kausalya in her regal pomp and state,
And Kaikeyi like a bond-slave must upon her rival wait !

Wilt thou do her due obeisance as we humble women do,
Will thy proud and princely Bharat as his brother's henchman go,

Will thy Bharat's gentle consort, fairest princess in this land,
In her tears and in her anguish wait on Sita's proud command ? "

With a woman's scornful anger Manthara proclaimed her grief,
With a mother's love for Rama thus Kaikeyi answered brief :

" What inspires thee, wicked woman, thus to rail in bitter tone,
Shall not Rama, best and eldest, fill his father's royal throne,

What alarms thee, crooked woman, in the happy rites begun,
Shall not Rama guard his brothers as a father guards his son ?

And when Rama's reign is over, shall not Gods my Bharat speed,
And by law and ancient custom shall not younger son succeed,

In the present bliss of Rama and in Bharat's future hope,
What offends thee, senseless woman, wherefore dost thou idly mope ?

Dear is Rama as my Bharat, ever duteous in his ways,
Rama honours Queen Kausalya, loftier honour to me pays,

Rama's realm is Bharat's kingdom, ruling partners they shall prove,
For himself than for his brothers Rama owns no deeper love ! ''

Scorn and anger shook her person and her bosom heaved a sigh,
As in wilder, fiercer accents Manthara thus made reply :

'' What insensate rage or madness clouds thy heart and blinds thine
     eye,
Courting thus thy own disaster, courting danger dread and high,

What dark folly clouds thy vision to the workings of thy foe,
Heedless thus to seek destruction and to sink in gulf of woe ?

Know, fair queen, by law and custom, son ascends the throne of pride,
Rama's son succeedeth Rama, luckless Bharat steps aside,

Brothers do not share a kingdom, nor can one by one succeed,
Mighty were the civil discord if such custom were decreed !

For to stop all war and tumult, thus the ancient laws ordain,
Eldest son succeeds his father, younger children may not reign,

Bharat barred from Rama's empire, vainly decked with royal grace,
Friendless, joyless, long shall wander, alien from his land and race !

Thou hast borne the princely Bharat, nursed him from thy gentle
     breast,
To a queen and to a mother need a prince's claims be pressed,

To a thoughtless heedless mother must I Bharat's virtues plead,
Must the Queen Kaikeyi witness Queen Kausalya's son succeed ?

Trust thy old and faithful woman who hath nursed thee, youthful
     queen,
And in great and princely houses many darksome deeds hath seen,

Trust my word, the wily Rama for his spacious empire's good,
Soon will banish friendless Bharat and secure his peace with blood !

Thou hast sent the righteous Bharat to thy ancient father's land,
And Satrughna young and valiant doth beside his brother stand,

Young in years and generous-hearted, they will grow in mutual love,
As the love of elder Rama doth in Lakshman's bosom move.

Young companions grow in friendship, and our ancient legends tell,
Weeds protect a forest monarch which the woodman's axe would fell,

Crownéd Rama unto Lakshman will a loving brother prove,
But for Bharat and Satrughná, Rama's bosom owns no love,

And a danger thus ariseth if the elder wins the throne,
Haste thee, heedless Queen Kaikeyi, save the younger and thy son !

Speak thy mandate to thy husband, let thy Bharat rule at home,
In the deep and pathless jungle let the banished Rama roam,

This will please thy ancient father and thy father's kith and kin,
This will please the righteous people, Bharat knows no guile or sin !

Speak thy mandate to thy husband, win thy son a happy fate,
Doom him not to Rama's service or his unrelenting hate,

Let not Rama in his rancour shed a younger brother's blood,
As the lion slays the tiger in the deep and echoing wood !

With the magic of thy beauty thou hast won thy monarch's heart,
Queen Kausalya's bosom rankles with a woman's secret smart,

Let her not with woman's vengeance turn upon her prouder foe,
And as crownéd Rama's mother venge her in Kaikeyi's woe,

Mark my word, my child Kaikeyi, much these ancient eyes have seen,
Rama's rule is death to Bharat, insult to my honoured queen ! "

Like a slow but deadly poison worked the ancient nurse's tears,
And a wife's undying impulse mingled with a mother's fears,

Deep within Kaikeyi's bosom worked a woman's jealous thought,
Speechless in her scorn and anger mourner's dark retreat she sought.

V

The Queen's Demand

Rama shall be crowned at sunrise, so did royal bards proclaim,
Every rite arranged and ordered, Dasa-ratha homeward came,

To the fairest of his consorts, dearest to his ancient heart,
Came the king with eager gladness joyful message to impart,

Radiant as the Lord of Midnight, ere the eclipse casts its gloom,
Came the old and ardent monarch heedless of his darksome doom !

Through the shady palace garden where the peacock wandered free,
Lute and lyre poured forth their music, parrot flew from tree to tree,

Through the corridor of creepers, painted rooms by artists done,
And the halls where scented *Champak* and the flaming *Asok* shone,

Through the portico of splendour graced by silver, tusk and gold,
Radiant with his thought of gladness walked the monarch proud
  and bold.

Through the lines of scented blossoms which by limpid waters shone,
And the rooms with seats of silver, ivory bench and golden throne,

Through the chamber of confection, where each viand wooed the taste,
Every object in profusion as in regions of the blest,

Through Kaikeyi's inner closet lighted with a softened sheen,
Walked the king with eager longing,—but Kaikeyi was not seen !

Thoughts of love and gentle dalliance woke within his ancient heart,
And the magic of her beauty and the glamour of her art,

With a soft desire the monarch vainly searched the vanished fair,
Found her not in royal chamber, found her not in gay parterre !

Filled with love and longing languor loitered not the radiant queen,
In her soft voluptuous chamber, in the garden, grove or green,

And he asked the faithful warder of Kaikeyi loved and lost,
She who served him with devotion and his wishes never crost,

Spake the warder in his terror that the queen with rage distraught,
Weeping silent tears of anguish had the mourner's chamber sought !

Thither flew the stricken monarch ; on the bare and unswept ground,
Trembling with tumultuous passion was the Queen Kaikeyi found,

On the cold uncovered pavement sorrowing lay the weeping wife,
Young wife of an ancient husband, dearer than his heart and life !

Like a bright and blossoming creeper rudely severed from the earth,
Like a fallen fair *Apsara*, beauteous nymph of heavenly birth,

Like a female forest-ranger bleeding from the hunter's dart,
Whom her mate the forest-monarch soothes with soft endearing art,

Lay the queen in tears of anguish ! And with sweet and gentle word
To the lotus-eyéd lady softly spake her loving lord :

" Wherefore thus, my Queen and Empress, sorrow-laden is thy heart,
Who with daring slight or insult seeks to cause thy bosom smart ?

If some unknown ailment pains thee, evil spirit of the air,
Skilled physicians wait upon thee, priests with incantations fair,

If from human foe some insult, wipe thy tears and doom his fate,
Rich reward or royal vengeance shall upon thy mandate wait !

Wilt thou doom to death the guiltless, free whom direst sins debase,
Wilt thou lift the poor and lowly or the proud and great disgrace,

Speak, and I and all my courtiers Queen Kaikeyi's hest obey,
For thy might is boundless, Empress, limitless thy regal sway !

Rolls my chariot-wheel revolving from the sea to farthest sea,
And the wide earth is my empire, monarchs list my proud decree,

Nations of the eastern regions and of Sindhu's western wave,
Brave Saurashtras and the races who the ocean's dangers brave,

Vangas, Angas and Magadhas, warlike Matsyas of the west,
Kasis and the southern races, brave Kosalas first and best,

Nations of my world-wide empire, rich in corn and sheep and kine,
All shall serve my Queen Kaikeyi and their treasures all are thine,

Speak, command thy king's obedience, and thy wrath will melt away,
Like the melting snow of winter 'neath the sun's reviving ray ! "

Blinded was the ancient husband as he lifted up her head,
Heedless oath and word he plighted that her wish should be obeyed,

Scheming for a fatal purpose, inly then Kaikeyi smiled,
And by sacred oath and promise bound the monarch love-beguiled :

" Thou hast given, Dasa-ratha, troth and word and royal oath,
Three and thirty Gods be witness, watchers of the righteous truth,

Sun and Moon and Stars be witness, Sky and Day and sable Night,
Rolling Worlds and this our wide Earth, and each dark and unseen
    wight,

Witness Rangers of the forest, Household Gods that guard us both,
Mortal beings and Immortal,—witness ye the monarch's oath,

Ever faithful to his promise, ever truthful in his word,
Dasa-ratha grants my prayer, Spirits and the Gods have heard !

Call to mind, O righteous monarch, days when in a bygone strife,
Warring with thy foes immortal thou hadst almost lost thy life,

With a woman's loving tendance poor Kaikeyi cured thy wound,
Till from death and danger rescued, thou wert by a promise bound,

Two rewards my husband offered, what my loving heart might seek,
Long delayed their wished fulfilment,—now let poor Kaikeyi speak,

And if royal deeds redeem not what thy royal lips did say,
Victim to thy broken promise Queen Kaikeyi dies to-day !

By these rites ordained for Rama,—such the news my menials bring,—
Let my Bharat, and not Rama, be anointed Regent King,

Wearing skins and matted tresses, in the cave or hermit's cell,
Fourteen years in Dandak's forests let the elder Rama dwell,

These are Queen Kaikeyi's wishes, these are boons for which I pray,
I would see my son anointed, Rama banished on this day ! "

VI

THE KING'S LAMENT

" Is this torturing dream or madness, do my feeble senses fail,
O'er my darkened mind and bosom doth a fainting fit prevail ? "

So the stricken monarch pondered and in hushed and silent fear,
Looked on her as on a tigress looks the dazed and stricken deer,

Lying on the unswept pavement still he heaved the choking sigh,
Like a wild and hissing serpent quelled by incantations high !

Sobs convulsive shook his bosom and his speech and accent failed,
And a dark and deathlike faintness o'er his feeble soul prevailed,

Stunned awhile remained the monarch, then in furious passion woke,
And his eyeballs flamed with redfire, to the queen as thus he spoke :

" Traitress to thy king and husband, fell destroyer of thy race,
Wherefore seeks thy ruthless rancour Rama rich in righteous grace,

Traitress to thy kith and kindred, Rama loves thee as thy own,
Wherefore then with causeless vengeance as a mother hate thy son ?

Have I courted thee, Kaikeyi, throned thee in my heart of truth,
Nursed thee in my home and bosom like a snake of poisoned tooth,

Have I courted thee, Kaikeyi, placed thee on Ayodhya's throne,
That my Rama, loved of people, thou shouldst banish from his own ?

Banish far my Queen Kausalya, Queen Sumitra saintly wife,
Wrench from me my ancient empire, from my bosom wrench my life,

But with brave and princely Rama never can his father part,
Till his ancient life is ended, cold and still his beating heart !

Sunless roll the world in darkness, rainless may the harvests thrive,
But from righteous Rama severed, never can his sire survive,

Feeble is thy aged husband, few and brief on earth his day,
Lend me, wife, a woman's kindness, as a consort be my stay !

Ask for other boon, Kaikeyi, aught my sea-girt empire yields,
Wealth or treasure, gem or jewel, castled town or smiling fields,

Ask for other gift, Kaikeyi, and thy wishes shall be given,
Stain me not with crime unholy in the eye of righteous Heaven ! "

Coldly spake the Queen Kaikeyi : " If thy royal heart repent,
Break thy word and plighted promise, let thy royal faith be rent,

Ever known for truth and virtue, speak to peers and monarchs all,
When from near and distant regions they shall gather in thy hall,

Speak if so it please thee, monarch, of thy evil-destined wife,
How she loved with wife's devotion, how she served and saved thy
    life,

How on plighted promise trusting for a humble boon she sighed,
How a monarch broke his promise, how a cheated woman died ! "

" Fair thy form," resumed the monarch, " beauty dwells upon thy
    face,
Woman's winsome charms bedeck thee, and a woman's peerless grace,

Wherefore then within thy bosom wakes this thought of cruel wile,
And what dark and loathsome spirit stains thy heart with blackest
    guile ?

Ever since the day, Kaikeyi, when a gentle bride you came,
By a wife's unfailing duty you have won a woman's fame,

Wherefore now this cruel purpose hath a stainless heart defiled,
Ruthless wish to send my Rama to the dark and pathless wild ?

Wherefore, darkly-scheming woman, on unrighteous purpose bent,
Doth thy cruel causeless vengeance on my Rama seek a vent,

Wherefore seek by deeds unholy for thy son the throne to win,
Throne which Bharat doth not covet,—blackened by his mother's sin?

Shall I see my banished Rama mantled in the garb of woe,
Reft of home and kin and empire to the pathless jungle go,

Shall I see disasters sweeping o'er my empire dark and deep,
As the forces of a foeman o'er a scattered army sweep ?

Shall I hear assembled monarchs in their whispered voices say,
Weak and foolish in his dotage, Dasa-ratha holds his sway,

Shall I say to righteous elders when they blame my action done,
That by woman's mandate driven I have banished thus my son ?

Queen Kausalya, dear-loved woman ! she who serves me as a slave,
Soothes me like a tender sister, helps me like a consort brave,

As a fond and loving mother tends me with a watchful care,
As a daughter ever duteous doth obeisance sweet and fair,

When my fond and fair Kausalya asks me of her banished son,
How shall Dasa-ratha answer for the impious action done,

How can husband, cold and cruel, break a wife's confiding heart,
How can father, false and faithless, from his best and eldest part ? "

Coldly spake the Queen Kaikeyi : " If thy royal heart repent,
Break thy word and plighted promise, let thy royal faith be rent,

Truth-abiding is our monarch, so I heard the people say,
And his word is all inviolate, stainless virtue marks his sway,

Let it now be known to nations,—righteous Dasa-ratha lied,
And a trusting, cheated woman broke her loving heart and died ! "

Darker grew the shades of midnight, coldly shone each distant star,
Wilder in the monarch's bosom raged the struggle and the war :

" Starry midnight, robed in shadows ! give my wearied heart relief,
Spread thy sable covering mantle o'er an impious monarch's grief,

Spread thy vast and inky darkness o'er a deed of nameless crime,
Reign perennial o'er my sorrows heedless of the lapse of time,

May a sinful monarch perish ere the dawning of the day,
O'er a dark life sin-polluted, beam not morning's righteous ray ! "

VII

The Sentence

Morning came and duteous Rama to the palace bent his way,
For to make his salutation and his due obeisance pay,

And he saw his aged father shorn of kingly pomp and pride,
And he saw the Queen Kaikeyi sitting by her consort's side.

Duteously the righteous Rama touched the ancient monarch's feet,
Touched the feet of Queen Kaikeyi with a son's obeisance meet,

" Rama ! " cried the feeble monarch, but the tear bedimmed his eye,
Sorrow choked his failing utterance and his bosom heaved a sigh,

Rama started in his terror at his father's grief or wrath,
Like a traveller in the jungle crossed by serpent in his path !

Reft of sense appeared the monarch, crushed beneath a load of pain,
Heaving oft a sigh of sorrow as his heart would break in twain,

Like the ocean tempest-shaken, like the sun in eclipse pale,
Like a crushed repenting *rishi* when his truth and virtue fail !

Breathless mused the anxious Rama,—what foul action hath he done,
What strange anger fills his father, wherefore greets he not his son ?

" Speak, my mother," uttered Rama," what strange error on my part,
Unremembered sin or folly fills with grief my father's heart,

Gracious unto me is father with a father's boundless grace,
Wherefore clouds his altered visage, wherefore tears bedew his face ?

Doth a piercing painful ailment rack his limbs with cruel smart,
Doth some secret silent anguish wring his torn and tortured heart,

Bharat lives with brave Satrughna in thy father's realms afar,
Hath some cloud of dark disaster crossed their bright auspicious star?

Duteously the royal consorts on the loving monarch wait,
Hath some woe or dire misfortune dimmed the lustre of their fate,

I would yield my life and fortune ere I wound my father's heart,
Hath my unknown crime or folly caused his ancient bosom smart ?

Ever dear is Queen Kaikeyi to her consort and her king,
Hath some angry accent escaped thee thus his royal heart to wring,

Speak, my ever-loving mother, speak the truth, for thou must know,
What distress or deep disaster pains his heart and clouds his brow ? "

Mother's love nor woman's pity moved the deep-determined queen,
As in cold and cruel accents thus she spake her purpose keen :

" Grief nor woe nor sudden ailment pains thy father loved of old,
But he fears to speak his purpose to his Rama true and bold,

And his loving accents falter some unloving wish to tell,
Till you give your princely promise, you will serve his mandate well !

Listen more, in bygone seasons,—Rama thou wert then unborn,—
I had saved thy royal father, he a gracious boon had sworn,

But his feeble heart repenting is by pride and passion stirred,
He would break his royal promise as a caitiff breaks his word,

Years have passed and now the monarch would his ancient word
    forego,
He would build a needless causeway when the waters ceased to flow !

Truth inspires each deed attempted and each word by monarchs
    spoke,
Not for thee, though loved and honoured, should a royal vow be broke,

If the true and righteous Rama binds him by his father's vow,
I will tell thee of the anguish which obscures his royal brow,

If thy feeble bosom falter and thy halting purpose fail,
Unredeemed is royal promise and unspoken is my tale ! "

" Speak thy word," exclaimed the hero, "and my purpose shall not fail,
Rama serves his father's mandate and his bosom shall not quail,

Poisoned cup or death untimely,—what the cruel fates decree,—
To his king and to his father Rama yields obedience free,

Speak my father's royal promise, hold me by his promise tied,
Rama speaks and shall not palter, for his lips have never lied."

Cold and clear Kaikeyi's accents fell as falls the hunter's knife,
" Listen then to word of promise and redeem it with thy life,

Wounded erst by foes immortal, saved by Queen Kaikeyi's care,
Two great boons your father plighted and his royal words were fair,

I have sought their due fulfilment,—brightly shines my Bharat's star,
Bharat shall be Heir and Regent, Rama shall be banished far !

If thy father's royal mandate thou wouldst list and honour still,
Fourteen years in Dandak's forest live and wander at thy will,

Seven long years and seven, my Rama, thou shalt in the jungle dwell,
Bark of trees shall be thy raiment and thy home the hermit's cell,

Over fair Kosala's empire let my princely Bharat reign,
With his cars and steeds and tuskers, wealth and gold and arméd men !

Tender-hearted is the monarch, age and sorrow dim his eye,
And the anguish of a father checks his speech and purpose high,

For the love he bears thee, Rama, cruel vow he may not speak,
I have spoke his will and mandate, and thy true obedience seek."

Calmly Rama heard the mandate, grief nor anger touched his heart,
Calmly from his father's empire and his home prepared to part.

BOOK III

DASA-RATHA-VIYOGA

(*The Death of the King*)

THE first six days of Rama's wanderings are narrated in this
Book. Sita and the faithful Lakshman accompanied Rama
in his exile, and the loyal people of Ayodhya followed their exiled
prince as far as the banks of the Tamasa river, where they halted
on the first night. Rama had to steal away at night to escape the
citizens, and his wanderings during the following days give us beautiful glimpses of forest life in holy hermitages. Thirty centuries have
passed since the age of the Kosalas and Videhas, but every step of the
supposed journey of Rama is well known in India to this day, and
is annually traversed by thousands of devoted pilgrims. The past
is not dead and buried in India, it lives in the hearts of millions
of faithful men and faithful women, and shall live for ever.

On the third day of their exile, Rama and his wife and brother
crossed the Ganges ; on the fourth day they came to the hermitage
of Bharad-vaja, which stood where Allahabad now stands, on the
confluence of the Ganges and the Jumna ; on the fifth day they
crossed the Jumna, the southern shores of which were then covered
with woods ; and on the sixth day they came to the hill of Chitra-
kuta, where they met the saint Valmiki, the reputed author of this
Epic. " We have often looked," says a writer in *Calcutta Review*,
vol. xxii, " on that green hill : it is the holiest spot of that sect of
the Hindu faith who devote themselves to this incarnation of Vishnu.
The whole neighbourhood is Rama's country. Every headland has
some legend, every cavern is connected with his name, some of the
wild fruits are still called Sita-phal, being the reputed food of the
exile. Thousands and thousands annually visit the spot, and round
the hill is raised a footpath on which the devotee, with naked feet,
treads full of pious awe."

Grief for the banished Rama pressed on the ancient heart of
Dasa-ratha. The feeble old king pined away and died, remember-
ing and recounting on his death-bed how in his youth he had caused
sorrow and death to an old hermit by killing his son. Scarcely any
passage in the Epic is more touching than this old sad story told
by the dying monarch.

Tha portions translated in this Book form the whole or the
main portions of Sections xxvi., xxvii., xxxi., xxxix., xl., xlvi.,
lii., liv., lv., lvi., lxiii., and lxiv. of Book ii. of the original text.

I

WOMAN'S LOVE

" Dearly loved, devoted Sita !   daughter of a royal line,
Part we now, for years of wand'ring in the pathless woods is mine,

For my father, promise-fettered, to Kaikeyi yields the sway,
And she wills her son anointed,—fourteen years doth Rama stray,

But before I leave thee, Sita, in the wilderness to rove,
Yield me one more tender token of thy true and trustful love !

Serve my crownéd brother, Sita, as a faithful, duteous dame,
Tell him not of Rama's virtues, tell him not of Rama's claim,

Since my royal father willeth,—Bharat shall be regent-heir,
Serve him with a loyal duty, serve him with obeisance fair,

Since my royal father willeth,—years of banishment be mine,
Brave in sorrow and in suffering, woman's brightest fame be thine !

Keep thy fasts and vigils, Sita, while thy Rama is away,
Faith in Gods and faith in virtue on thy bosom hold their sway,

In the early watch of morning to the Gods for blessings pray,
To my father Dasa-ratha honour and obeisance pay,

To my mother, Queen Kausalya, is thy dearest tendance due,
Offer her thy consolation, be a daughter fond and true !

Queen Kaikeyi and Sumitra equal love and honour claim,
With a soothing soft endearment sweetly serve each royal dame,

Cherish Bharat and Satrughna with a sister's watchful love,
And a mother's true affection and a mother's kindness prove !

Listen, Sita, unto Bharat speak no heedless angry word,
He is monarch of Kosala and of Raghu's race is lord,

Crownéd kings our willing service and our faithful duty own,
Dearest sons they disinherit, cherish strangers near the throne !

Bharat's will with deep devotion and with faultless faith obey,
Truth and virtue on thy bosom ever hold their gentle sway,

And to please each dear relation, gentle Sita, be it thine,
Part we love! for years of wand'ring in the pathless woods is mine!"

Rama spake, and soft-eyed Sita, ever sweet in speech and word,
Stirred by loving woman's passion boldly answered thus her lord:

" Do I hear my husband rightly, are these words my Rama spake,
And her banished lord and husband will the wedded wife forsake ?

Lightly I dismiss the counsel which my lord hath lightly said,
For it ill beseems a warrior and my husband's princely grade !

For the faithful woman follows where her wedded lord may lead,
In the banishment of Rama, Sita's exile is decreed,

Sire nor son nor loving brother rules the wedded woman's state,
With her lord she falls or rises, with her consort courts her fate,

If the righteous son of Raghu wends to forests dark and drear,
Sita steps before her husband wild and thorny paths to clear !

Like the tasted refuse water cast thy timid thoughts aside,
Take me to the pathless jungle, bid me by my lord abide,

Car and steed and gilded palace, vain are these to woman's life,
Dearer is her husband's shadow to the loved and loving wife !

For my mother often taught me and my father often spake,
That her home the wedded woman doth beside her husband make,

As the shadow to the substance, to her lord is faithful wife,
And she parts not from her consort till she parts with fleeting life !

Therefore bid me seek the jungle and in pathless forests roam,
Where the wild deer freely ranges and the tiger makes his home,

Happier than in father's mansions in the woods will Sita rove,
Waste no thought on home or kindred, nestling in her husband's love!

World-renowned is Rama's valour, fearless by her Rama's side,
Sita will still live and wander with a faithful woman's pride,

And the wild fruit she will gather from the fresh and fragrant wood,
And the food by Rama tasted shall be Sita's cherished food !

Bid me seek the sylvan greenwoods, wooded hills and plateaus high,
Limpid rills and crystal *nullas* as they softly ripple by,

And where in the lake of lotus tuneful ducks their plumage lave,
Let me with my loving Rama skim the cool translucent wave !

Years will pass in happy union,—happiest lot to woman given,—
Sita seeks not throne or empire, nor the brighter joys of heaven,

Heaven conceals not brighter mansions in its sunny fields of pride,
Where without her lord and husband faithful Sita would reside !

Therefore let me seek the jungle where the jungle-rangers rove,
Dearer than the royal palace, where I share my husband's love,

And my heart in sweet communion shall my Rama's wishes share,
And my wifely toil shall lighten Rama's load of woe and care ! "

Vainly gentle Rama pleaded dangers of the jungle life,
Vainly spake of toil and trial to a true and tender wife !

II

BROTHER'S FAITHFULNESS

Tears bedewed the face of Lakshman as he heard what Sita said,
And he touched the feet of Rama and in gentle accents prayed :

" *If my elder and his lady to the pathless forests wend,*
Armed with bow and ample quiver Lakshman will on them attend,

Where the wild deer range the forest and the lordly tuskers roam,
And the bird of gorgeous plumage nestles in its jungle home,

Dearer far to me those woodlands where my elder Rama dwells,
Than the homes of bright Immortals where perennial bliss prevails !

Grant me then thy sweet permission,—faithful to thy glorious star,
Lakshman shall not wait and tarry when his Rama wanders far,

Grant me then thy loving mandate,—Lakshman hath no wish to stay,
None shall bar the faithful younger when the elder leads the way ! "

" Ever true to deeds of virtue, duteous brother, faithful friend,
Dearer than his life to Rama, thou shall not to forests wend,

Who shall stay by Queen Kausalya, Lakshman, if we both depart,
Who shall stay by Queen Sumitra, she who nursed thee on her
    heart ?

For the king our aged father, he who ruled the earth and main,
Is a captive to Kaikeyi, fettered by her silken chain,

Little help Kaikeyi renders to our mothers in her pride,
Little help can Bharat offer, standing by his mother's side.

Thou alone can'st serve Kausalya when for distant woods I part,
When the memory of my exile rankles in her sorrowing heart,

Thou alone can'st serve Sumitra, soothe her sorrows with thy love,
Stay by them, my faithful Lakshman, and thy filial virtues prove,

Be this then they sacred duty, tend our mothers in their woe,
Little joy or consolation have they left on earth below ! "

Spake the hero : " Fear no evil, well is Rama's prowess known,
And to mighty Rama's mother Bharat will obeisance own,

Nathless if the pride of empire sways him from the righteous path,
Blood will venge the offered insult and will quench our filial wrath !

But a thousand peopled hamlets Queen Kausalya's hests obey,
And a thousand arméd champions own her high and queenly sway,

Aye, a thousand village-centres Queen Sumitra's state maintain,
And a thousand swords like Lakshman's guard her proud and pros-
    perous reign !

All alone with gentle Sita thou shalt track thy darksome way,
Grant it, that thy faithful Lakshman shall protect her night and day,

Grant it, with his bow and quiver Lakshman shall the forests roam,
And his axe shall fell the jungle, and his hands shall rear the home !

Grant it, in the deepest woodlands he shall seek the forest fruit,
Berries dear to holy hermits and the sweet and luscious root,

And when with thy meek-eyed Sita thou shalt seek the mountain crest,
Grant it, Lakshman ever duteous watch and guard thy nightly rest ! "

Words of brother's deep devotion Rama heard with grateful heart,
And with Sita and with Lakshman for the woods prepared to part :

" Part we then from loving kinsmen, arms and mighty weapons bring,
Bows of war which Lord Varuna rendered to Videha's king,

Coats of mail to sword impervious, quivers which can never fail,
And the rapiers bright as sunshine, golden-hilted, tempered well,

Safely rest these goodly weapons in our great preceptor's hall,
Seek and bring them, faithful brother, for methinks we need them all!"

Rama spake; his valiant brother then the wondrous weapons brought,
Wreathed with fresh and fragrant garlands and with gold and
    jewels wrought,

" Welcome, brother," uttered Rama, "stronger thus to woods we go,
Wealth and gold and useless treasure to the holy priests bestow,

To the son of saint Vasishtha, to each sage is honour due,
Then we leave our father's mansions, to our father's mandate true ! "

III

MOTHER'S BLESSINGS

Tears of sorrow and of suffering flowed from Queen Kausalya's eye,
As she saw departing Sita for her blessings drawing nigh,

And she clasped the gentle Sita and she kissed her moistened head,
And her tears like summer tempest choked the loving words she said :

" Part we, dear devoted daughter, to thy husband ever true,
With a woman's whole affection render love to husband's due !

False are women loved and cherished, gentle in their speech and word,
When misfortune's shadows gather, who are faithless to their lord,

Who through years of sunny splendour smile and pass the livelong
    day,
When misfortune's darkness thickens, from their husband turn away,

Who with changeful fortune changing oft ignore the plighted word,
And forget a woman's duty, woman's faith to wedded lord,

Who to holy love inconstant from their wedded consort part,
Manly deed nor manly virtue wins the changeful woman's heart !

But the true and righteous woman, loving spouse and changeless wife,
Faithful to her lord and consort holds him dearer than her life,

Ever true and righteous Sita, follow still my godlike son,
Like a God to thee is Rama in the woods or on the throne ! "

" I shall do my duty, mother," said the wife with wifely pride,
" Like a God to me is Rama, Sita shall not leave his side,

From the Moon will part his lustre ere I part from wedded lord,
Ere from faithful wife's devotion falter in my deed or word,

For the stringless lute is silent, idle is the wheel-less car,
And no wife the loveless consort, inauspicious is her star !

Small the measure of affection which the sire and brother prove,
Measureless to wedded woman is her lord and husband's love,

True to Law and true to Scriptures, true to woman's plighted word,
Can I ever be, my mother, faithless, loveless to my lord ? "

Tears of joy and mingled sorrow filled the Queen Kausalya's eye,
As she marked the faithful Sita true in heart, in virtue high,

And she wept the tears of sadness when with sweet obeisance due,
Spake with hands in meekness folded Rama ever good and true :

" Sorrow not, my loving mother, trust in virtue's changeless beam,
Swift will fly the years of exile like a brief and transient dream,

Girt by faithful friends and forces, blest by righteous Gods above,
Thou shalt see thy son returning to thy bosom and thy love ! "

Unto all the royal ladies Rama his obeisance paid,
For his failings unremembered, blessings and forgiveness prayed,

And his words were soft and gentle, and they wept to see him go,
Like the piercing cry of curlew rose the piercing voice of woe,

And in halls where drum and tabor rose in joy and regal pride,
Voice of grief and lamentation sounded far and sounded wide !

Then the true and faithful Lakshman parted from each weeping dame,
And to sorrowing Queen Sumitra with his due obeisance came,

And he bowed to Queen Sumitra and his mother kissed his head,
Stilled her anguish-laden bosom and in trembling accents said :

" Dear devoted duteous Lakshman, ever to thy elder true,
When thy elder wends to forest, forest-life to thee is due,

Thou hast served him true and faithful in his glory and his fame,
This is Law for true and righteous,—serve him in his woe and shame,

This is Law for race of Raghu known on earth for holy might,
Bounteous in their sacred duty, brave and warlike in the fight !

Therefore tend him as thy father, as thy mother tend his wife,
And to thee, like fair Ayodhya be thy humble forest life,

Go, my son, the voice of Duty bids my gallant Lakshman go,
Serve thy elder with devotion and with valour meet thy foe !

IV

CITIZENS' LAMENT

Spake Sumantra chariot-driver waiting by the royal car,
" Haste thee, mighty-destined Rama, for we wander long and far,

Fourteen years in Dandak's forest shall the righteous Rama stray,
Such is Dasa-ratha's mandate, haste thee Rama and obey."

Queenly Sita bright-apparelled, with a strong and trusting heart,
Mounted on the car of splendour for the pathless woods to part,

And the king for needs providing gave her robes and precious store,
For the many years of exile in a far and unknown shore,

And a wealth of warlike weapons to the exiled princes gave,
Bow and dart and linkéd armour, sword and shield and lances brave.

Then the gallant brothers mounted on the gold-emblazoned car,
For unending was the journey and the wilderness was far,

Skilled Sumantra saw them seated, urged the swiftly-flying steed,
Faster than the speed of tempest was the noble coursers' speed.

And they parted for the forest ; like a long unending night,
Gloomy shades of grief and sadness deepened on the city's might,

Mute and dumb but conscious creatures felt the woe the city bore,
Horses neighed and shook their bright bells, elephants returned a roar!

Man and boy and maid and matron followed Rama with their eye,
As the thirsty seek the water when the parchéd fields are dry,

Clinging to the rapid chariot, by its side, before, behind,
Thronging men and wailing women wept for Rama good and kind :

" Draw the reins, benign Sumantra, slowly drive the royal car,
We would once more see our Rama, banished long and banished far,

Iron-hearted is Kausalya from her Rama thus to part,
Rends it not her mother's bosom thus to see her son depart ?

True is righteous-hearted Sita cleaving to her husband still,
As the ever present sunlight cleaves to Meru's golden hill,

Faithful and heroic Lakshman ! thou hast by thy brother stood,
And in duty still unchanging thou hast sought the pathless wood,

Fixed in purpose, true in valour, mighty boon to thee is given,
And the narrow path thou choosest is the righteous path to heaven! "

Thus they spake in tears and anguish as they followed him apace,
And their eyes were fixed on Rama, pride of Raghu's royal race,

Meanwhile ancient Dasa-ratha from his palace chamber came,
With each weeping queen and consort, with each woe-distracted dame!

And around the aged monarch rose the piercing voice of pain,
Like the wail of forest creatures when the forest-king is slain,

And the faint and feeble monarch was with age and anguish pale,
Like the darkened moon at eclipse when his light and radiance fail !

Rama saw his ancient father with a faltering footstep go,
Used to royal pomp and splendour, stricken now by age and woe,

Saw his mother faint and feeble to the speeding chariot hie,
As the mother-cow returneth to her young that loiters by,

Still she hastened to the chariot, " Rama ! Rama ! " was her cry,
And a throb was in her bosom and a tear was in her eye !

" Speed, Sumantra," uttered Rama, " from this torture let me part,
Speed, my friend, this sight of sadness breaks a much-enduring heart,

Heed not Dasa-ratha's mandate, stop not for the royal train,
Parting slow is lengthened sorrow like the sinner's lengthened pain !"

Sad Sumantra urged the coursers and the rapid chariot flew,
And the royal chiefs and courtiers round their fainting monarch drew,

And they spake to Dasa-ratha : " Follow not thy banished son,
He whom thou wouldst keep beside thee comes not till his task is
   done ! "

Dasa-ratha, faint and feeble, listened to these words of pain,
Stood and saw his son departing,—saw him not on earth again !

V

CROSSING THE TAMASA : THE CITIZENS' RETURN

Evening's thickening shades descended on Tamasa's distant shore,
Rama rested by the river, day of toilsome journey o'er,

And Ayodhya's loving people by the limpid river lay,
Sad and sorrowing they had followed Rama's chariot through the day!

" Soft-eyed Sita, faithful Lakshman," thus the gentle Rama said,
" Hail the first night of our exile mantling us in welcome shade,

Weeps the lone and voiceless forest, and in darksome lair and nest,
Feathered bird and forest creature seek their midnight's wonted rest,

Weeps methinks our fair Ayodhya to her Rama ever dear,
And perchance her men and women shed for us a silent tear,

Loyal men and faithful women, they have loved their ancient king,
And his anguish and our exile will their gentle bosoms wring !

Most I sorrow for my father and my mother loved and lost,
Stricken by untimely anguish, by a cruel fortune crost,

But the good and righteous Bharat gently will my parents tend,
And with fond and filial duty tender consolation lend,

Well I know his stainless bosom and his virtues rare and high,
He will soothe our parents' sorrow and their trickling tear will dry !

Faithful Lakshman, thou hast nobly stood by us when sorrows fell,
Guard my Sita by thy valour, by thy virtues tend her well,

Wait on her while from this river Rama seeks his thirst to slake,
On this first night of his exile food nor fruit shall Rama take,

Thou Sumantra, tend the horses, darkness comes with close of day,
Weary was the endless journey, weary is our onward way ! "

Store of grass and welcome fodder to the steeds the driver gave,
Gave them rest and gave them water from Tamasa's limpid wave,

And performing night's devotions, for the princes made their bed,
By the softly rippling river 'neath the tree's umbrageous shade.

On a bed of leaf and verdure Rama and his Sita slept,
Faithful Lakshman with Sumantra nightly watch and vigils kept,

And the stars their silent lustre on the weary exiles shed,
And on wood and rolling river night her darksome mantle spread.

Early woke the righteous Rama and to watchful Lakshman spake :
" Mark the slumb'ring city people, still their nightly rest they take,

They have left their homes and children, followed us with loyal hear',
They would take us to Ayodhya, from their princes loth to part !

Speed, my brother, for the people wake not till the morning's star,
Speed by night the silent chariot, we may travel fast and far,

So my true and loving people see us not by dawn of day,
Follow not through wood and jungle Rama in his onward way,

For a monarch meek in suffering should his burden bravely bear,
And his true and faithful people may not ask his woe to share ! "

Lakshman heard the gentle mandate, and Sumantra yoked the steed,
Fresh with rest and grateful fodder, matchless in their wondrous
    speed,

Rama with his gentle consort and with Lakshman true and brave,
Crossed beneath the silent starlight dark Tamasa's limpid wave.

On the farther bank a pathway, fair to view and far and wide,
Stretching onwards to the forests spanned the spacious country-side,

" Leave the broad and open pathway," so the gentle Rama said,
" Follow yet a track diverging, so the people be misled.

Then returning to the pathway we shall march ere break of day,
So our true and faithful people shall not know our southward way."

Wise Sumantra hastened northward, then returning to the road,
By his master and his consort and the valiant Lakshman stood,

Raghu's sons and gentle Sita mounted on the stately car,
And Sumantra drove the coursers travelling fast and travelling far.

Morning dawned, the waking people by Tamasa's limpid wave,
Saw not Rama and his consort, saw not Lakshman young and brave,

And the tear suffused their faces and their hearts with anguish burned,
Sorrow-laden and lamenting to their cheerless homes returned.

VI

CROSSING THE GANGES. BHARAD-VAJA'S HERMITAGE

Morning dawned, and far they wandered, by their people loved and
  lost,
Drove through grove and flowering woodland, rippling rill and river
  crost,

Crossed the sacred Vedasruti on their still unending way,
Crossed the deep and rapid Gumti where the herds of cattle stray,

All the toilsome day they travelled, evening fell o'er wood and lea,
And they came where sea-like Ganga rolls in regal majesty,

'Neath a tall Ingudi's shadow by the river's zephyrs blest,
Second night of Rama's exile passed in sleep and gentle rest.

Morning dawned, the royal chariot Rama would no further own,
Sent Sumantra and the coursers back to fair Ayodhya's town,

Doffing then their royal garments Rama and his brother bold
Coats of bark and matted tresses wore like anchorites of old.

Guha, chief of wild Nishadas, boat and needed succour gave,
And the princes and fair Sita ventured on the sacred wave.

And by royal Rama bidden strong Nishadas plied the oar,
And the strong boat quickly bounding left fair Ganga's northern shore.

" Goddess of the mighty Ganga ! " so the pious Sita prayed,
" Exiled by his father's mandate, Rama seeks the forest shade,

Ganga ! o'er the three worlds rolling, bride and empress of the sea,
And from BRAHMA's sphere descended ! banished Sita bows to thee.

May my lord return in safety, and a thousand fattened kine,
Gold and gifts and gorgeous garments, pure libations shall be thine,

And with flesh and corn I worship unseen dwellers on thy shore,
May my lord return in safety, fourteen years of exile o'er ! "

On the southern shore they journeyed through the long and weary day,
Still through grove and flowering woodland held their long and weary
    way,

And they slayed the deer of jungle and they spread their rich repast,
Third night of the princes' exile underneath a tree was past.

Morning dawned, the soft-eyed Sita wandered with the princes brave,
To the spot where ruddy Ganga mingles with dark Jumna's wave,

And they crost the shady woodland, verdant lawn and grassy mead,
Till the sun was in its zenith, Rama then to Lakshman said :

" Yonder mark the famed Prayaga, spot revered from age to age,
And the line of smoke ascending speaks some *rishi's* hermitage,

There the waves of ruddy Ganga with the dark blue Jumna meet,
And my ear the sea-like voices of the mingling waters greet.

Mark the monarchs of the forest severed by the hermit's might,
And the logs of wood and fuel for the sacrificial rite,

Mark the tall trees in their blossom and the peaceful shady grove,
There the sages make their dwelling, thither, Lakshman, let us rove."

Slowly came the exile-wand'rers, when the sun withdrew his rays,
Where the vast and sea-like rivers met in sisters' sweet embrace,

And the *asram's* peaceful dwellers, bird of song and spotted deer,
Quaked to see the princely strangers in their warlike garb appear !

Rama stepped with valiant Lakshman, gentle Sita followed close,
Till behind the screening foliage hermits' peaceful dwellings rose,

And they came to Bharad-vaja, anchorite and holy saint,
Girt by true and faithful pupils on his sacred duty bent.

Famed for rites and lofty penance was the anchorite of yore,
Blest with more than mortal vision, deep in more than mortal lore,

And he sat beside the altar for the *agni-hotra* rite,
Rama spake in humble accents to the man of holy might :

" We are sons of Dasa-ratha and to thee our homage bring,
With my wife, the saintly Sita, daughter of Videha's king,

Exiled by my royal father in the wilderness I roam,
And my wife and faithful brother make the pathless woods their
  home,

We would through these years of exile in some holy *asram* dwell,
And our food shall be the wild fruit and our drink from crystal well,

We would practise pious penance still on sacred rites intent,
Till our souls be filled with wisdom and our years of exile spent ! "

Pleased the ancient Bharad-vaja heard the prince's humble tale,
And with kind and courteous welcome royal strangers greeted well,

And he brought the milk and *arghya* where the guests observant stood,
Crystal water from the fountain, berries from the darksome wood,

And a low and leafy cottage for their dwelling-place assigned,
As a host receives a stranger, welcomed them with offerings kind.

In the *asram's* peaceful courtyard fearless browsed the jungle deer,
All unharmed the bird of forest pecked the grain collected near,

And by holy men surrounded 'neath the trees' umbrageous shade,
In his pure and peaceful accents *rishi* Bharad-vaja said :

" Not unknown or unexpected, princely strangers, have ye come,
I have heard of sinless Rama's causeless banishment from home,

Welcome to a hermit's forest, be this spot your place of rest,
Where the meeting of the rivers makes our sacred *asram* blest,

Live amidst these peaceful woodlands, still on sacred rites intent
Till your souls be filled with wisdom and your years of exile spent ! "

" Gracious are thy accents, *rishi*," Rama answered thus the sage,
" But fair towns and peopled hamlets border on this hermitage,

And to see the banished Sita and to see us, much I fear,
Crowds of rustics oft will trespass on thy calm devotions here,

Far from towns and peopled hamlets, grant us, *rishi*, in thy grace,
Some wild spot where hid in jungle we may pass these years in peace."

" Twenty miles from this Prayaga," spake the *rishi* pond'ring well,
" Is a lonely hill and jungle where some ancient hermits dwell,

Chitra-kuta, Peak of Beauty, where the forest creatures stray,
And in every bush and thicket herds of lightsome monkeys play,

Men who view its towering summit are on lofty thoughts inclined,
Earthly pride nor earthly passions cloud their pure and peaceful mind,

Hoary-headed ancient hermits, hundred autumns who have done,
By their faith and lofty penance heaven's eternal bliss have won,

Holy is the fair seclusion for thy purpose suited well,
Or if still thy heart inclineth, here in peace and comfort dwell ! "

Spake the *rishi* Bharad-vaja, and with every courteous rite,
Cheered his guests with varied converse till the silent hours of night,

Fourth night of the princes' exile in Prayaga's hermitage,
Passed the brothers and fair Sita honoured by Prayaga's Sage.

VII

CROSSING THE JUMNA—VALMIKI'S HERMITAGE

Morning dawned, and faithful Sita with the brothers held her way,
Where the dark and eddying waters of the sacred Jumna stray,

Pondering by the rapid river long the thoughtful brothers stood,
Then with stalwart arms and axes felled the sturdy jungle wood,

Usira of strongest fibre, slender bamboo smooth and plain,
Jambu branches intertwining with the bent and twisting cane,

And a mighty raft constructed, and with creepers scented sweet,
Lakshman for the gentle Sita made a soft and pleasant seat.

Then the rustic bark was floated, framed with skill of woodman's craft,
By her loving lord supported Sita stepped upon the raft,

And her raiments and apparel Rama by his consort laid,
And the axes and the deerskins, bow and dart and shining blade,

Then with stalwart arms the brothers plied the bending bamboo oar,
And the strong raft gaily bounding left for Jumna's southern shore.

" Goddess of the glorious Jumna ! " so the pious Sita prayed,
" Peaceful be my husband's exile in the forest's darksome shade,

May he safely reach Ayodhya, and a thousand fattened kine,
Hundred jars of sweet libation, mighty Jumna, shall be thine,

Grant that from the woods returning he may see his home again,
Grant that honoured by his kinsmen he may rule his loving men ! "

On her breast her arms she folded while the princes plied the oar,
And the bright bark bravely bounding reached the wooded southern
    shore.

And the wanderers from Ayodhya on the river's margin stood,
Where the unknown realm extended mantled by unending wood,

Gallant Lakshman with his weapons went before the path to clear,
Soft-eyed Sita followed gently, Rama followed in the rear.

Oft from tree and darksome jungle, Lakshman ever true and brave,
Plucked the fruit or smiling blossom and to gentle Sita gave,

Oft to Rama turned his consort, pleased and curious evermore,
Asked the name of tree or creeper, fruit or flower unseen before.

Still with brotherly affection Lakshman brought each dewy spray,
Bud or blossom of wild beauty from the woodland bright and gay,

Still with eager joy and pleasure Sita turned her eye once more,
Where the tuneful swans and *saras* flocked on Jumna's sandy shore.

Two miles thus they walked and wandered and the belt of forest
    passed,
Slew the wild deer of the jungle, spread on leaves their rich repast,

Peacocks flew around them gaily, monkeys leaped on branches bent,
Fifth night of their endless wanderings in the forest thus they spent.

" Wake, my love, and list the warblings and the voices of the wood,"
Thus spake Rama when the morning on the eastern mountains stood,

Sita woke and gallant Lakshman, and they sipped the sacred wave,
To the hill of Chitra-kuta held their way serene and brave.

" Mark, my love," so Rama uttered, "every bush and tree and flower,
Tinged by radiant light of morning sparkles in a golden shower,

Mark the flaming flower of *Kinsuk* and the *Vilwa* in its pride,
Luscious fruits in wild profusion ample store of food provide,

Mark the honeycombs suspended from each tall and stately tree,
How from every virgin blossom steals her store the faithless bee !

Oft the lone and startled wild cock sounds its clarion full and clear,
And from flowering fragrant forests peacocks send the answering
    cheer,

Oft the elephant of jungle ranges in this darksome wood,
For yon peak is Chitra-kuta loved by saints and hermits good,

Oft the chanted songs of hermits echo through its sacred grove,
Peaceful on its shady uplands, Sita, we shall live and rove ! "

Gently thus the princes wandered through the fair and woodland scene,
Fruits and blossoms lit the branches, feathered songsters filled the
    green,

Anchorites and ancient hermits lived in every sylvan grove,
And a sweet and sacred stillness filled the woods with peace and love !

Gently thus the princes wandered to the holy hermitage,
Where in lofty contemplation lived the mighty Saint and Sage,

Heaven inspired thy song, Valmiki !   Ancient Bard of ancient day,
Deeds of virtue and of valour live in thy undying lay !

And the Bard received the princes with a father's greetings kind,
Bade them live in Chitra-kuta with a pure and peaceful mind,

To the true and faithful Lakshman, Rama then his purpose said,
And of leaf and forest timber Lakshman soon a cottage made.

" So our sacred *Sastras* sanction," thus the righteous Rama spake,
" Holy offering we should render when our dwelling-home we make,

Slay the black buck, gallant Lakshman, and a sacrifice prepare,
For the moment is auspicious and the day is bright and fair."

Lakshman slew a mighty black-buck, with the antlered trophy came,
Placed the carcass consecrated by the altar's blazing flame,

Radiant round the mighty offering tongues of red fire curling shone,
And the buck was duly roasted and the tender meat was done.

Pure from bath, with sacred *mantra* Rama did the holy rite,
And invoked the bright Immortals for to bless the dwelling site,

To the kindly VISWA-DEVAS, and to RUDRA fierce and strong,
And to VISHNU Lord of Creatures, Rama raised the sacred song.

Righteous rite was duly rendered for the forest-dwelling made,
And with true and deep devotion was the sacred *mantra* prayed,

And the worship of the Bright Ones purified each earthly stain,
Pure-souled Rama raised the altar and the *chaitya's* sacred fane.

Evening spread its holy stillness, bush and tree its magic felt,
As the Gods in BRAHMA'S mansions, exiles in their cottage dwelt,

In the woods of Chitra-kuta where the Malyavati flows,
Sixth day of their weary wand'rings ended in a sweet repose.

VIII

TALE OF THE HERMIT'S SON

Wise Sumantra chariot-driver came from Ganga's sacred wave,
And unto Ayodhya's monarch, banished Rama's message gave,

Dasa-ratha's heart was shadowed by the deepening shade of night,
As the darkness of the eclipse glooms the sun's meridian light !

On the sixth night,—when his Rama slept in Chitra-kuta's bower,—
Memory of an ancient sorrow flung on him its fatal power,

Of an ancient crime and anguish, unforgotten, dark and dread,
Through the lapse of years and seasons casting back its death-like
    shade !

And the gloom of midnight deepened, Dasa-ratha sinking fast,
To Kausalya sad and sorrowing spake his memories of the past :

" Deeds we do in life, Kausalya, be they bitter, be they sweet,
Bring their fruit and retribution, rich reward or suffering meet.

Heedless child is he, Kausalya, in his fate who doth not scan
Retribution of his *karma*, sequence of a mighty plan !

Oft in madness and in folly we destroy the mango grove,
Plant the gorgeous gay *palasa* for the red flower that we love,

Fruitless as the red *palasa* is the *karma* I have sown,
And my barren lifetime withers through the deed which is my own !

Listen to my tale, Kausalya, in my days of youth renowned,
I was called a *sabda-bedhi*, archer prince who shot by sound,

I could hit the unseen target, by the sound my aim could tell,—
Blindly drinks a child the poison, blindly in my pride I fell !

I was then my father's Regent, thou a maid to me unknown,
Hunting by the fair Sarayu in my car I drove alone,

Buffalo or jungle tusker might frequent the river's brink,
Nimble deer or watchful tiger stealing for his nightly drink,

Stalking with a hunter's patience, loitering in the forests drear,
Sound of something in the water struck my keen and listening ear,

In the dark I stood and listened, some wild beast the water drunk,
'Tis some elephant, I pondered, lifting water with its trunk.

I was called a *sabda-bedhi*, archer prince who shot by sound,
On the unseen fancied tusker dealt a sure and deadly wound,

Ah ! too deadly was my arrow and like hissing cobra fell,
On my startled ear and bosom smote a voice of human wail,

Dying voice of lamentation rose upon the midnight high,
Till my weapons fell in tremor and a darkness dimmed my eye !

Hastening with a nameless terror soon I reached Sarayu's shore,
Saw a boy with hermit's tresses, and his pitcher lay before,

Weltering in a pool of red blood, lying on a gory bed,
Feebly raised his voice the hermit, and in dying accents said :

' What offence, O mighty monarch, all-unknowing have I done,
That with quick and kingly justice slayest thus a hermit's son ?

Old and feeble are my parents, sightless by the will of fate,
Thirsty in their humble cottage for their duteous boy they wait,

And thy shaft that kills me, monarch, bids my ancient parents die,
Helpless, friendless, they will perish, in their anguish deep and high !

Sacred lore and lifelong penance change not mortal's earthly state,
Wherefore else they sit unconscious when their son is doomed by fate,

Or if conscious of my danger, could they dying breath recall,
Can the tall tree save the sapling doomed by woodman's axe to fall ?

Hasten to my parents, monarch, soothe their sorrow and their ire,
For the tears of good and righteous wither like the forest fire,

Short the pathway to the *asram*, soon the cottage thou shalt see,
Soothe their anger by entreaty, ask their grace and pardon free !

But before thou goest, monarch, take, O take thy torturing dart,
For it rankles in my bosom with a cruel burning smart,

And it eats into my young life as the river's rolling tide
By the rains of summer swollen eats into its yielding side.'

Writhing in his pain and anguish thus the wounded hermit cried,
And I drew the fatal arrow, and the holy hermit died !

Darkly fell the thickening shadows, stars their feeble radiance lent,
As I filled the hermit's pitcher, to his sightless parents went,

Darkly fell the moonless midnight, deeper gloom my bosom rent,
As with faint and falt'ring footsteps to the hermits slow I went.

Like two birds bereft of plumage, void of strength, deprived of flight,
Were the stricken ancient hermits, friendless, helpless, void of sight,

Lisping in their feeble accents still they whispered of their child,
Of the stainless boy whose red blood Dasa-ratha's hands defiled !

And the father heard my footsteps, spake in accents soft and kind :
' Come, my son, to waiting parents, wherefore dost thou stay behind,

Sporting in the rippling water didst thou midnight's hour beguile,
But thy faint and thirsting mother anxious waits for thee the while,

Hath my heedless word or utterance caused thy boyish bosom smart,
But a feeble father's failings may not wound thy filial heart,

Help of helpless, sight of sightless, and thy parents' life and joy,
Wherefore art thou mute and voiceless, speak, my brave and beauteous
    boy ! '

Thus the sightless father welcomed cruel slayer of his son,
And an anguish tore my bosom for the action I had done,

Scarce upon the sonless parents could I lift my aching eye,
Scarce in faint and faltering accents to the father make reply,

For a tremor shook my person and my spirit sank in dread,
Straining all my utmost prowess, thus in quavering voice I said :

' Not thy son, O holy hermit, but a Kshatra warrior born,
Dasa-ratha stands before thee by a cruel anguish torn,

For I came to slay the tusker by Sarayu's wooded brink,
Buffalo or deer of jungle stealing for his midnight drink,

And I heard a distant gurgle, some wild beast the water drunk,—
So I thought,—some jungle tusker lifting water with its trunk,

And I sent my fatal arrow on the unknown, unseen prey,
Speeding to the spot I witnessed,—there a dying hermit lay !

From his pierced and quivering bosom then the cruel dart I drew,
And he sorrowed for his parents as his spirit heavenward flew,

Thus unconscious, holy father, I have slayed thy stainless son,
Speak my penance, or in mercy pardon deed unknowing done ! '

Slow and sadly by their bidding to the fatal spot I led,
Long and loud bewailed the parents by the cold unconscious dead,

And with hymns and holy water they performed the funeral rite,
Then with tears that burnt and withered, spake the hermit in his
    might :

' *Sorrow for a son beloved is a father's direst woe,*
Sorrow for a son beloved, Dasa-ratha, thou shalt know !

See the parents weep and perish, grieving for a slaughtered son,
Thou shalt weep and thou shalt perish for a loved and righteous son !

Distant is the expiation,—but in fulness of the time,
Dasa-ratha's death in anguish cleanses Dasa-ratha's crime ! '

Spake the old and sightless prophet ; then he made the funeral pyre,
And the father and the mother perished in the lighted fire,

Years have gone and many seasons, and in fulness of the time,
Comes the fruit of pride and folly and the harvest of my crime !

Rama eldest born and dearest, Lakshman true and faithful son,
Ah ! forgive a dying father and a cruel action done,

Queen Kaikeyi, thou hast heedless brought on Raghu's race this stain,
Banished are the guiltless children and thy lord and king is slain !

Lay thy hands on mine, Kausalya, wipe thy unavailing tear,
Speak a wife's consoling accents to a dying husband's ear,

Lay thy hands on mine, Sumitra, vision falls my closing eyes,
And for brave and banished Rama wings my spirit to the skies !

Hushed and silent passed the midnight, feebly still the monarch sighed,
Blessed Kausalya and Sumitra, blest his banished sons, and died.

BOOK IV

RAMA-BHARATA-SAMBADA

(*The Meeting of the Princes*)

THE scene of this Book is laid at Chitra-kuta. Bharat returning from the kingdom of the Kaikeyas heard of his father's
death and his brother's exile, and refused the throne which had
been reserved for him. He wandered through the woods and
jungle to Chitra-kuta, and implored Rama to return to Ayodhya
and seat himself on the throne of his father. But Rama had given
his word, and would not withdraw from it.

Few passages in the Epic are more impressive than Rama's wise
and kindly advice to Bharat on the duties of a ruler, and his firm
refusal to Bharat's passionate appeal to seat himself on the throne.
Equally touching is the lament of Queen Kausalya when she meets
Sita in the dress of an anchorite in the forest.

But one of the most curious passages in the whole Epic is the
speech of Jabali the Sceptic, who denied heaven and a world hereafter. In ancient India as in ancient Greece there were different
schools of philosophers, some of them orthodox and some of them
extremely heterodox, and the greatest latitude of free thought was
permitted. In Jabali, the poet depicts a free-thinker of the broad-
est type. He ridicules the ideas of Duty and of Future Life with a
force of reasoning which a Greek sophist and philosopher could not
have surpassed. But Rama answers with the fervour of a righteous,
truth-loving, God-fearing man.

All persuasion was in vain, and Bharat returned to Ayodhya
with Rama's sandals, and placed them on the throne, as an emblem
of Rama's sovereignty during his voluntary exile. Rama himself
then left Chitra-kuta and sought the deeper forests of Dandak, so
that his friends and relations might not find him again during his
exile. He visited the hermitage of the Saint Atri; and the ancient
and venerable wife of Atri welcomed the young Sita, and robed her
in rich raiments and jewels, on the eve of her departure for the un-
explored wildernesses of the south.

The portions translated in this Book are the whole or the main
portions of Sections xcix., c., ci., civ., cviii., cix., cxii., and
cxix. of Book ii. of the original text.

I

THE MEETING OF THE BROTHERS

Sorrowing for his sire departed Bharat to Ayodhya came,
But the exile of his brother stung his noble heart to flame,

Scorning sin-polluted empire, travelling with each widowed queen,
Sought through wood and trackless jungle Chitra-kuta's peaceful
scene.

Royal guards and Saint Vasishtha loitered with the dames behind,
Onward pressed the eager Bharat, Rama's hermit-home to find,

Nestled in a jungle thicket, Rama's cottage rose in sight,
Thatched with leaves and twining branches, reared by Lakshman's
faithful might.

Faggots hewn of gnarléd branches, blossoms culled from bush and
tree,
Coats of bark and russet garments, *kusa* spread upon the lea,

Store of horns and branching antlers, fire-wood for the dewy night,—
Spake the dwelling of a hermit suited for a hermit's rite.

" May the scene," so Bharat uttered, " by the righteous *rishi* told,
Markalvati's rippling waters, Chitra-kuta's summit bold,

Mark the dark and trackless forest where the untamed tuskers roam,
And the deep and hollow caverns where the wild beasts make their
home,

Mark the spacious wooded uplands, wreaths of smoke obscure the
sky,
Hermits feed their flaming altars for their worship pure and high.

Done our weary work and wand'ring, righteous Rama here we meet,
Saint and king and honoured elder !   Bharat bows unto his feet,

Born a king of many nations, he hath forest refuge sought,
Yielded throne and mighty kingdom for a hermit's humble cot,

Honour unto righteous Rama, unto Sita true and bold,
Theirs be fair Kosala's empire, crown and sceptre, wealth and gold!"

Stately *Sal* and feathered palm-tree on the cottage lent their shade,
Strewn upon the sacred altar was the grass of *kusa* spread,

Gaily on the walls suspended hung two bows of ample height,
And their back with gold was pencilled, bright as INDRA'S bow of
   might,

Cased in broad unfailing quivers arrows shone like light of day,
And like flame-tongued fiery serpents cast a dread and lurid ray,

Resting in their golden scabbards lay the sword of warriors bold,
And the targets broad and ample bossed with rings of yellow gold,

Glove and gauntlet decked the cottage safe from fear of hostile men,
As from creatures of the forest is the lion's lordly den !

Calm in silent contemplation by the altar's sacred fire,
Holy in his pious purpose though begirt by weapons dire,

Clad in deer-skin pure and peaceful, poring on the sacred flame,
In his bark and hermit's tresses like an anchorite of fame,

Lion-shouldered, mighty-arméd, but with gentle lotus eye,
Lord of wide earth ocean-girdled, but intent on penance high,

Godlike as the holy BRAHMA, on a skin of dappled deer
Rama sat with meek-eyed Sita, faithful Lakshman loitered near !

" Is this he whom joyous nations called to fair Ayodhya's throne,
Now the friend of forest-rangers wandering in the woods alone,

Is this he who robed in purple made Ayodhya's mansions bright,
Now in jungle bark and deer-skin clad as holy anchorite,

Is this he whose wreathéd ringlets fresh and holy fragrance shed,
Now a hermit's matted tresses cluster round his royal head,

Is this he whose royal *yajnas* filled the earth with righteous fame,
Now inured to hermit's labour by the altar's sacred flame,

Is this he whose brow and forehead royal gem and jewel graced,
Heir to proud Kosala's empire, eldest, noblest, and the best ? "

Thus lamented pious Bharat, for his heart was anguish-rent,
As before the feet of Rama he in loving homage bent,

" *Arya !* " in his choking accents this was all that Bharat said,
" *Arya !* " spake the young Satrughna and he bent his holy head !

Rama to his loving bosom raised his brothers from his feet,
Ah, too deep is love for utterance when divided brothers meet,

Faithful Guha, brave Sumantra, bowed to Rama's righteous feet,
And a joy and mingled sadness filled the hermit's calm retreat !

II

BHARAT'S ENTREATY AND RAMA'S REPLY

"Speak, my true, my faithful Bharat," so the righteous Rama cried,
" Wherefore to this jungle dwelling hast thou from Ayodhya hied,

Speak, my fond and loving brother, if our father bade thee come,
Leaving throne and spacious empire in this wilderness to roam ?

Heir and Regent of Kosala ! Dost thou tend our father well,
And obey the lofty mandate from his royal lips that fell,

And the ancient Dasa-ratha, glorious still in regal might,
Doth he pass his bright life's evening in each pure and holy rite ?

Doth my mother, Queen Kausalya, still for Rama wet her eye,
And the gentle Queen Sumitra for her banished Lakshman sigh,

Doth the peerless Queen Kaikeyi pass her days in duties fair,
Guard her Bharat's mighty empire, tend him with a mother's care ?

Is each holy rite and homage to the Gods and Fathers done,
Is the honour due to elders rendered by each duteous son,

Do thy warriors guard thy kingdom as of yore with matchless skill,
And with counsel deep and duteous do thy min'sters serve thy will ?

Rich thy fields in corn and produce fed by rivers broad and deep,
Rich thy green unending pastures with the kine and fattened sheep,

Tend the herdsman and his cattle, tend the tiller of the soil,
Watch and help with all thy bounty workmen in their peaceful toil,

For the monarch's highest duty is to serve his people's weal
And the ruler's richest glory is to labour and to heal !

Guard thy forts with sleepless caution with the engines of the war,
With the men who shoot the arrow and who drive the flying car,

Guard Kosala's royal treasure, make thy gifts of wealth and food,
Not to lords and proud retainers, but to worthy and the good !

Render justice pure and spotless as befits thy royal line,
And to save the good and guiltless, Bharat, be it ever thine,

For the tears of suffering virtue wither like the thunder levin,
And they slay our men and cattle like the wrath of righteous heaven,

Fruitful be thy lore of Veda, fruitful be each pious rite,
Be thy queen a fruitful mother, be thy empire full of might ! "

Weeping, weeping, Bharat answered Dasa-ratha's eldest son,
" Dasa-ratha walks the bright sky, for his earthly task is done !

For impelled by Queen Kaikeyi to the woods he bade thee go,
And his spotless fame was clouded and his bosom sank in woe,

And my mother, late repenting, weeps her deed of deepest shame,
Weeps her wedded lord departed, and a woman's tarnished fame !

Thou alone canst wipe this insult by a deed of kindness done,—
Rule o'er Dasa-ratha's empire, Dasa-ratha's eldest son,

Weeping queens and loyal subjects supplicate thy noble grace,—
Rule o'er Raghu's ancient empire, son of Raghu's royal race !

For our ancient Law ordaineth and thy Duty makes it plain,
Eldest-born succeeds his father as the king of earth and main,

By the fair Earth loved and welcomed, Rama, be her wedded lord,
As by planet-jewelled Midnight is the radiant Moon adored !

And thy father's ancient min'sters and thy courtiers faithful still,
Wait to do thy righteous mandate and to serve thy royal will,

As a pupil, as a brother, as a slave, I seek thy grace,—
Come and rule thy father's empire, king of Raghu's royal race ! "

Weeping, on the feet of Rama, Bharat placed his lowly head,
Weeping for his sire departed, tears of sorrow Rama shed,

Then he raised his loving brother with an elder's deathless love,
Sorrow wakes our deepest kindness and our holiest feelings prove !

" But I may not," answered Rama, "seek Ayodhya's ancient throne,
For a righteous father's mandate duteous son may not disown,

And I may not, gentle brother, break the word of promise given,
To a king and to a father who is now a saint in heaven !

Not on thee, nor on thy mother, rests the censure or the blame,
Faithful to his father's wishes Rama to the forest came,

For the son and duteous consort serve the father and the lord,
Higher than an empire's glory is a father's spoken word !

All inviolate is his mandate,—on Ayodhya's jewelled throne,
Or in pathless woods and jungle Rama shall his duty own,

All inviolate is the blessing by a loving mother given,
For she blessed my life in exile like a pitying saint of heaven !

Thou shalt rule the kingdom, Bharat, guard our loving people well,
Clad in wild bark and in deer-skin I shall in the forests dwell,

So spake saintly Dasa-ratha in Ayodhya's palace hall,
And a righteous father's mandate duteous son may not recall ! "

III

KAUSALYA'S LAMENT AND RAMA'S REPLY

Slow and sad with Saint Vasishtha, with each widowed royal dame,
Unto Rama's hermit-cottage ancient Queen Kausalya came,

And she saw him clad in wild bark like a hermit stern and high,
And an anguish smote her bosom and a tear bedewed her eye.

Rama bowed unto his mother and each elder's blessings sought,
Held their feet in salutation with a holy reverence fraught,

And the queens with loving fingers, with a mother's tender care,
Swept the dust of wood and jungle from his head and bosom fair,

Lakshman too in loving homage bent before each royal dame,
And they blessed the faithful hero spotless in his righteous fame.

Lastly came the soft-eyed Sita with obeisance soft and sweet,
And with hands in meekness folded bent her tresses to their feet,

Pain and anguish smote their bosoms, round their Sita as they prest,
As a mother clasps a daughter, clasped her in their loving breast !

Torn from royal hall and mansions, ranger of the darksome wood,
Reft of home and kith and kindred by her forest hut she stood !

" Hast thou, daughter of Videha," weeping thus Kausalya said,
" Dwelt in woods and leafy cottage and in pathless jungle strayed,

Hast thou, Rama's royal consort, lived a homeless anchorite,
Pale with rigid fast and penance, worn with toil of righteous rite ?

But thy sweet face, gentle Sita, is like faded lotus dry,
And like lily parched by sunlight, lustreless thy beauteous eye,

Like the gold untimely tarnished is thy sorrow-shaded brow,
Like the moon by shadows darkened is thy form of beauty now !

And an anguish scathes my bosom like the withering forest fire,
Thus to see thee, duteous daughter, in misfortunes deep and dire,

Dark is wide Kosala's empire, dark is Raghu's royal house,
When in woods my Rama wanders and my Rama's royal spouse ! ''

Sweetly, gentle Sita answered, answered Rama fair and tall,
That a righteous father's mandate duteous son may not recall !

IV

JABALI'S REASONING AND RAMA'S REPLY

Jabali a learned Brahman and a Sophist skilled in word,
Questioned Faith and Law and Duty, spake to young Ayodhya's
    lord:

"Wherefore, Rama, idle maxims cloud thy heart and warp thy mind,
Maxims which mislead the simple and the thoughtless human kind ?

Love nor friendship doth a mortal to his kith or kindred own,
Entering on his wide earth friendless, and departing all alone,

Foolishly upon the father and the mother dotes the son,
Kinship is an idle fancy,—save thyself thy kith is none !

In the wayside inn he halteth who in distant lands doth roam,
Leaves it with the dawning daylight for another transient home,

Thus on earth are kin and kindred, home and country, wealth and
    store,
We but meet them on our journey, leave them as we pass before !

Wherefore for a father's mandate leave thy empire and thy throne,
Pass thy days in trackless jungle sacrificing all thy own,

Wherefore to Ayodhya's city, as to longing wife's embrace,
Speed'st thou not to rule thy empire, lord of Raghu's royal race ?

Dasa-ratha claims no duty, and this will is empty word,
View him as a foreign monarch, of thy realm thou art the lord,

Dasa-ratha is departed, gone where all the mortals go,
For a dead man's idle mandate wherefore lead this life of woe ?

Ah ! I weep for erring mortals who on erring duty bent
Sacrifice their dear enjoyment till their barren life is spent,

Who to Gods and to the Fathers vainly still their offerings make,
Waste of food ! for God nor Father doth our pious homage take !

And the food by one partaken, can it nourish other men,
Food bestowed upon a Brahman, can it serve our Fathers then ?

Crafty priests have forged these maxims and with selfish objects say,
Make thy gifts and do thy penance, leave thy worldly wealth and
    pray !

There is no Hereafter, Rama, vain the hope and creed of men,
Seek the pleasures of the present, spurn illusions poor and vain,

Take the course of sense and wisdom, cast all idle faith aside,
Take the kingdom Bharat offers, rule Ayodhya in thy pride ! "

" Fair thy purpose," answered Rama, " false thy reason leads astray,
Tortuous wisdom brings no profit, virtue shuns the crooked way,

For the deed proclaims the hero from the man of spacious lies,
Marks the true and upright *Arya* from the scheming worldly-wise !

If assuming virtue's mantle I should seek the sinful path,
Gods who judge our secret motives curse me with their deepest
    wrath,

And thy counsel helps not, *rishi*, mansions of the sky to win,
And a king his subjects follow adding deeper sin to sin !

Sweep aside thy crafty reasoning, Truth is still our ancient way,
Truth sustains the earth and nations and a monarch's righteous
    sway,

Mighty Gods and holy sages find in Truth their haven shore,
Scorning death and dark destruction, Truth survives for evermore !

Deadlier than the serpent's venom is the venom of a lie,
From the false, than from the cobra, men with deeper terror fly,

Dearer than the food to mortals, Truth as nourishment is given,
Truth sustains the wide creation, Truth upholds the highest heaven,

Vain were gifts and sacrifices, rigid penances were vain,
Profitless the holy *Vedas* but for Truth which they sustain,

Gifts and rites and rigid penance have no aim or purpose high,
Save in Truth which rules the wide earth and the regions of the sky !

I have plighted truth and promise and my word may not unsay,
Fourteen years in pathless forests father's mandate I obey,

And I seek no spacious reasons my relinquished throne to win,
Gods nor Fathers nor the *Vedas* counsel tortuous paths of sin !

Pardon, *rishi*, still unchanging shall remain my promise given
To my mother Queen Kaikeyi, to my father now in heaven,

Pardon, *rishi*, still in jungle we shall seek the forest fare,
Worship Gods who watch our actions, and pervade the earth and air !

Unto AGNI, unto VAYU, shall my constant prayers run,
I shall live like happy INDRA, hundred sacrifices done,

And the deep and darksome jungle shall be Rama's royal hall,
For a righteous father's mandate duteous son may not recall ! "

V

THE SANDALS

Tears nor sighs nor sad entreaty Rama's changeless purpose shook,
Till once more with hands conjoinéd Bharat to his elder spoke :

" Rama, true to royal mercy, true to duties of thy race,
Grant this favour to thy mother, to thy brother grant this grace,

Vain were my unaided efforts to protect our father's throne,
Town and hamlet, lord and tiller, turn to thee and thee alone !

Unto Rama, friends and kinsmen, chiefs and warriors, turn in pain,
And each city chief and elder, and each humble village swain,

Base thy empire strong, unshaken, on a loyal nation's will,
With thy worth and with thy valour serve thy faithful people still ! "

Rama raised the prostrate Bharat to his ever-loving breast,
And in voice of tuneful *hansa* thus his gentle speech addrest :

" Trust me, Bharat, lofty virtue, strength and will to thee belong,
Thou could'st rule a worldwide empire in thy faith and purpose
    strong,

And our father's ancient min'sters, ever faithful, wise and deep,
They shall help thee with their counsel and thy ancient frontiers keep.

List ! the Moon may lose his lustre, Himalaya lose his snow,
Heaving Ocean pass his confines surging from the caves below,

But the truth-abiding Rama will not move from promise given,
He hath spoke and will not palter, help him righteous Gods in
    heaven ! "

Blazing like the Sun in splendour, beauteous like the Lord of Night,
Rama vowed his Vow of Duty, changeless in his holy might !

" Humble token," answered Bharat, " still I seek from Rama's hand,
Token of his love and kindness, token of his high command,

From thy feet cast forth those sandals, they shall decorate the throne,
They shall nerve my heart to duty and shall safely guard thy own,

They shall to a loyal nation absent monarch's will proclaim,
Watch the frontiers of the empire and the people's homage claim ! "

Rama gave the loosened sandals as his younger humbly prayed,
Bharat bowed to them in homage and his parting purpose said :

" Not alone will banished Rama barks and matted tresses wear,
Fourteen years the crownéd Bharat will in hermit's dress appear,

Henceforth Bharat dwells in palace guised as hermit of the wood,
In the sumptuous hall of feasting wild fruit is his only food,

Fourteen years shall pass in waiting, weary toil and penance dire
Then, if Rama comes not living, Bharat dies upon the pyre ! "

VI

The Hermitage of Atri

With the sandals of his elder Bharat to Ayodhya went,
Rama sought for deeper forests on his arduous duty bent,

Wandering with his wife and Lakshman slowly sought the hermitage,
Where resided saintly Atri, Vedic Bard and ancient sage.

Anasuya, wife of Atri, votaress of Gods above,
Welcomed Sita in her cottage, tended her with mother's love,

Gave her robe and holy garland, jewelled ring and chain of gold,
Heard the tale of love and sadness which the soft-eyed Sita told :

How the monarch of Videha held the plough and tilled the earth,
From the furrow made by ploughshare infant Sita sprang to birth,

How the monarch of Videha welcomed kings of worth and pride,
Rama 'midst the gathered monarchs broke the bow and won the
    bride,

How by Queen Kaikeyi's mandate Rama lost his father's throne,
Sita followed him in exile in the forest dark and lone !

Softly from the lips of Sita words of joy and sorrow fell,
And the pure-souled pious priestess wept to hear the tender tale,

And she kissed her on the forehead, held her on her ancient breast,
And in mother's tender accents thus her gentle thoughts exprest :

" Sweet the tale you tell me, Sita, of thy wedding and thy love,
Of the true and tender Rama, righteous as the Gods above,

And thy wifely deep devotion fills my heart with purpose high,
Stay with us my gentle daughter for the night shades gather nigh.

Hastening from each distant region feathered songsters seek their
    nest,
Twitter in the leafy thickets ere they seek their nightly rest,

Hastening from their pure ablutions with their pitcher smooth and
    fair,
In their dripping barks the hermits to their evening rites repair,

And in sacred *agni-hotra* holy anchorites engage,
And a wreath of smoke ascending marks the altar of each sage.

Now a deeper shadow mantles bush and brake and trees around,
And a thick and inky darkness falls upon the distant ground,

Midnight prowlers of the jungle steal beneath the sable shade,
But the tame deer by the altar seeks his wonted nightly bed.

Mark ! how by the stars encircled sails the radiant Lord of Night,
With his train of silver glory streaming o'er the azure height,

And thy consort waits thee, Sita, but before thou leavest, fair,
Let me deck thy brow and bosom with these jewels rich and rare,

Old these eyes and grey these tresses, but a thrill of joy is mine,
Thus to see thy youth and beauty in this gorgeous garment shine !"

Pleased at heart the ancient priestess clad her in apparel meet,
And the young wife glad and grateful bowed to Anasuya's feet,

Robed and jewelled, bright and beauteous, sweet-eyed Sita softly
     came,
Where with anxious heart awaited Rama prince of righteous fame.

With a wifely love and longing Sita met her hero bold,
Anasuya's love and kindness in her grateful accents told,

Rama and his brother listened of the grace by Sita gained,
Favours of the ancient priestess, pious blessings she had rained.

In the *rishi's* peaceful *asram* Rama passed the sacred night,
In the hushed and silent forest silvered by the moon's pale light,

Daylight dawned, to deeper forests Rama went serene and proud,
As the sun in midday splendour sinks within a bank of cloud !

BOOK V

PANCHAVATI

(*On the Banks of the Godavari*)

THE wanderings of Rama in the Deccan, his meeting with Saint Agastya, and his residence on the banks of the Godavari river, are narrated in this Book. The reader has now left Northern India and crossed the Vindhya mountains ; and the scene of the present and succeeding five Books is laid in the Deccan and Southern India. The name of Agastya is connected with the Deccan, and many are the legends told of this great Saint, before whom the Vindhya mountains bent in awe, and by whose might the Southern ocean was drained. It is likely that some religious teacher of that name first penetrated beyond the Vindhyas, and founded the first Aryan settlement in the Deccan, three thousand years ago. He was pioneer, discoverer and settler,—the Indian Columbus who opened out Southern India to Aryan colonization and Aryan religion.

Two *yojanas* from Agastya's hermitage, Rama built his forest dwelling in the woods of Panchavati, near the sources of the Godavari river, and within a hundred miles from the modern city of Bombay. There he lived with his wife and brother in peace and piety, and the Book closes with the description of an Indian winter morning, when the brothers and Sita went for their ablutions to the Godavari, and thought of their distant home in Oudh. The description of the peaceful forest-life of the exiles comes in most appropriately on the eve of stirring events which immediately succeed, and which give a new turn to the story of the Epic. We now stand therefore at the turning point of the poet's narrative ; he has sung of domestic incidents and of peaceful hermitages so far ; he sings of dissensions and wars hereafter.

The portions translated in this Book form Sections i., xii., xiii., xv., and xvi. of Book iii. of the original text.

I

THE HERMITAGE OF AGASTYA

Righteous Rama, soft-eyed Sita, and the gallant Lakshman stood
In the wilderness of Dandak,—trackless, pathless, boundless wood,

But within its gloomy gorges, dark and deep and known to few,
Humble homes of hermit sages rose before the princes' view.

Coats of bark and scattered *kusa* spake their peaceful pure abode,
Seat of pious rite and penance which with holy splendour glowed,

Forest songsters knew the *asram* and the wild deer cropt its blade,
And the sweet-voiced sylvan wood-nymph haunted oft its holy
shade,

Brightly blazed the sacred altar, vase and ladle stood around,
Fruit and blossom, skin and faggot, sanctified the holy ground.

From the broad and bending branches ripening fruits in clusters
hung,
And with gifts and rich libations hermits raised the ancient song,

Lotus and the virgin lily danced upon the rippling rill,
And the golden sunlight glittered on the greenwoods calm and still,

And the consecrated woodland by the holy hermits trod,
Shone like BRAHMA's sky in lustre, hallowed by the grace of God !

Rama loosened there his bow-string and the peaceful scene surveyed,
And the holy sages welcomed wanderers in the forest shade,

Rama bright as Lord of Midnight, Sita with her saintly face,
Lakshman young and true and valiant, decked with warrior's peerless grace !

Leafy hut the holy sages to the royal guests assigned,
Brought them fruit and forest blossoms, blessed them with their
blessings kind,

" Raghu's son," thus spake the sages, " helper of each holy rite,
Portion of the royal INDRA, fount of justice and of might,

On thy throne or in the forest, king of nations, lord of men,
Grant us to thy kind protection in this hermit's lonely den ! "

Homely fare and jungle produce were before the princes laid,
And the toil-worn, tender Sita slumbered in the *asram's* shade.

Thus from grove to grove they wandered, to each haunt of holy sage,
Sarabhanga's sacred dwelling and Sutikshna's hermitage,

Till they met the Saint Agastya, mightiest Saint of olden time,
Harbinger of holy culture in the wilds of Southern clime !

" Eldest born of Dasa-ratha, long and far hath Rama strayed,"—
Thus to pupil of Agastya young and gallant Lakshman said,—

" With his faithful consort Sita in these wilds he wanders still,
I am righteous Rama's younger, duteous to his royal will,

And we pass these years of exile to our father's mandate true,
Fain to mighty Saint Agastya we would render homage due ! "

Listening to his words the hermit sought the shrine of Sacred Fire,
Spake the message of the princes to the Saint and ancient Sire :

" Righteous Rama, valiant Lakshman, saintly Sita seek this shade,
And to see thee, radiant *rishi*, have in humble accents prayed."

" Hath he come," so spake Agastya, " Rama prince of Raghu's race,
Youth for whom this heart hath thirsted, youth endued with
    righteous grace,

Hath he come with wife and brother to accept our greetings kind,
Wherefore came ye for permission, wherefore linger they behind ? "

Rama and the soft-eyed Sita were with gallant Lakshman led,
Where the dun deer free and fearless roamed within the holy shade,

Where the shrines of great Immortals stood in order thick and close,
And by bright and blazing altars chanted songs and hymns arose.

BRAHMA and the flaming AGNI, VISHNU lord of heavenly light,
INDRA and benign VIVASAT ruler of the azure height,

SOMA and the radiant BHAGA, and KUVERA lord of gold,
And VIDHATRI great Creator worshipped by the saints of old,

VAYU breath of living creatures, YAMA monarch of the dead,
And VARUNA with his fetters which the trembling sinners dread,

Holy Spirit of GAYATRI goddess of the morning prayer,
VASUS and the hooded NAGAS, golden-winged GARUDA fair,

KARTIKEYA heavenly leader strong to conquer and to bless,
DHARMA god of human duty and of human righteousness,

Shrines of all these bright Immortals ruling in the skies above,
Filled the pure and peaceful forest with a calm and holy love !

Girt by hermits righteous-hearted then the Saint Agastya came,
Rich in wealth of pious penance, rich in learning and in fame,

Mighty-arméd Rama marked him radiant like the midday sun,
Bowed and rendered due obeisance with each act of homage done,

Valiant Lakshman tall and stately to the great Agastya bent,
With a woman's soft devotion Sita bowed unto the saint.

Saint Agastya raised the princes, greeted them in accents sweet,
Gave them fruit and herb and water, offered them the honoured seat,

With libations unto AGNI offered welcome to each guest,
Food and drink beseeming hermits on the wearied princes pressed.

" False the hermits," spake Agastya, " who to guests their dues deny,
Hunger they in life hereafter—like the speaker of a lie.

And a royal guest and wanderer doth our foremost honour claim,
Car-borne kings protect the wide earth by their prowess and their
fame,

By these fruits and forest blossoms be our humble homage shewn,
By some gift, of Rama worthy, be Agastya's blessings known !

Take this bow, heroic Rama,—need for warlike arms is thine,—
Gems of more than earthly radiance on the goodly weapon shine,

Worshipper of righteous VISHNU ! VISHNU'S wondrous weapon take,
Heavenly artist VISWA-KARMAN shaped this bow of heavenly make !

Take this shining dart of BRAHMA radiant like a tongue of flame,
Sped by good and worthy archer never shall it miss its aim,

And this INDRA'S ample quiver filled with arrows true and keen,
Filled with arrows still unfailing in the battle's dreadful scene !

Take this sabre golden-hilted in its case of burnished gold,
Not unworthy of a monarch and a warrior true and bold,

Impious foes of bright Immortals know these weapons dread and dire,
Mowing down the ranks of foemen, scathing like the forest fire !

Be these weapons thy companions,—Rama, thou shalt need them oft,—
Meet and conquer still thy foemen like the Thunder-God aloft ! "

II

THE COUNSEL OF AGASTYA

" Pleased am I," so spake Agastya, " in these forests dark and wild,
Thou hast come to seek me, Rama, with the saintly Janak's child,

But like pale and drooping blossom severed from the parent tree,
Far from home in toil and trouble, faithful Sita follows thee,

True to wedded lord and husband she hath followed Raghu's son,
With a woman's deep devotion woman's duty she hath done !

How unlike the fickle woman, true while Fame and Fortune smile,
Faithless when misfortunes gather, loveless in her wicked wile,

How unlike the changeful woman, false as light the lightnings fling,
Keen as sabre, quick as tempest, swift as bird upon its wing !

Dead to Fortune's frown or favour, Sita still in truth abides,
As the star of Arundhati in her mansion still resides,

Rest thee with thy gentle consort, farther still she may not roam,
Holier were this hermit's forest as the saintly Sita's home ! "

" Great Agastya ! " answered Rama, " blesséd is my banished life,
For thy kindness to an exile and his friendless homeless wife,

But in wilder, gloomier forests lonesome we must wander still,
Where a deeper, darker shadow settles on the rock and rill."

" Be it so," Agastya answered, " two short *yojans* from this place,
Wild is Panchavati's forest where unseen the wild deer race,

Godavari's limpid waters through its gloomy gorges flow,
Fruit and root and luscious berries on its silent margin grow,

Seek that spot and with thy brother build a lonesome leafy home,
Tend thy true and toil-worn Sita, farther still she may not roam !

Not unknown to me the mandate by thy royal father given,
Not unseen thy endless wanderings destined by the will of Heaven,

Therefore Panchavati's forest marked I for thy woodland stay,
Where the ripening wild fruit clusters and the wild bird trills his lay,

Tend thy dear devoted Sita and protect each pious rite,
Matchless in thy warlike weapons peerless in thy princely might !

Mark yon gloomy *Mahua* forest stretching o'er the boundless lea,
Pass that wood and turning northward seek an old *Nyagrodha* tree,

Then ascend a sloping upland by a steep and lofty hill,
Thou shalt enter Panchavati, blossom-covered, calm and still ! "

Bowing to the great Agastya, Rama left the mighty sage,
Bowing to each saint and hermit, Lakshman left the hermitage,

And the princes tall and stately marched where Panchavati lay,
Soft-eyed Sita followed meekly where her Rama led the way !

III

The Forest of Panchavati

Godavari's limpid waters in her gloomy gorges strayed,
Unseen rangers of the jungle nestled in the darksome shade !

" Mark the woodlands," uttered Rama, " by the Saint Agastya told,
Panchavati's lonesome forest with its blossoms red and gold,

Skilled to scan the wood and jungle, Lakshman, cast thy eye around,
For our humble home and dwelling seek a low and level ground,

Where the river laves its margin with a soft and gentle kiss,
Where my sweet and soft-eyed Sita may repose in sylvan bliss,

Where the lawn is fresh and verdant and the *kusa* young and bright,
And the creeper yields her blossoms for our sacrificial rite."

" Little can I help thee, brother," did the duteous Lakshman say,
"Thou art prompt to judge and fathom, Lakshman listens to obey!"

" Mark this spot," so answered Rama, leading Lakshman by the
          hand,
" Soft the lawn of verdant *kusa*, beauteous blossoms light the land,

Mark the smiling lake of lotus gleaming with a radiance fair,
Wafting fresh and gentle fragrance o'er the rich and laden air,

Mark each scented shrub and creeper bending o'er the lucid wave,
Where the bank with soft caresses Godavari's waters lave !

Tuneful ducks frequent this margin, *Chakravakas* breathe of love,
And the timid deer of jungle browse within the shady grove,

And the valleys are resonant with the peacock's clarion cry,
And the trees with budding blossoms glitter on the mountains high,

And the rocks in well-marked strata in their glittering lines appear,
Like the streaks of white and crimson painted on our tuskers fair !

Stately *Sal* and feathered palm-tree guard this darksome forest-land,
Golden date and flowering mango stretch afar on either hand,

Asok thrives and blazing *Kinsuk*, *Chandan* wafts a fragrance rare,
Aswa-karna and *Khadira* by the *Sami* dark and fair,

Beauteous spot for hermit-dwelling joyous with the voice of song,
Haunted by the timid wild deer and by black buck fleet and strong ! "

Foe-compelling faithful Lakshman heard the words his elder said,
And by sturdy toil and labour stately home and dwelling made,

Spacious was the leafy cottage walled with moistened earth and soft,
Pillared with the stately bamboo holding high the roof aloft,

Interlacing twigs and branches, corded from the ridge to eaves,
Held the thatch of reed and branches and of jungle grass and leaves,

And the floor was pressed and levelled and the toilsome task was done,
And the structure rose in beauty for the righteous Raghu's son !

To the river for ablutions Lakshman went of warlike fame,
With a store of fragrant lotus and of luscious berries came,

Sacrificing to the Bright Gods sacred hymns and *mantras* said,
Proudly then unto his elder shewed the home his hand had made.

In her soft and grateful accents gentle Sita praised his skill,
Praised a brother's loving labour, praised a hero's dauntless will,

Rama clasped his faithful Lakshman in a brother's fond embrace,
Spake in sweet and kindly accents with an elder's loving grace :

" How can Rama, homeless wand'rer, priceless love like thine
    requite,
Let him hold thee in his bosom, soul of love and arm of might,

And our father good and gracious, in a righteous son like thee,
Lives again and treads the bright earth, from the bonds of YAMA
    free ! "

Thus spake Rama, and with Lakshman and with Sita child of love,
Dwelt in Panchavati's cottage as the Bright Gods dwell above !

IV

WINTER IN PANCHAVATI

Came and passed the golden autumn in the forest's gloomy shade,
And the northern blasts of winter swept along the silent glade,

When the chilly night was over, once at morn the prince of fame,
For his morning's pure ablutions to the Godavari came.

Meek-eyed Sita softly followed with the pitcher in her arms,
Gallant Lakshman spake to Rama of the Indian winter's charms :

" Comes the bright and bracing winter to the royal Rama dear,
Like a bride the beauteous season doth in richest robes appear,

Frosty air and freshening zephyrs wake to life each mart and plain,
And the corn in dewdrop sparkling makes a sea of waving green,

But the village maid and matron shun the freezing river's shore,
By the fire the village elder tells the stirring tale of yore !

With the winter's ample harvest men perform each pious rite,
To the Fathers long departed, to the Gods of holy might,

With the rite of *agrayana* pious men their sins dispel,
And with gay and sweet observance songs of love the women tell,

And the monarchs bent on conquest mark the winter's cloudless glow,
Lead their bannered cars and forces 'gainst the rival and the foe !

Southwards rolls the solar chariot, and the cold and widowed North
Reft of ' bridal mark ' and joyance coldly sighs her sorrows forth,

Southward rolls the solar chariot, Himalaya, ' home of snow,'
True to name and appellation doth in whiter garments glow,

Southward rolls the solar chariot, cold and crisp the frosty air,
And the wood of flower dismantled doth in russet robes appear !

Star of Pushya rules December and the night with rime is hoar,
And beneath the starry welkin in the woods we sleep no more,

And the pale moon mist-enshrouded sheds a faint and feeble beam,
As the breath obscures the mirror, winter mist obscures her gleam,

Hidden by the rising vapour faint she glistens on the dale,
Like our sun-embrownéd Sita with her toil and penance pale !

Sweeping blasts from western mountains through the gorges whistle
     by
And the *saras* and the curlew raise their shrill and piercing cry,

Boundless fields of wheat and barley are with dewdrops moist and
     wet,
And the golden rice of winter ripens like the clustering date,

Peopled marts and rural hamlets wake to life and cheerful toil,
And the peaceful happy nations prosper on their fertile soil !

Mark the sun in morning vapours—like the moon subdued and pale—
Brightening as the day advances piercing through the darksome veil,

Mark his gay and golden lustre sparkling o'er the dewy lea,
Mantling hill and field and forest, painting bush and leaf and tree,

Mark it glisten on the green grass, on each bright and bending blade,
Lighten up the long-drawn vista, shooting through the gloomy glade !

Thirst-impelled the lordly tusker still avoids the freezing drink,
Wild duck and the tuneful *hansa* doubtful watch the river's brink,

From the rivers wrapped in vapour unseen cries the wild curlew,
Unseen rolls the misty streamlet o'er its sandbank soaked in dew,

And the drooping water-lily bends her head beneath the frost,
Lost her fresh and fragrant beauty and her tender petals lost !

Now my errant fancy wanders to Ayodhya's distant town,
Where in hermit's barks and tresses Bharat wears the royal crown,

Scorning regal state and splendour, spurning pleasures loved of yore,
Spends his winter day in penance, sleeps at night upon the floor,

Aye ! perchance Sarayu's waters seeks he now, serene and brave,
As we seek, when dawns the daylight, Godavari's limpid wave !

Rich of hue, with eye of lotus, truthful, faithful, strong of mind,
For the love he bears thee, Rama, spurns each joy of baser kind,

' False he proves unto his father who is led by mother's wile,'—
Vain this ancient impious adage—Bharat spurns his mother's guile,

Bharat's mother Queen Kaikeyi, Dasa-ratha's royal spouse,
Deep in craft, hath brought disaster on Ayodhya's royal house ! "

" Speak not thus," so Rama answered, " on Kaikeyi cast no blame,
Honour still the righteous Bharat, honour still the royal dame,

Fixed in purpose and unchanging still in jungle wilds I roam,
But thy accents, gentle Lakshman, wake a longing for my home !

And my loving mem'ry lingers on each word from Bharat fell,
Sweeter than the draught of nectar, purer than the crystal well,

And my righteous purpose falters, shaken by a brother's love,
May we meet again our brother, if it please the Gods above ! "

Waked by love, a silent tear-drop fell on Godavari's wave,
True once more to righteous purpose Rama's heart was calm and
    brave,

Rama plunged into the river 'neath the morning's crimson beam,
Sita softly sought the waters as the lily seeks the stream,

And they prayed to Gods and Fathers with each rite and duty done,
And they sang the ancient *mantra* to the red and rising Sun,

With her lord, in loosened tresses Sita to her cottage came,
As with RUDRA wanders UMA in Kailasa's hill of fame !

BOOK VI

SITA-HARANA

(*Sita Lost*)

WE exchange the quiet life of Rama in holy hermitages for the more stirring incidents of the Epic in this Book. The love of a Raksha princess for Rama and for Lakshman is rejected with scorn, and smarting under insult and punishment she fires her brother Ravan, the king of Ceylon, with a thirst for vengeance. The dwellers of Ceylon are described in the Epic as monsters of various forms, and able to assume different shapes at will. Ravan sends Maricha in the shape of a beautiful deer to tempt away Rama and Lakshman from the cottage, and then finds his chance for stealing away the unprotected Sita.

The misfortunes of our lives, according to Indian thinkers, are but the results of our misdeeds ; calamities are brought about by our sins. And thus we find in the Indian Epic, that a dark and foul suspicion against Lakshman crossed the stainless mind of Sita, and words of unmerited insult fell from her gentle lips, on the eve of the great calamity which clouded her life ever after. It was the only occasion on which the ideal woman of the Epic harboured an unjust thought or spoke an angry word ; and it was followed by a tragic fate which few women on earth have suffered. To the millions of men and women in India, Sita remains to this day the ideal of female love and female devotion ; her dark suspicions against Lakshman sprang out of an excess of her affection for her husband ; and her tragic fate and long trial proved that undying love.

The portions translated in this Book form the whole or the main portions of Sections xvii., xviii., xliii., xlv., xlvi., xlvii., and xlix. of Book iii. of the original text.

I

SURPA-NAKHA IN LOVE

As the Moon with starry Chitra dwells in azure skies above,
In his lonesome leafy cottage Rama dwelt in Sita's love,

And with Lakshman strong and valiant, quick to labour and obey,
Tales of bygone times recounting Rama passed the livelong day.

And it so befell, a maiden, dweller of the darksome wood,
Led by wand'ring thought or fancy once before the cottage stood,

Surpa-nakha, Raksha maiden, sister of the Raksha lord,
Came and looked with eager longing till her soul was passion-stirred !

Looked on Rama lion-chested, mighty-arméd, lotus-eyed,
Stately as the jungle tusker, with his crown of tresses tied,

Looked on Rama lofty-fronted, with a royal visage graced,
Like KANDARPA young and lustrous, lotus-hued and lotus-faced !

What though she a Raksha maiden, poor in beauty plain in face,
Fell her glances passion-laden on the prince of peerless grace,

What though wild her eyes and tresses, and her accents counselled
    fear,
Soft-eyed Rama fired her bosom, and his sweet voice thrilled her ear,

What though bent on deeds unholy, holy Rama won her heart,
And, for love makes bold a female, thus did she her thoughts impart :

" Who be thou in hermit's vestments, in thy native beauty bright,
Friended by a youthful woman, arméd with thy bow of might,

Who be thou in these lone regions where the Rakshas hold their sway,
Wherefore in a lonely cottage in this darksome jungle stay ? "

With his wonted truth and candour Rama spake sedate and bold,
And the story of his exile to the Raksha maiden told :

" Dasa-ratha of Ayodhya ruled with INDRA's godlike fame,
And his eldest, first-born Rama, by his mandate here I came,

Younger Lakshman strong and valiant doth with me these forests
    roam,
And my wife, Videha's daughter, Sita makes with me her home.

Duteous to my father's bidding, duteous to my mother's will,
Striving in the cause of virtue in the woods we wander still.

Tell me, female of the forest, who thou be and whence thy birth,
Much I fear thou art a Raksha wearing various forms on earth ! "

" Listen," so spake Surpa-nakha, "if my purpose thou wouldst know,
I am Raksha, Surpa-nakha, wearing various shapes below.

Know my brothers, royal Ravan, Lanka's lord from days of old,
Kumbha-karna dread and dauntless, and Bibhishan true and bold,

Khara and the doughty Dushan with me in these forests stray,
But by Rama's love emboldened I have left them on the way !

Broad and boundless is my empire and I wander in my pride,
Thee I choose as lord and husband,—cast thy human wife aside,

Pale is Sita and misshapen, scarce a warrior's worthy wife,
To a nobler, lordlier female consecrate thy gallant life !

Human flesh is food of Rakshas ! weakling Sita I will slay,
Slay that boy thy stripling brother,—thee as husband I obey,

On the peaks of lofty mountains, in the forests dark and lone,
We shall range the boundless woodlands and the joys of dalliance
    prove ! "

II

SURPA-NAKHA PUNISHED

Rama heard her impious purpose and a gentle smile repressed,
To the foul and forward female thus his mocking words addressed :

" List, O passion-smitten maiden ! Sita is my honoured wife,
With a rival loved and cherished cruel were thy wedded life !

But no consort follows Lakshman, peerless is his comely face,
Dauntless is his warlike valour, matchless is his courtly grace,

And he leads no wife or consort to this darksome woodland grove,
With no rival to thy passion seek his ample-hearted love ! "

Surpa-nakha passion-laden then on Lakshman turned her eye,
But in merry mocking accents smiling Lakshman made reply :

" Ruddy in thy youthful beauty like the lotus in her pride,
I am slave of royal Rama, would'st thou be a vassal's bride ?

Rather be his younger consort, banish Sita from his arms,
Spurning Sita's faded beauty let him seek thy fresher charms,

Spurning Sita's faded graces let him brighter pleasures prove,
Wearied with a woman's dalliance let him court a Raksha's love ! "

Wrath of unrequited passion raged like madness in her breast,
Torn by anger strong as tempest thus her answer she addrest :

" Are these mocking accents uttered, Rama, to insult my flame,
Feasting on her faded beauty dost thou still revere thy dame ?

But beware a Raksha's fury and an injured female's wrath,
Surpa-nakha slays thy consort, bears no rival in her path ! "

Fawn-eyed Sita fell in terror as the Raksha rose to slay,
So beneath the flaming meteor sinks Rohini's softer ray,

And like Demon of Destruction furious Surpa-nakha came,
Rama rose to stop the slaughter and protect his helpless dame.

" Brother, we have acted wrongly, for with those of savage breed,
Word in jest is courting danger,—this the penance of our deed,

Death perchance or death-like stupor hovers o'er my lovéd dame,
Let me wake to life my Sita, chase this female void of shame ! "

Lakshman's anger leaped like lightning as the female hovered near,
With his sword the wrathful warrior cleft her nose and either ear,

Surpa-nakha in her anguish raised her accents shrill and high,
And the rocks and wooded valleys answered back the dismal cry,

Khara and the doughty Dushan heard the far-resounding wail,
Saw her red disfigured visage, heard her sad and woeful tale !

III

RAMA'S DEPARTURE

Vainly fought the vengeful Khara, doughty Dushan vainly bled,
Rama and the valiant Lakshman strewed the forest with the dead,

Till the humbled Surpa-nakha to her royal brother hied,
Spake her sorrows unto Ravan and Maricha true and tried.

Shape of deer unmatched in beauty now the deep Maricha wore,
Golden tints upon his haunches, sapphire on his antlers bore,

Till the woodland-wand'ring Sita marked the creature in his pride,
Golden was his neck of beauty, silver-white his flank and side !

" Come, my lord and gallant Lakshman," thus the raptur'd Sita
    spake,
" Mark the deer of wondrous radiance browsing by the forest
    brake ! "

" Much my heart misgives me, sister," Lakshman hesitated still,
" 'Tis some deep deceitful Raksha wearing every shape at will,

Monarchs wand'ring in this forest, hunting in this lonely glen,
Oft waylaid by artful Rakshas are by deep devices slain,

Bright as day-god or *Gandharva*, woodland scenes they love to stray,
Till they fall upon the heedless, quick to slaughter and to slay,

Trust me, not in jewelled lustre forest creatures haunt the green,
'Tis some *maya* and illusion, trust not what thy eyes have seen ! "

Vainly spake the watchful Lakshman in the arts of Rakshas skilled,
For with forceful fascination Sita's inmost heart was thrilled,

" Husband, good and ever gracious," sweetly thus implored the wife,
" I would tend this thing of beauty,—sharer of my forest life !

I have witnessed in this jungle graceful creatures passing fair,
Chowri and the gentle roebuck, antelope of beauty rare,

I have seen the lithesome monkey sporting in the branches' shade,
Grizzly bear that feeds on *Mahua*, and the deer that crops the blade,

I have marked the stately wild bull dash into the deepest wood,
And the *Kinnar* strange and wondrous as in sylvan wilds he stood,

But these eyes have never rested on a form so wondrous fair,
On a shape so full of beauty, decked with tints so rich and rare !

Bright his bosom gem-bespangled, soft the lustre of his eye,
Lighting up the gloomy jungle as the Moon lights up the sky,

And his gentle voice and glances and his graceful steps and light,
Fill my heart with eager longing and my soul with soft delight !

If alive that beauteous object thou canst capture in thy way,
As thy Sita's sweet companion in these woodlands he will stay,

And when done our days of exile, to Ayodhya will repair,
Dwell in Sita's palace chamber nursed by Sita's tender care,

And our royal brother Bharat oft will praise his strength and speed,
And the queens and royal mothers pause the gentle thing to feed !

If alive this wary creature be it, husband, hard to take,
Slay him and his skin of lustre cherish for thy Sita's sake,

i will as a golden carpet spread the skin upon the grass,
Sweet memento of this forest when our forest days will pass !

Pardon if an eager longing which befits a woman ill,
And an unknown fascination doth my inmost bosom fill,

As I mark his skin bespangled and his antlers' sapphire ray,
And his coat of starry radiance glowing in the light of day ! "

Rama bade the faithful Lakshman with the gentle Sita stay,
Long through woods and gloomy gorges vainly held his cautious way,

Vainly set the snare in silence by the lake and in the dale,
'Scaping every trap, Maricha, pierced by Rama's arrows fell,

Imitating Rama's accents uttered forth his dying cry :
" Speed, my faithful brother Lakshman, helpless in the woods I
 die ! "

IV

LAKSHMAN'S DEPARTURE

" Heardst that distant cry of danger ? " questioned Sita in distress,
" Woe, to me ! who in my frenzy sent my lord to wilderness,

Speed, brave Lakshman, help my Rama, doleful was his distant cry
And my fainting bosom falters and a dimness clouds my eye !

To the dread and darksome forest with thy keenest arrows speed,
Help thy elder and thy monarch, sore his danger and his need,

For perchance the cruel Rakshas gather round his lonesome path,
As the mighty bull is slaughtered by the lions in their wrath ! "

Spake the hero : " Fear not, Sita ! Dwellers of the azure height,
Rakshas nor the jungle-rangers match the peerless Rama's might,

Rama knows no dread or danger, and his mandate still I own,
And I may not leave thee, Lady, in this cottage all alone !

Cast aside thy causeless terror ; in the sky or earth below,
In the nether regions, Rama knows no peer or equal foe,

He shall slay the deer of jungle, he shall voice no dastard cry,
'Tis some trick of wily Rakshas in this forest dark and high !

Sita, thou hast heard my elder bid me in this cottage stay,
Lakshman may not leave thee, Lady, for this duty—to obey.

Ruthless Rakshas roam the forest to revenge their leader slain,
Various are their arts and accents ; chase thy thought of causeless
    pain ! ''

Sparkled Sita's eye in anger, frenzy marked her speech and word,
For a woman's sense is clouded by the danger of her lord :

'' Markest thou my Rama's danger with a cold and callous heart,
Courtest thou the death of elder in thy deep deceitful art,

In thy semblance of compassion dost thou hide a cruel craft,
As in friendly guise the foeman hides his death-compelling shaft,

Following like a faithful younger in this dread and lonesome land,
Seekest thou the death of elder to enforce his widow's hand ?

False thy hope as foul thy purpose ! Sita is a faithful wife,
Sita follows saintly Rama, true in death as true in life ! ''

Quivered Lakshman's frame in anguish and the tear stood in his eye,
Fixed in faith and pure in purpose, calm and bold he made reply :

'' Unto me a Queen and Goddess,—as a mother to a son,—
Answer to thy heedless censure patient Lakshman speaketh none,

Daughter of Videha's monarch,—pardon if I do thee wrong,—
Fickle is the faith of woman, poison-dealing is her tongue !

And thy censure, trust me, Lady, scathes me like a burning dart,
Free from guile is Lakshman's purpose, free from sin is Lakshman's
    heart,

Witness ye my truth of purpose, unseen dwellers of the wood,
Witness, I for Sita's safety by my elder's mandate stood,

Duteous to my queen and elder, I have toiled and worked in vain,
Dark suspicion and dishonour cast on me a needless stain !

Lady ! I obey thy mandate, to my elder now I go,
Guardian Spirits of the forest watch thee from each secret foe,

Omens dark and signs of danger meet my pained and aching sight,
May I see thee by thy Rama, guarded by his conquering might ! ''

V

RAVAN'S COMING

Ravan watched the happy moment burning with a vengeful spite.
Came to sad and sorrowing Sita in the guise of anchorite,

Tufted hair and russet garment, sandals on his feet he wore,
And depending from his shoulders on a staff his vessel bore.

And he came to lonely Sita, for each warlike chief was gone,
As the darkness comes to evening lightless from the parted Sun,

And he cast his eyes on Sita, as a *graha* casts its shade
On the beauteous star Rohini when the bright Moon's glories fade.

Quaking Nature knew the moment ; silent stood the forest trees,
Conscious of a deed of darkness fell the fragrant forest breeze,

Godavari's troubled waters trembled 'neath his lurid glance,
And his red eye's fiery lustre sparkled in the wavelets' dance !

Mute and still were forest creatures when in guise of anchorite,
Unto Sita's lonely cottage pressed the Raksha in his might,

Mute and voiceless was the jungle as he cast on her his eye,
As across the star of Chitra, planet Sani walks the sky !

Ravan stood in hermit's vestments,—vengeful purpose unrevealed,—
As a deep and darksome cavern is by grass and leaf concealed,

Ravan stood sedate and silent, and he gazed on Rama's queen,
Ivory brow and lip of coral, sparkling teeth of pearly sheen !

Lighting up the lonely cottage, Sita sat in radiance high,
As the Moon with streaks of silver fills the lonely midnight sky,

Lighting up the gloomy woodlands with her eyes serenely fair,
With her bark-clad shape of beauty mantled by her raven hair !

Ravan fired by impure passion fixed on her his lustful eye,
And the light that lit his glances gave his holy texts the lie,

Ravan in his flattering accents, with a soft and soothing art,
Praised the woman's peerless beauty to subdue the woman's heart :

" Beaming in thy golden beauty, robed in sylvan russet dress,
Wearing wreath of fragrant lotus like a nymph of wilderness,

Art thou *Sri* or radiant *Gauri*, maid of Fortune or of Fame,
Nymph of Love or sweet Fruition, what may be thy sacred name ?

On thy lips of ruddy coral teeth of tender jasmine shine,
In thy eyes of limpid lustre dwells a light of love divine,

Tall and slender, softly rounded, are thy limbs of beauty rare,
Like the swelling fruit of *tala* heaves thy bosom sweetly fair !

Smiling lips that tempt and ravish, lustre that thy dark eyes beam,
Crush my heart, as rolling waters crush the margin of the stream.

And thy wealth of waving tresses mantles o'er thy budding charms,
And thy waist of slender beauty courts a lover's circling arms !

Goddess or Gandharva maiden wears no brighter form or face,
Woman seen by eyes of mortals owns not such transcendent grace,

Wherefore then, in lonesome forest, nymph or maiden, make thy stay,
Where the jungle creatures wander and the Rakshas hold their sway?

Royal halls and stately mansions were for thee a meeter home,
And thy steps should grace a palace, not in pathless forest roam,

Blossoms rich, not thorn of jungle, decorate a lady's bower,
Silken robes, not sylvan garments, heighten Beauty's potent power !

Lady of the sylvan forest ! other destiny is thine,—
As a bride beloved and courted in thy bridal garments shine,

Choose a loved and lordly suitor who shall wait on thee in pride,
Choose a hero worth thy beauty, be a monarch's queenly bride !

Speak thy lineage, heaven-descended ! who may be thy parents high,
Rudras or the radiant *Maruts, Vasus* leaders of the sky,

All unworthy is this forest for a nymph or heavenly maid,
Beasts of prey infest the jungle, Rakshas haunt its gloomy shade,

Lions dwell in lovely caverns, tuskers ford the silent lake,
Monkeys sport on pendant branches, tigers steal beneath the brake,

Wherefore then this dismal forest doth thy fairy face adorn,
Who art thou and whence descended, nymph or maid or goddess-
    born ? "

VI

Ravan's Wooing

" Listen, Brahman ! " answered Sita,—unsuspecting in her mind
That she saw a base betrayer in a hermit seeming kind,—

" I am born of royal Janak, ruler of Videha's land,
Rama prince of proud Kosala by his valour won my hand.

Years we passed in peaceful pleasure in Ayodhya's happy clime,
Rich in every rare enjoyment gladsome passed our happy time,

Till the monarch Dasa-ratha,—for his days were almost done,—
Wished to crown the royal Rama as his Heir and Regent son.

But the scheming Queen Kaikeyi claimed a long-forgotten boon,
That my consort should be exiled and her son should fill the throne,

She would take no rest or slumber, nourishment of drink or food,
Till her Bharat ruled the empire, Rama banished to the wood !

Five and twenty righteous summers graced my good and gracious
    lord,
True to faith and true to duty, true in purpose, deed, and word,

Loved of all his loyal people, rich in valour and in fame,
For the rite of consecration Rama to his father came.

Spake Kaikeyi to my husband :—' List thy father's promise fair,
Bharat shall be ruling monarch, do thou to the woods repair,'—

Ever gentle, ever duteous, Rama listened to obey,
And through woods and pathless jungles we have held our lonely way.

This, O pious-hearted hermit, is his story of distress,
And his young and faithful brother follows him in wilderness,

Lion in his warlike valour, hermit in his saintly vow,
Lakshman with his honoured elder wanders through the forest now.

Rest thee here, O holy Brahman, rich in piety and fame,
Till the forest-ranging brothers greet thee with the forest game,

Speak, if so it please thee, father, what great *rishi* claims thy birth,
Wherefore in this pathless jungle wand'rest friendless on this earth."

" Brahman nor a righteous *rishi*," royal Ravan made reply,
" Leader of the wrathful Rakshas, Lanka's lord and king am I,

He whose valour quells the wide-world, Gods above and men below,
He whose proud and peerless prowess Rakshas and Asuras know !

But thy beauty's golden lustre, Sita, wins my royal heart,
Be a sharer of my empire, of my glory take a part,

Many queens of queenly beauty on the royal Ravan wait,
Thou shalt be their reigning empress, thou shalt own my regal state !

Lanka girt by boundless ocean is of royal towns the best,
Seated in her pride and glory on a mountain's towering crest,

And in mountain paths and woodlands thou shalt with thy Ravan
stray,
Not in Godavari's gorges through the dark and dreary day,

And five thousand gay-dressed damsels shall upon my Sita wait,
Queen of Ravan's true affection, proud partaker of his state ! "

Sparkled Sita's eyes in anger and a tremor shook her frame,
As in proud and scornful accents answered thus the royal dame :

'' Knowest thou Rama great and godlike, peerless hero in the strife,
Deep, uncompassed, like the ocean ?—I am Rama's wedded wife !

Knowest thou Rama proud and princely, sinless in his saintly life,
Stately as the tall *Nyagrodha ?*—I am Rama's wedded wife !

Mighty-arméd, mighty-chested, mighty with his bow and sword,
Lion midst the sons of mortals,—Rama is my wedded lord !

Stainless as the Moon in glory, stainless in his deed and word,
Rich in valour and in virtue,—Rama is my wedded lord !

Sure thy fitful life is shadowed by a dark and dreadful fate,
Since in frenzy of thy passion courtest thou a warrior's mate,

Tear the tooth of hungry lion while upon the calf he feeds,
Touch the fang of deadly cobra while his dying victim bleeds,

Aye, uproot the solid mountain from its base of rocky land,
Ere thou win the wife of Rama stout of heart and strong of hand !

Pierce thy eye with point of needle till it racks thy tortured head,
Press thy red tongue cleft and bleeding on the razor's shining blade,

Hurl thyself upon the ocean from a towering peak and high,
Snatch the orbs of day and midnight from their spheres in azure sky,

Tongues of flaming conflagration in thy flowing dress enfold,
Ere thou take the wife of Rama to thy distant dungeon hold,

Ere thou seek to insult Rama unrelenting in his wrath,
O'er a bed of pikes of iron tread a softer easier path ! "

VII

RAVAN'S TRIUMPH

Vain her threat and soft entreaty, Ravan held her in his wrath,
As the planet Budha captures fair Rohini in his path,

By his left hand tremor-shaken, Ravan held her streaming hair,
By his right the ruthless Raksha lifted up the fainting fair !

Unseen dwellers of the woodlands watched the dismal deed of shame,
Marked the mighty-arméd Raksha lift the poor and helpless dame,

Seat her on his car celestial yoked with asses winged with speed,
Golden in its shape and radiance, fleet as INDRA's heavenly steed !

Angry threat and sweet entreaty Ravan to her ears addressed,
As the struggling fainting woman still he held upon his breast,

Vain his threat and vain entreaty, " Rama ! Rama ! " still she cried,
To the dark and distant forest where her noble lord had hied.

Then arose the car celestial o'er the hill and wooded vale,
Like a snake in eagle's talons Sita writhed with piteous wail,

Dim and dizzy, faint and faltering, still she sent her piercing cry,
Echoing through the boundless woodlands, pealing to the upper sky ؛

" Save me, mighty-arméd Lakshman, stainless in thy heart and deed,
Save a faithful wife and woman from a Raksha's lust and greed,

True and faithful was thy warning,—false and foul the charge I made,
Pardon, friend, an erring sister, pardon words a woman said !

Help me, ever righteous Rama, duty bade thee yield thy throne,
Duty bids thee smite the sinful, save the wife who is thy own,

Thou art king and stern chastiser of each deed of sin and shame,
Hurl thy vengeance on the Raksha who insults thy faithful dame !

Deed of sin, unrighteous Ravan, brings in time its dreadful meed,
As the young corn grows and ripens from the small and living seed,

For this deed of insult, Ravan, in thy heedless folly done,
Death of all thy race and kindred thou shalt reap from Raghu's son !

Darksome woods of Panchavati, Janasthana's smiling vale,
Flowering trees and winding creepers, murmur to my lord this tale,

Sweet companions of my exile, friends who cheered my woodland
    stay,
Speak to Rama, that his Sita ruthless Ravan bears away !

Towering peaks and lofty mountains, wooded hills sublime and high,
Far-extending gloomy ranges heaving to the azure sky,

In your voice of pealing thunder to my lord and consort say,
Speak of Rama, that his Sita ruthless Ravan bears away !

Unseen dwellers of the woodlands, spirits of the rock and fell,
Sita renders you obeisance as she speaks her sad farewell,

Whisper to my righteous Rama when he seeks his homeward way,
Speak to Rama, that his Sita ruthless Ravan bears away !

Ah, my Rama, true and tender ! thou hast loved me as thy life,
From the foul and impious Raksha thou shalt still redeem thy wife,

Ah, my Rama, mighty-arméd ! vengeance soon shall speed thy way,
When thou hearest helpless Sita is by Ravan torn away !

And thou royal bird, Jatayu, witness Ravan's deed of shame,
Witness how he courts destruction, stealing Rama's faithful dame,

Rama and the gallant Lakshman soon shall find their destined prey,
When they know that trusting Sita is by Ravan torn away ! "

Vainly wept the anguished Sita ; vain Jatayu in his wrath,
Fought with beak and bloody talons to impede the Raksha's path,

Pierced and bleeding fell the vulture; Ravan fled with Rama's bride,
Where amidst the boundless ocean Lanka rose in towering pride !

BOOK VII
KISHKINDHA

(In the Nilgiri Mountains)

RAMA'S wanderings in the Nilgiri mountains, and his alliance with Sugriva the chief of these regions, form the subject of the Book. With that contempt for aboriginal races which has marked civilized conquerors in all ages, the poet describes the dwellers of these regions as monkeys and bears. But the modern reader sees through these strange epithets; and in the description of the social and domestic manners, the arts and industries, the sacred rites and ceremonies, and the civic and political life of the Vanars, the reader will find that the poet even imports Aryan customs into his account of the dwellers of Southern India. They formed an alliance with Rama, they fought for him and triumphed with him, and they helped him to recover his wife form the king of Ceylon.

The portions translated in this Book from Sections v., xv., xvi., xxvi., a portion of Section xxviii., and an abstract of Sections xl. to xliii. of Book iv. of the original text.

I

FRIENDS IN MISFORTUNE

Long and loud lamented Rama by his lonesome cottage door,
Janasthana's woodlands answered, Panchavati's echoing shore,

Long he searched in wood and jungle, mountain crest and pathless plain,
Till he reached the Malya mountains stretching to the southern main.

There Sugriva king of Vanars, Hanuman his henchman brave,
Banished from their home and empire lived within the forest cave,

To the exiled king Sugriva, Hanuman his purpose told,
As he marked the pensive Rama wand'ring with his brother bold :

" Mark the sons of Dasa-ratha banished from their royal home,
Duteous to their father's mandate in these pathless forests roam,

89

Great was monarch Dasa-ratha famed for sacrifice divine,
Raja-suya, Aswa-medha, and for gift of gold and kine,

By a monarch's stainless duty people's love the monarch won,
By a woman's false contrivance banished he his eldest son !

True to duty, true to virtue, Rama passed his forest life,
Till a false perfidious Raksha stole his fair and faithful wife,

And the anguish-stricken husband seeks thy friendship and thy aid,
Mutual sorrow blends your fortunes, be ye friends in mutual need ! "

Bold Sugriva heard the counsel, and to righteous Rama hied,
And the princes of Ayodhya with his greetings gratified :

" *Well I know thee, righteous Rama, soul of piety and love,*
And thy duty to thy father and thy faith in God above,

Fortune favours poor Sugriva, Rama courts his humble aid,
In our deepest direst danger be our truest friendship made !

Equal is our fateful fortune,—I have lost a queenly wife,
Banished from Kishkindha's empire here I lead a forest life,

Pledge of love and true alliance, Rama, take this proffered hand,
Banded by a common sorrow we shall fall or stoutly stand ! "

Rama grasped the hand he offered, and the tear was in his eye,
And they swore undying friendship o'er the altar blazing high,

Hanuman with fragrant blossoms sanctified the sacred rite,
And the comrades linked by sorrow walked around the altar's light,

And their word and troth they plighted : " In our happiness and woe
We are friends in thought and action, we will face our common foe ! "

And they broke a leafy *Sal* tree, spread it underneath their feet,
Rama and his friend Sugriva sat upon the common seat,

And a branch of scented *Chandan* with its tender blossoms graced,
Hanuman as seat of honour for the faithful Lakshman placed.

" Listen, Rama," spake Sugriva, " reft of kingdom, reft of wife,
Fleeing to these rugged mountains I endure a forest life,

For my tyrant brother Bali rules Kishkindha all alone,
Forced my wife from my embraces, drove me from my father's
    throne,

Trembling in my fear and anguish I endure a life of woe,
Render me my wife and empire from my brother and my foe ! "

" Not in vain they seek my succour," so the gallant Rama said,
" Who with love and offered friendship seek my counsel and my aid,

Not in vain these glistening arrows in my ample quiver shine,
Bali dies the death of tyrants, wife and empire shall be thine !

Quick as INDRA'S *forkéd lightning are these arrows feather-plumed,*
Deadly as the hissing serpent are these darts with points illumed,

And this day shall not be ended ere it sees thy brother fall,
As by lurid lightning severed sinks the crest of mountain tall ! "

II

THE COUNSEL OF TARA

Linked in bonds of faithful friendship Rama and Sugriva came,
Where in royal town Kishkindha, Bali ruled with warlike fame,

And a shout like troubled ocean's or like tempest's deafening roar
Spake Sugriva's mighty challenge to the victor king once more !

Bali knew that proud defiance shaking sky and solid ground,
And like sun by eclipse shaded, dark and pale he looked around,

And his teeth were set in anger and a passion lit his eye,
As a tempest stirs a torrent when its lilies scattered lie,

And he rose in wrath terrific with a thought of vengeance dread,
And the firm earth shook and trembled 'neath his proud and haughty
    tread !

But the true and tender Tara held her husband and her lord,
And a woman's deeper wisdom spake in woman's loving word :

" Wherefore like a rain-fed torrent swells thy passion in its sway,
Thoughts of wrath like withered blossoms from thy bosom cast away,

Wait till dawns another morning, wait till thou dost truly know,
With what strength and added forces comes again thy humbled foe.

Crushed in combat faint Sugriva fled in terror and in pain,
Trust me, not without a helper comes he to the fight again,

Trust me, lord, that loud defiance is no coward's falt'ring cry,
Conscious strength not hesitation speaks in voice so proud and high !

Much my woman's heart misgives me, not without a mighty aid,
Not without a daring comrade comes Sugriva to this raid,

Not with feeble friend Sugriva seeks alliance in his need,
Nor invokes a powerless chieftain in his lust and in his greed.

Mighty is his royal comrade,—listen, husband, to my word,
What my son in forest confines from his messengers hath heard,—

Princes from Ayodhya's country peerless in the art of war,
Rama and the valiant Lakshman in these forests wander far,

Much I fear, these matchless warriors have their aid and counsel lent
Conscious of his strength Sugriva hath this proud defiance sent !

To his foes resistless Rama is a lightning from above,
To his friends a tree of shelter, soul of tenderness and love,

Dearer than his love of glory is his love to heal and bless,
Dearer than the crown and empire is his hermit's holy dress,

Not with such, my lord and husband, seek a vain unrighteous strife,
For, like precious ores in mountains, virtues dwell in Rama's life.

Make Sugriva thy companion, make him Regent and thy Heir,
Discord with a younger brother rends an empire broad and fair,

Make thy peace with young Sugriva, nearest and thy dearest kin,
Brother's love is truest safety, brother's hate is deadliest sin !

Trust me, monarch of Kishkindha, trust thy true and faithful wife,
Thou shalt find no truer comrade than Sugriva in thy life,

Wage not then a war fraternal, smite him not in sinful pride,
As a brother and a warrior let him stand by Bali's side.

Listen to thy Tara's counsel if to thee is Tara dear,
If thy wife is true in duty scorn not Tara's wifely tear,

Not with Rama prince of virtue wage a combat dread and high,
Not with Rama prince of valour, peerless like the Lord of sky ! "

III

THE FALL OF BALI

Star-eyed Tara softly counselled pressing to her consort's side,
Mighty Bali proudly answered with a warrior's lofty pride:

" Challenge of a humbled foeman and a younger's haughty scorn
May not, shall not, tender Tara, by a king be meekly borne !

Bali turns not from encounter even with his dying breath,
Insult from a foe, unanswered, is a deeper stain than death,

And Sugriva's quest for combat Bali never shall deny,
Though sustained by Rama's forces and by Rama's prowess high !

Free me from thy sweet embraces and amidst thy maids retire,
Woman's love and soft devotion woman's timid thoughts inspire,

Fear not, Tara, blood of brother Bali's honour shall not stain,
I will quell his proud presumption, chase him from this realm again,

Free me from thy loving dalliance, midst thy damsels seek thy place,
Till I come a happy victor to my Tara's fond embrace ! "

Slow and sad with sweet obeisance Tara stepped around her lord,
Welling tear-drops choked her accents as she prayed in stifled word,

Slow and sad with swelling bosom Tara with her maids retired,
Bali issued proud and stately with the thought of vengeance fired !

Hissing like an angry cobra, city's lofty gates he past,
And his proud and angry glances fiercely all around he cast,

Till he saw the bold Sugriva, gold-complexioned, red with ire,
Girded for the dubious combat, flaming like the forest fire !

Bali braced his warlike garments and his hand he lifted high,
Bold Sugriva raised his right arm with a proud and answering cry,

Bali's eyes were red as copper and his chain was burnished gold,
To his brother bold Sugriva thus he spake in accents bold :

" Mark this iron fist, intruder, fatal is its vengeful blow,
Crushed and smitten thou shalt perish and to nether world shalt go,"

" Nay that fate awaits thee, Bali," spake Sugriva armed for strife,
" When this right arm smites thy forehead, from thy bosom rends
    thy life ! "

Closed the chiefs in fatal combat, each resistless in his pride,
And like running rills from mountains poured their limbs the purple
    tide,

Till Sugriva quick uprooting *Sal* tree from the jungle wood,
As the dark cloud hurls the lightning, hurled it where his brother
stood,

Staggering 'neath the blow terrific Bali reeled and almost fell,
As a proud ship overladen reels upon the ocean's swell !

But with fiercer rage and fury Bali in his anguish rose,
And with mutual blows they battled,—brothers and relentless foes,

Like the sun and moon in conflict or like eagles in their fight,
Still they fought with cherished hatred and an unforgotten spite,

Till with mightier force and fury Bali did his younger quell,
Faint Sugriva fiercely struggling 'neath his brother's prowess fell !

Still the wrathful rivals wrestled with their bleeding arms and knees,
With their nails like claws of tigers and with riven rocks and trees,

And as INDRA battles Vritra in the tempest's pealing roar,
Blood-stained Bali, red Sugriva, strove and struggled, fought and
tore,

Till Sugriva faint and falt'ring fell like Vritra from the sky,
To his comrade and his helper turned his faint and pleading eye !

Ah ! those soft and pleading glances smote the gentle Rama's heart,
On his bow of ample stature Rama raised the fatal dart,

Like the fatal disc of YAMA was his proudly circled bow,
Like a snake of deadly poison flew his arrow swift and low,

Wingéd dwellers of the forest heard the twang with trembling fear,
Echoing woods gave back the accent, lightly fled the startled deer,

And as INDRA's flag is lowered when the Aswin winds prevail,
Lofty Bali pierced and bleeding by that fatal arrow fell !

IV

THE CONSECRATION OF SUGRIVA

Tears of love the tender Tara on her slaughtered hero shed,
E'en Sugriva's bosom melted when he saw his brother dead,

And each Vanar chief and warrior, *maha-matra*, lord and peer,
Gathered round the sad Sugriva wet with unavailing tear !

And they girt the victor Rama and they praised his wond'rous might,
As the heavenly *rishis* gather circling Brahma's throne of light,

Hanuman of sun-like radiance, lofty as a hill of gold,
Clasped his hands in due obeisance, spake in accents calm and bold :

" By thy prowess, peerless Rama, prince Sugriva is our lord,
To his father's throne and empire, to his father's town restored,

Cleansed by bath and fragrant unguents and in royal garments gay,
He shall with his gold and garlands homage to the victor pay,

To the rock-bound fair Kishkindha do thy friendly footsteps bend,
And as monarch of the Vanars consecrate thy grateful friend ! "

" Fourteen years," so Rama answered, " by his father's stern
    command,
In a city's sacred confines banished Rama may not stand,

Friend and comrade, brave Sugriva, enter thou the city wall,
And assume the royal sceptre in thy father's royal hall.

Gallant Angad, son of Bali, is in regal duties trained,
Ruling partner of thy empire be the valiant prince ordained,

Eldest son of eldest brother,—such the maxim that we own,—
Worthy of his father's kingdom, doth ascend his father's throne.

Listen ! 'tis the month of *Sravan*, now begins the yearly rain,
In these months of wind and deluge thoughts of vengeful strife were
    vain,

Enter then thy royal city, fair Kishkindha be thy home,
With my ever faithful Lakshman let me in these mountains roam.

Spacious is yon rocky cavern fragrant with the mountain air,
Bright with lily and with lotus, watered by a streamlet fair,

Here we dwell till month of *Kartik* when the clouded sky will clear,
And the time of war and vengeance on our foeman shall be near."

Bowing to the victor's mandate brave Sugriva marched in state,
And the host of thronging Vanars entered by the city gate,

Prostrate chiefs with due obeisance rendered homage, one and all,
And Sugriva blessed his people, stepped within the palace hall.

And they sprinkled sacred water from the vases jewel-graced,
And they waved the fan of *chowri*, raised the sun-shade silver-laced,

And they spread the gold and jewel, grain and herb and fragrant *ghee*,
Sapling twigs and bending branches, blossoms from the flowering tree,

Milk-white garments gem-bespangled, and the *Chandan's* fragrant dye,
Wreaths and spices, snow-white lilies, lotus azure as the sky,

Jatarupa and *Priyangu*, honey, curd and holy oil,
Costly sandals gilt and jewelled, tiger-skin the hunter's spoil !

Decked in gold and scented garlands, robed in radiance rich and rare,
Sweetly stepped around Sugriva sixteen maidens passing fair,

Priests received the royal bounty, gift and garment gold-belaced,
And they lit the holy altar with the sacred *mantra* graced,

And they poured the sweet libation on the altar's lighted flame,
And on throne of royal splendour placed the chief of royal fame !

On a high and open terrace with auspicious garlands graced,
Facing eastward, in his glory was the brave Sugriva placed,

Water from each holy river, from each *tirtha* famed of old,
From the broad and boundless ocean, was arranged in jars of gold,

And from vase and horn of wild bull, on their monarch and their lord,
Holy consecrating water chiefs and loyal courtiers poured.

Gaya and the great Gavaksha, Gandha-madan proud and brave,
Hanuman held up the vases, Jambaman his succour gave,

And they laved the king Sugriva as Immortals in the sky
Consecrate the star-eyed INDRA in his mansions bright and high,

And a shout of joy and triumph, like the pealing voice of war,
Spake Sugriva's consecration to the creatures near and far !

Duteous still to Rama's mandate, as his first-born and his own,
King Sugriva named young Angad sharer of his royal throne,

Gay and bannered town Kishkindha hailed Sugriva's gracious word,
Tender Tara wiped her tear-drops bowing to a younger lord !

V

THE RAINS IN THE NILGIRI MOUNTAINS

" Mark the shadowing rain and tempest," Rama to his brother said,
As on Malya's cloud-capped ranges in their hermit-guise they strayed,

" Massive clouds like rolling mountains gather thick and gather high,
Lurid lightnings glint and sparkle, pealing thunders shake the sky,

Pregnant with the ocean moisture by the solar ray instilled,
Now the skies like fruitful mothers are with grateful waters filled !

Mark the folds of cloudy masses, ladder-like of smooth ascent,
One could almost reach the Sun-god, wreath him with a wreath of
    scent,

And when glow these heavy masses red and white with evening's
    glow,
One could almost deem them sword-cuts branded by some heavenly
    foe !

Mark the streaks of golden lustre lighting up the checkered sky,
Like a lover *chandan*-painted in each breeze it heaves a sigh,

And the earth is hot and feverish, moistened with the tears of rain,
Sighing like my anguished Sita when she wept in woe and pain !

Fresh and sweet like draught of nectar is the rain-besprinkled breeze,
Fragrant with the *ketak* blossom, scented by the camphor trees,

Fresh and bold each peak and mountain bathed in soft descending
    rain,
So they sprinkle holy water when they bless a monarch's reign !

Fair and tall as holy hermits, stand yon shadow-mantled hills,
Murmuring *mantras* with the zephyr, robed in threads of sparkling
    rills,

Fair and young as gallant coursers neighing forth their thunder cries,
Lashed by golden whips of lightning are the dappled sunlit skies !

Ah, my lost and loving Sita ! writhing in a Raksha's power,
As the lightning shakes and quivers in this dark tempestuous shower,

Shadows thicken on the prospect, flower and leaf are wet with rain,
And each passing object, Lakshman, wakes in me a thought of pain !

Joyously from throne and empire with my Sita I could part,
As the stream erodes its margin, Sita's absence breaks my heart,

Rain and tempest cloud the prospect as they cloud my onward path,
Dubious is my darksome future, mighty is my foeman's wrath !

Ravan monarch of the Rakshas,—so Jatayu said and died,—
In some unknown forest fastness doth my sorrowing Sita hide,

But Sugriva true and faithful seeks the Raksha's secret hold,
Firm in faith and fixed in purpose we will face our foeman bold ! "

VI

THE QUEST FOR SITA

Past the rains, the marshalled Vanars gathered round Sugriva bold,
And unto a gallant chieftain thus the king his purpose told :

" Brave in war and wise in counsel ! take ten thousand of my best,
Seek the hiding-place of Ravan in the regions of the East.

Seek each ravine rock and forest and each shadowy hill and cave,
Far where bright Sarayu's waters mix with Ganga's ruddy wave,

And where Jumna's dark blue waters ceaseless roll in regal pride,
And the Sone through leagues of country spreads its torrents far and
    wide.

Seek where in Videha's empire castled towns and hamlets shine,
In Kosala and in Malwa and by Kasi's sacred shrine,

Magadh rich in peopled centres, Pundra region of the brave,
Anga rich in corn and cattle on the eastern ocean wave.

Seek where clans of skilful weavers dwell upon the eastern shore,
And from virgin mines of silver miners work the sparkling ore.

In the realms of uncouth nations, in the islets of the sea,
In the mountains of the ocean, wander far and wander free ! "

Next to Nila son of AGNI, Jambaman VIDHATA'S son,
Hanuman the son of MARUT, famed for deeds of valour done,

Unto Gaya and Gavaksha, Gandha-madan true and tried,
Unto Angad prince and regent, thus the brave Sugriva cried :

" Noblest, bravest of our chieftains, greatest of our race are ye,
Seek and search the Southern regions, rock and ravine, wood and
    tree,

Search the thousand peaks of Vindhya lifting high its misty head,
Through the gorges of Narmada rolling o'er its rocky bed,

By the gloomy Godavari and by Krishna's wooded stream,
Through Utkala's sea-girt forests tinged by morning's early gleam.

Search the towns of famed Dasarna and Avanti's rocky shore,
And the uplands of Vidarbha and the mountains of Mysore,

Land of Matsyas and Kalingas and Kausika's regions fair,
Trackless wilderness of Dandak seek with anxious toil and care.

Search the empire of the Andhras, of the sister-nations three,—
Cholas, Cheras and the Pandyas dwelling by the southern sea,

Pass Kaveri's spreading waters, Malya's mountains towering brave,
Seek the isle of Tamra-parni, gemmed upon the ocean wave ! "

To Susena chief and elder,—Tara's noble sire was he,—
Spake Sugriva with obeisance and in accents bold and free :

" Take my lord, a countless army of the bravest and the best,
Search where beats the sleepless ocean on the regions of the West.

Search the country of Saurashtras, of Bahlikas strong and brave,
And each busy mart and seaport on the western ocean wave,

Castles girt by barren mountains, deserts by the sandy sea,
Forests of the fragrant *ketak*, regions of the *tamal* tree !

Search the ocean port of Pattan shaded by its fruitful trees,
Where the feathery groves of cocoa court the balmy western breeze,

Where on peaks of Soma-giri lordly lions wander free,
Where the waters of the Indus mingle with the mighty sea ! "

Lastly to the valiant chieftain Satavala strong and brave,
For the quest of saintly Sita thus his mighty mandate gave :

" Hie thee, gallant Satavala, with thy forces wander forth,
To the peaks of Himalaya, to the regions of the North !

Mlechchas and the wild Pulindas in the rocky regions dwell,
Madra chiefs and mighty Kurus live within each fertile vale,

Wild Kambojas of the mountains, Yavanas of wondrous skill,
Sakas swooping from their gorges, Pattanas of iron will !

Search the woods of *devadaru* mantling Himalaya's side,
And the forests of the *lodhra* spreading in their darksome pride,

Search the land of Soma-srama where the gay *Gandharvas* dwell
In the tableland of Kala search each rock and ravine well !

Cross the snowy Himalaya, and Sudarsan's holy peak,
Deva-sakha's wooded ranges which the feathered songsters seek,

Cross the vast and dreary region void of stream or wooded hill,
Till you reach the white Kailasa, home of Gods, serene and still !

Pass Kuvera's pleasant regions, search the Krauncha mountain well,
And the land where warlike females and the horse-faced women
dwell,

Halt not till you reach the country where the Northern Kurus
rest,
Utmost confines of the wide earth, home of Gods and Spirits
blest ! "

BOOK VIII

SITA-SANDESA

(*Sita Discovered*)

AMONG the many chiefs sent by Sugriva in different directions in search of Sita, Hanuman succeeded in the quest and discovered Sita in Ceylon. Ceylon is separated from India by a broad channel of the sea, and Hanuman leaped, or rather flew through the air, across the channel, and lighted on the island. Sita, scorning the proposals of Ravan, was kept in confinement in a garden of *Asoka* trees, surrounded by a terrible guard of Raksha females ; and in this hard confinement she remained true and faithful to her lord. Hanuman gave her a token from Rama, and carried back to Rama a token which she sent of her undying affection and truth.

The portions translated in this Book form the whole of the main portions of Sections xv., xxxi., xxxvi., and lxvi. of Book v. of the original text.

I

SITA IN THE ASOKA GARDEN

Crossed the ocean's boundless waters, Hanuman in duty brave,
Lighted on the emerald island girded by the sapphire wave,

And in tireless quest of Sita searched the margin of the sea,
In a dark *Asoka* garden hid himself within a tree.

Creepers threw their clasping tendrils round the trees of ample height,
Stately palm and feathered cocoa, fruit and blossom pleased the sight,

Herds of tame and gentle creatures in the grassy meadow strayed,
Kokils sang in leafy thicket, birds of plumage lit the shade,

Limpid lakes of scented lotus with their fragrance filled the air,
Homes and huts of rustic beauty peeped through bushes green and fair,

Blossoms rich in tint and fragrance in the checkered shadow gleamed,
Clustering fruits of golden beauty in the yellow sunlight beamed !

Brightly shone the red *Asoka* with the morning's golden ray,
Karnikara and *Kinsuka* dazzling as the light of day,

Brightly grew the flower of *Champak* in the vale and on the reef,
Punnaga and *Saptaparna* with its seven-fold scented leaf,

Rich in blossoms many tinted, grateful to the ravished eye,
Gay and green and glorious Kanka was like garden of the sky,

Rich in fruit and laden creeper and in beauteous bush and tree,
Flower-bespangled golden Lanka was like gem-bespangled sea!

Rose a palace in the woodlands girt by pillars strong and high,
Snowy-white like fair Kailasa cleaving through the azure sky,

And its steps were ocean coral and its pavement yellow gold,
White and gay and heaven-aspiring rose the structure high and bold!

By the rich and royal mansion Hanuman his eyes did rest,
On a woman sad and sorrowing in her sylvan garments drest,

Like the moon obscured and clouded, dim with shadows deep and
     dark,
Like the smoke-enshrouded red fire, dying with a feeble spark,

Like the tempest-pelted lotus by the wind and torrent shaken,
Like the beauteous star Rohini by a *graha* overtaken!

Fasts and vigils paled her beauty, tears bedimmed her tender grace,
Anguish dwelt within her bosom, sorrow darkened on her face,

And she lived by Rakshas guarded, as a faint and timid deer,
Severed from her herd and kindred when the prowling wolves are
     near,

And her raven locks ungathered hung behind in single braid,
And her gentle eye was lightless, and her brow was hid in shade!

" This is she ! the peerless princess, Rama's consort loved and lost,
This is she ! the saintly Sita, by a cruel fortune crost,"

Hanuman thus thought and pondered : " On her graceful form I spy,
Gems and gold by sorrowing Rama oft depicted with a sigh,

On her ears the golden pendants and the tiger's sharpened tooth,
On her arms the jewelled bracelets, tokens of unchanging truth,

On her pallid brow and bosom still the radiant jewels shine,
Rama with a sweet affection did in early days entwine !

Hermit's garments clothe her person, braided is her raven hair,
Matted bark of trees of forest drape her neck and bosom fair,

And a dower of dazzling beauty still bedecks her peerless face,
Though the shadowing tinge of sorrow darkens all her earlier grace !

This is she ! the soft-eyed Sita, wept with unavailing tear,
This is she ! the faithful consort, unto Rama ever dear,

Unforgetting and unchanging, truthful still in deed and word,
Sita in her silent suffering sorrows for her absent lord,

Still for Rama lost but cherished, Sita heaves the choking sigh,
Sita lives for righteous Rama, for her Rama she would die ! "

II

THE VOICE OF HOPE

Hanuman from leafy shelters lifts his voice in sacred song,
Till the tale of Rama's glory Lanka's woods and vales prolong :

" Listen, Lady, to my story ;—Dasa-ratha famed in war,
Rich in steeds and royal tuskers, arméd men and battle car,

Ruled his realm in truth and virtue, in his bounty ever free,
Of the mighty race of Raghu mightiest king and monarch he,

Robed in every royal virtue, great in peace in battle brave,
Blest in bliss of grateful nations, blest in blessings which he gave !

And his eldest-born and dearest, Rama soul of righteous might,
Shone, as mid the stars resplendent shines the radiant Lord of Night,

True unto his sacred duty, true unto his kith and kin,
Friend of piety and virtue, punisher of crime and sin,

Loved in all his spacious empire, peopled mart and hermit's den,
With a truer deeper kindness Rama loved his subject men !

Dasa-ratha, promise-fettered, then his cruel mandate gave,
Rama with his wife and brother lived in woods and rocky cave,

And he slayed the deer of jungle and he slept in leafy shade,
Stern destroyer of the Rakshas in the pathless forests strayed,

Till the monarch of the Rakshas,—fraudful is his impious life,—
Cheated Rama in the jungle, from his cottage stole his wife !

Long lamenting lone and weary Rama wandered in the wood,
Searched for Sita in the jungle where his humble cottage stood,

Godavari's gloomy gorges, Krishna's dark and wooded shore,
And the ravine, rock and valley, and the cloud-capped mount áin
    hoar !

Then he met the sad Sugriva in wild Malya's dark retreat,
Won for him his father's empire and his father's royal seat,

Now Sugriva's countless forces wander far and wander near,
In the search of stolen Sita still unto his Rama dear !

I am henchman of Sugriva and the mighty sea have crost,
In the quest of hidden Sita, Rama's consort loved and lost,

And methinks that form of beauty, peerless shape of woman's grace,
Is my Rama's dear-loved consort, Rama's dear-remembered face ! "

Hushed the voice: the ravished Sita cast her wond'ring eyes around,
Whence that song of sudden gladness, whence that soul-entrancing
    sound ?

Dawning hope and rising rapture overflowed her widowed heart,
Is it dream's deceitful whisper which the cruel Fates impart ?

III

RAMA'S TOKEN

" 'Tis no dream's deceitful whisper ! " Hanuman spake to the
    dame,
As from darksome leafy shelter he to Rama's consort came,

" Rama's messenger and vassal, token from thy lord I bring,
Mark this bright ring, jewel-lettered with the dear name of thy king,

For the loved and cherished Sita is to Rama ever dear,
And he sends his loving message and his force is drawing near ! "

Sita held that tender token from her loved and cherished lord,
And once more herself she fancied to his loving arms restored,

And her pallid face was lighted and her soft eye sent a spark,
As the Moon regains her lustre freed from *Rahu's* shadows dark !

And with voice of deep emotion in each softly whispered word,
Spake her thoughts in gentle accents of her consort and her lord:

" Messenger of love of Rama ! Dauntless is thy deed and bold,
Thou hast crossed the boundless ocean to the Raksha's castled hold,

Thou hast crossed the angry billows which confess no monarch's
    sway,
O'er the face of rolling waters found thy unresisted way,

Thou hast done what living mortal never sought to do before,
Dared the Raksha in his island, Ravan in his sea-girt shore !

Speak, if Rama lives in safety in the woods or by the hill,
And if young and gallant Lakshman faithful serves his brother still,

Speak, if Rama in his anger and his unforgiving ire,
Hurls destruction on my captor like the world-consuming fire,

Speak, if Rama in his sorrow wets his pale and drooping eye,
If the thought of absent Sita wakes within his heart a sigh !

Doth my husband seek alliance with each wild and warlike chief,
Striving for a speedy vengeance and for Sita's quick relief,

Doth he stir the warlike races to a fierce and vengeful strife,
Dealing death to ruthless Rakshas for this insult on his wife,

Doth he still in fond remembrance cherish Sita loved of yore,
Nursing in his hero-bosom tender sorrows evermore !

Didst thou hear from far Ayodhya, from Kausalya royal dame,
From the true and tender Bharat prince of proud and peerless fame,

Didst thou hear if royal Bharat leads his forces to the fight,
Conquering Ravan's scattered army in his all-resistless might,

Didst thou hear if brave Sugriva marshals Vanars in his wrath,
And the young and gallant Lakshman seeks to cross the ocean path?"

Hanuman with due obeisance placed his hand upon his head,
Bowed unto the queenly Sita and in gentle accents said :

" Trust me, Lady, valiant Rama soon will greet his saintly wife,
E'en as INDRA greets his goddess, SACHI dearer than his life,

Trust me, Sita, conquering Rama comes with panoply of war,
Shaking Lanka's sea-girt mountains, slaying Rakshas near and far !

He shall cross the boundless ocean with the battle's dread array,
He shall smite the impious Ravan and the cruel Rakshas slay,

Mighty Gods and strong Asuras shall not hinder Rama's path,
When at Lanka's gates he thunders with his more than godlike wrath,

Deadly YAMA, all-destroying, pales before his peerless might,
When his red right arm of vengeance wrathful Rama lifts to smite !

By the lofty Mandar mountains, by the fruit and root I seek,
By the cloud-obstructing Vindhyas, and by Malya's towering peak,

I will swear, my gentle Lady, Rama's vengeance draweth nigh,
Thou shalt see his beaming visage like the Lord of Midnight Sky,

Firm in purpose Rama waiteth on the Prasra-vana hill,
As upon the huge Airavat, INDRA, motionless and still !

Flesh of deer nor forest honey tasteth Rama true and bold,
Till he rescues cherished Sita from the Raksha's castled hold,

Thoughts of Sita leave not Rama dreary day or darksome night,
Till his vengeance deep and dreadful crushes Ravan in his might,

Forest flower nor scented.creeper pleases Rama's anguished heart,
Till he wins his wedded consort by his death-compelling dart ! "

IV

SITA'S TOKEN

Token from her raven tresses Sita to the Vanar gave,
Hanuman with dauntless valour crossed once more the ocean wave,

Where in Prasra-vana's mountain Rama with his brother stayed,
Jewel from the brow of Sita by her sorrowing consort laid,

Spake of Ravan's foul endearment and his loathsome loving word,
Spake of Sita's scorn and anger and her truth unto her lord,

Tears of sorrow and affection from the warrior's eyelids start,
As his consort's loving token Rama presses to his heart !

" As the mother-cow, Sugriva, yields her milk beside her young,
Welling tears upon this token yields my heart by anguish wrung,

Well I know this dear-loved jewel sparkling with the ray of heaven,
Born in sea, by mighty INDRA to my Sita's father given,

Well I know this tender token, Janak placed it on her hair,
When she came my bride and consort decked in beauty rich and rare,

Well I know this sweet memorial, Sita wore it on her head,
And her proud and peerless beauty on the gem a lustre shed !

Ah, methinks the gracious Janak stands again before my eye,
With a father's fond affection, with a monarch's stature high,

Ah, methinks my bride and consort, she who wore it on her brow,
Stands again before the altar, speaks again her loving vow,

Ah, the sad, the sweet remembrance ! ah, the happy days gone by,
Once again, O loving vision, wilt thou gladden Rama's eye !

Speak again, my faithful vassal, how my Sita wept and prayed,
Like the water to the thirsty, dear to me what Sita said,

Did she send this sweet remembrance as a blessing from above,
As a true and tender token of a woman's changeless love,

Did she waft her heart's affection o'er the billows of the sea,
Wherefore came she not in person from her foes and fetters free ?

Hanuman, my friend and comrade, lead me to the distant isle,
Where my soft-eyed Sita lingers midst the Rakshas dark and vile,

Where my true and tender consort like a lone and stricken deer,
Girt by Rakshas stern and ruthless sheds the unavailing tear,

Where she weeps in ceaseless anguish, sorrow-stricken, sad and pale,
Like the Moon by dark clouds shrouded then her light and lustre fail !

Speak again, my faithful henchman, loving message of my wife,
Like some potent drug her accents renovate my fainting life,

Arm thy forces, friend Sugriva, Rama shall not brook delay,
While in distant Lanka's confines Sita weeps the livelong day,

Marshal forth thy bannered forces, cross the ocean in thy might,
Rama speeds on wings of vengeance Lanka's impious lord to smite ! "

BOOK IX

RAVANA-SABHA

(The Council of War)

RAVAN was thoroughly frightened by the deeds of Hanuman. For Hanuman had not only penetrated into his island and discovered Sita in her imprisonment, but had also managed to burn down a great portion of the city before he left the island. Ravan called a Council of War, and as might be expected, all the advisers heedlessly advised war.

All but Bibhishan. He was the youngest brother of Ravan, and condemned the folly and the crime by which Ravan was seeking a war with the righteous and unoffending Rama. He advised that Sita should be restored to her lord and peace made with Rama. His voice was drowned in the cries of more violent advisers.

It is noticeable that Ravan's second brother, Kumbha-karna, also had the courage to censure his elder's action. But unlike Bibhishan he was determined to fight for his king whether he was right or wrong. There is a touch of sublimity in this blind and devoted loyalty of Kumbha-karna to the cause of his king and his country.

Bibhishan was driven from the court with indignity, and joined the forces of Rama, to whom he gave much valuable information about Lanka and its warriors.

The passages translated in this Book form Sections vi., viii., ix., portions of Sections xii. and xv., and the whole of Section xvi. of Book vi. of the original text.

I

RAVAN SEEKS ADVICE

Monarch of the mighty Rakshas, Ravan spake to warriors all,
Spake to gallant chiefs and princes gathered in his Council Hall:

" Listen, Princes, Chiefs, and Warriors ! Hanuman our land hath seen,
Stealing through the woods of Lanka unto Rama's prisoned queen,

And audacious in his purpose and resistless in his ire,
Burnt our turret tower and temple, wasted Lanka's town with fire !

Speak your counsel, gallant leaders, Ravan is intent to hear,
Triumph waits on fearless wisdom, speak your thoughts without a
fear,

Wisest monarchs act on counsel from his men for wisdom known,
Next are they who in their wisdom and their daring act alone,

Last, unwisest are the monarchs who nor death nor danger weigh,
Think not, ask not friendly counsel, by their passions borne away !

Wisest counsel comes from courtiers who in holy lore unite,
Next, when varying plans and reasons blending lead unto the right,

Last and worst, when stormy passions mark the hapless king's debate,
And his friends are disunited when his foe is at the gate !

Therefore freely speak your counsel and your monarch's task shall be
But to shape in deed and action what your wisest thoughts decree,

Speak with minds and hearts united, shape your willing monarch's
deed,
Counsel peace, or Ravan's forces to a war of vengeance lead,

Ere Sugriva's countless forces cross the vast and boundless main,
Ere the wrathful Rama girdles Lanka with a living chain ! "

II

PRAHASTA'S SPEECH

Dark and high as summer tempest mighty-armed Prahasta rose,
Spake in fierce and fiery accents hurling challenge on his foes :

"Wherefore, Ravan, quails thy bosom, gods against thee strive in vain,
Wherefore fear the feeble mortals, homeless hermits, helpless men ?

Hanuman approached in secret, stealing like a craven spy,
Not from one in open combat would alive the Vanar fly,

Let him come with all his forces, to the confines of the sea
I will chase the scattered army and thy town from foemen free !

Not in fear and hesitation Ravan should repent his deed,
While his gallant Raksha forces stand beside him in his need,

Not in tears and vain repentance Sita to his consort yield,
While his chieftains guard his empire in the battle's gory field ! "

III

DURMUKHA'S SPEECH

Durmukha of cruel visage and of fierce and angry word,
Rose within the Council Chamber, spake to Lanka's mighty lord :

" Never shall the wily foeman boast of insult on us flung,
Hanuman shall die a victim for the outrage and the wrong !

Stealing in unguarded Lanka through thy city's virgin gate,
He hath courted deep disaster and a dark untimely fate,

Stealing in the inner mansions where our dames and damsels dwell,
Hanuman shall die a victim,—tale of shame he shall not tell !

Need is none of Ravan's army, bid me seek the foe alone,
If he hides in sky or ocean or in nether regions thrown,

Need is none of gathered forces, Ravan's mandate I obey,
I will smite the bold intruder and his Vanar forces slay ! "

IV

VAJRA-DANSHTRA'S SPEECH

Iron-toothéd Vajra-danshtra then arose in wrath and pride,
And his blood-stained mace of battle held in fury by his side,

" Wherefore, Ravan, waste thy forces on the foemen poor and vile,
Hermit Rama and his brother, Hanuman of impious wile,

Bid me,—with this mace of battle proud Sugriva I will slay,
Chase the helpless hermit brothers to the forests far away !

Or to deeper counsel listen ! Varied shapes the Rakshas wear,
Let them wearing human visage. dressed as Bharat's troops appear,

Succour from his ruling brother Rama will in gladness greet,
Then with mace and blood-stained sabre we shall lay them at our feet,

Rock and javelin and arrow we shall on our foemen hail,
Till no poor surviving Vanar lives to tell the tragic tale ! "

V

SPEECH OF NIKUMBHA AND VAJRA-HANU

Then arose the brave Nikumbha,—Kumbha-karna's son was he,—
Spake his young heart's mighty passion in his accents bold and free :

" Need is none, O mighty monarch, for a battle or a war,
Bid me meet the homeless Rama and his brother wand'ring far,

Bid me face the proud Sugriva, Hanuman of deepest wile,
I will rid thee of thy foemen and of Vanars poor and vile ! "

Rose the chief with jaw of iron, Vajra-hanu fierce and young,
Licked his lips like hungry tiger with his red and lolling tongue :

" Wherefore, monarch, dream of battle ? Rakshas feed on human
        gore,
Let me feast upon thy foemen by the ocean's lonely shore,

Rama and his hermit brother, Hanuman who hides in wood,
Angad and the proud Sugriva soon shall be my welcome food ! "

VI

BIBHISHAN'S WARNING

Twenty warriors armed and girded in the Council Hall arose,
Thirsting for a war of vengeance, hurling challenge on the foes,

But Bibhishan deep in wisdom,—Ravan's youngest brother he,—
Spake the word of solemn warning, for his eye could farthest see :

" Pardon, king and honoured elder, if Bibhishan lifts his voice
'Gainst the wishes of the warriors and the monarch's fatal choice,

Firm in faith and strong in forces Rama comes with conqu'ring might,
Vain against a righteous warrior would unrighteous Ravan fight !

Think him not a common Vanar who transpassed the ocean wave,
Wrecked thy city tower and temple and a sign and warning gave,

Think him not a common hermit who Ayodhya ruled of yore,
Crossing India's streams and mountains, thunders now on Lanka's
shore !

What dark deed of crime or folly hath the righteous Rama done,
That you stole his faithful consort unprotected and alone,

What offence or nameless insult hath the saintly Sita given,
She who chained in Lanka's prison pleads in piteous tear to Heaven ?

Take my counsel, king and elder, Sita to her lord restore,
Wipe this deed of wrong and outrage, Rama's righteous grace implore,

Take my counsel, Raksha monarch, vain against him is thy might,
Doubly arméd is the hero,—he who battles for the right !

Render Sita to her Rama ere with vengeance swift and dire,
He despoils our peopled Lanka with his bow and brand and fire,

Render wife unto her husband ere in battle's dread array,
Rama swoops upon thy empire like a falcon on its prey,

Render to the lord his consort ere with blood of Rakshas slain,
Rama soaks the land of Lanka to the margin of the main !

Listen to my friendly counsel,—though it be I stand alone,—
Faithful friend but fiery foeman is this Dasa-ratha's son,

Listen to my voice of warning,—Rama's shafts are true and keen,
Flaming like the with'ring sunbeams on the summer's parchéd green,

Listen to my soft entreaty,—righteousness becomes the brave,
Cherish peace and cherish virtue and thy sons and daughters save ! "

VII

KUMBHA-KARNA'S DETERMINATION

Ravan's brother Kumbha-karna, from his wonted slumber woke,
Mightiest he of all the Rakshas, thus in solemn accents spoke :

" Truly speaks the wise Bibhishan ; ere he stole a hermit's wife,
Ravan should have thought and pondered, courted not a causeless
    strife,

Ere he did this deed of folly, Ravan should have counsel sought,
Tardy is the vain repentance when the work of shame is wrought !

Word of wisdom timely spoken saves from death and dangers dire,
Vain is grief for crime committed,—offerings to unholy fire,

Vain is hero's worth or valour if by foolish counsel led,
Toil and labour fail and perish save when unto wisdom wed,

And the foeman speeds in triumph o'er a heedless monarch's might,
As through gaps of Krauncha mountains *hansas* speed their southern
    flight !

Ravan, thou hast sought unwisely Sita in her calm retreat,
As the wild and heedless hunter feeds upon the poisoned meat.

Nathless, faithful Kumbha-karna will his loyal duty know,
He shall fight his monarch's battle, he shall face his brother's foe !

True to brother and to monarch, be he right or be he wrong,
Kumbha-karna fights for Lanka 'gainst her foemen fierce and strong,

Recks not if the mighty INDRA and VIVASVAT cross his path,
Or the wild and stormy MARUTS, AGNI in his fiery wrath !

For the Lord of Sky shall tremble when he sees my stature high,
And he hears his thunders echoed by my loud and answering cry,

Rama armed with ample quiver shall no second arrow send,
Ere I slay him in the battle and his limb from limb I rend !

Wiser heads than Kumbha-karna right and true from wrong may
    know,
Faithful to his race and monarch he shall face the haughty foe,

Joy thee in thy pleasure, Ravan, rule thy realm in regal pride,
When I slay the hermit Rama, widowed Sita be thy bride ! "

VIII

INDRAJIT'S ASSURANCE

Indrajit the son of Ravan then his lofty purpose told,
'Midst the best and boldest Rakshas none so gallant, none so bold :

" Wherefore, noble king and father, pale Bibhishan's counsel hear,
Scion of the race of Rakshas speaks not thus in dastard fear,

In this race of valiant Rakshas, known for deeds of glory done,
Feeble-hearted, faint in courage, save Bibhishan, there is none !

Matched with meanest of the Rakshas what are sons of mortal men,
What are homeless human brothers hiding in the hermit's den,

Shall we yield to weary wand'rers, driven from their distant home,
Chased from throne and father's kingdom in the desert woods to
    roam ?

Lord of sky and nether region, INDRA 'neath my weapon fell,
Pale Immortals know my valour and my warlike deeds can tell,

INDRA's tusker, huge Airavat, by my prowess overthrown,
Trumpeted its anguished accents, shaking sky and earth with groan,

Mighty Gods and dauntless Daityas fame of Indrajit may know,
And he yields not, king and father, to a homeless human foe ı "

IX

RAVAN'S DECISION

Anger swelled in Ravan's bosom as he cast his blood-red eye
On Bibhishan calm and fearless, and he spake in accents high :

" Rather dwell with open foemen or in homes where cobras haunt,
Than with faithless friends who falter and whom fears of danger
    daunt !

O, the love of near relations !—false and faithless, full of guile,—
How they sorrow at my glory, at my danger how they smile,

How they grieve with secret anguish when my loftier virtues shine,
How they harbour jealous envy when deserts and fame are mine,

How they scan with curious vision every fault that clouds my path,
How they wait with eager longing till I fall in Fortune's wrath !

Ask the elephants of jungle how their captors catch and bind,—
Not by fire and feeble weapons, but by treason of their kind,

Not by javelin or arrow,—little for these arms they care,—
But their false and fondling females lead them to the hunter's snare !

Long as nourishment and vigour shall impart the milk of cow,
Long as woman shall be changeful, hermits holy in their vow,

Aye, so long shall near relations hate us in their inner mind,
Mark us with a secret envy though their words be ne'er so kind !

Rain-drops fall upon the lotus but unmingling hang apart,
False relations round us gather but they blend not heart with heart,

Winter clouds are big with thunder but they shed no freshening rain,
False relations smile and greet us but their soothing words are vain,

Bees are tempted by the honey but from flower to flower they range,
False relations share our favour but in secret seek a change !

Lying is thy speech, Bibhishan, secret envy lurks within,
Thou wouldst rule thy elder's empire, thou wouldst wed thy elder's
    queen,

Take thy treason to the foemen,—brother's blood I may not shed,—
Other Raksha craven-hearted by my royal hands had bled ! ''

X

BIBHISHAN'S DEPARTURE

'' This to me ! '' Bibhishan answered, as with fiery comrades four,
Rose in arms the wrathful Raksha and in fury rushed before,

'' But I spare thee, royal Ravan, angry words thy lips have passed,
False and lying and unfounded is the censure thou hast cast !

True Bibhishan sought thy safety, strove to save his elder's reign,—
Speed thee now to thy destruction since all counsel is in vain,

Many are thy smiling courtiers who with honeyed speech beguile,—
Few are they with truth and candour speak their purpose void of
    guile !

Blind to reason and to wisdom, Ravan, seek thy destined fate,
For thy impious lust of woman, for thy dark unrighteous hate,

Blind to danger and destruction, deaf to word of counsel given,
By the flaming shafts of Rama thou shalt die by will of Heaven !

Yet, O ! yet, my king and elder, let me plead with latest breath,
'Gainst the death of race and kinsmen,'gainst my lord and brother's death,

Ponder yet, O Raksha monarch, save thy race and save thy own,
Ravan, part we now for ever,—guard thy ancient sea-girt throne ! "

BOOK X

YUDDHA

(The War in Ceylon)

RAMA crossed over with his army from India to Ceylon. There is a chain of islands across the strait, and the Indian poet supposes them to be the remains of a vast causeway which Rama built to cross over with his army.

The town of Lanka, the capital of Ceylon, was invested, and the war which followed was a succession of sallies by the great leaders and princes of Lanka. But almost every sally was repulsed, every chief was killed, and at last Ravan himself who made the last sally was slain and the war ended.

Among the numberless fights described in the original work, those of Ravan himself, his brother Kumbha-karna, and his son Indrajit, are the most important, and oftenest recited and listened to in India ; and these have been rendered into English in this Book. And the reader will mark a certain method in the poet's estimate of the warriors who took part in these battles.

First and greatest among the warriors was Rama ; he was never beaten by an open foe, never conquered in fair fight. Next to him, and to him only, was Ravan the monarch of Lanka ; he twice defeated Lakshman in battle, and never retreated except before Rama. Next to Rama and to Ravan stood their brothers, Lakshman and Kumbha-karna ; it is difficult to say who was the best of these two, for they fought only once, and it was a drawn battle. Fifth in order of prowess was Indrajit the son of Ravana, but he was the first in his magic art. Concealed in mists by his magic, he twice defeated both Rama and Lakshman ; but in his last battle he had to wage a face to face combat with Lakshman, and was slain. After these five warriors, pre-eminent for their prowess, various Vanars and Rakshas took their rank.

The war ended with the fall of Ravan and his funerals. The portions translated in this Book form the whole or portions of Sections xliv., xlviii., lix., lxvi., lxvii., and lxxiii., an abstract of Sections lxxv. to xci., and portions of Sections xciii., xcvi., ci., cii., ciii., cix., cx., and cxiii. of Book vi. of the original text.

I

INDRAJIT'S FIRST BATTLE—THE SERPENT-NOOSE

Darkly round the leaguered city Rama's countless forces lay,
Far as Ravan cast his glances in the dawning light of day,

Wrath and anguish shook his bosom and the gates he opened wide,
And with ranks of charging Rakshas sallied with a Raksha's pride !

All the day the battle lasted, endless were the tale to tell,
What unnumbered Vanars perished and what countless Rakshas fell,

Darkness came, the fiery foemen urged the still unceasing fight,
Struggling with a deathless hatred fiercer in the gloom of night !

Onward came resistless Rakshas, laid Sugriva's forces low,
Crushed the broken ranks of Vanars, drank the red blood of the foe,

Bravely fought the scattered Vanars facing still the tide of war,
Struggling with the charging tusker and the steed and battle car,

Till at last the gallant Lakshman and the godlike Rama came,
And they swept the hosts of Ravan like a sweeping forest flame,

And their shafts like hissing serpents on the falt'ring foemen fell,
Fiercer grew the sable midnight with the dying shriek and yell !

Dust arose like clouds of summer from each thunder-sounding car,
From the hoofs of charging coursers, from the elephants of war,

Streams of red blood warm and bubbling issued from the countless
slain,
Flooded battle's dark arena like the floods of summer rain,

Sound of trumpet and of bugle, drum and horn and echoing shell,
And the neigh of charging coursers and the tuskers' dying wail,

And the yell of wounded Rakshas and the Vanars' fierce delight,
Shook the earth and sounding welkin, waked the echoes of the night !

Six bright arrows Rama thundered from his weapon dark and dread,
Iron-toothéd Vajra-dranshtra and his fainting comrades fled,

Dauntless still the serried Rakshas, wave on wave succeeding came,
Perished under Rama's arrows as the moths upon the flame !

Indrajit the son of Ravan, Lanka's glory and her pride,
Matchless in his magic weapons came and turned the battle's tide,

What though Angad in his fury had his steeds and driver slayed,
Indrajit hid in the midnight battled from its friendly shade,

Shrouded in a cloud of darkness still he poured his darts like rain,
On young Lakshman and on Rama and on countless Vanars slain,

Matchless in his magic weapons, then he hurled his *Naga*-dart,
Serpent noose upon his foemen draining lifeblood from their heart !

Vainly then the royal brothers fought the cloud-enshrouded foe,
Vainly sought the unseen warrior dealing unresisted blow,

Fastened by a noose of *Naga* forced by hidden foe to yield,
Rama and the powerless Lakshman fell and fainted on the field !

II

SITA'S LAMENT

Indrajit ere dawned the morning entered in his father's hall,
Spake of midnight's darksome contest, Rama's death and Lakshman's fall,

And the proud and peerless Ravan clasped his brave and gallant son,'
Praised him for his skill and valour and his deed of glory done,

And with dark and cruel purpose bade his henchmen yoke his car,
Bade them take the sorrowing Sita to the gory field of war !

Soon they harnessed royal coursers and they took the weeping wife,
Where her Rama, pierced and bleeding, seemed bereft of sense and
life,

Brother lay beside his brother with their shattered mail and bow,
Arrows thick and dark with red blood spake the conquest of the foe,

Anguish woke in Sita's bosom and a dimness filled her eye,
And a widow's nameless sorrow burst in widow's mournful cry :

" Rama, lord and king and husband ! didst thou cross the billowy
sea,
Didst thou challenge death and danger, court thy fate to rescue me,

Didst thou hurl a fitting vengeance on the cruel Raksha force,
Till the hand of hidden foeman checked thy all-resistless course ?

Breathes upon the earth no warrior who could face thee in the fight,
Who could live to boast his triumph o'er thy world-subduing might,

But the will of Fate is changeless, Death is mighty in his sway,—
Peerless Rama, faithful Lakshman, sleep the sleep that knows no
    day !

But I weep not for my Rama nor for Lakshman young and brave,
They have done a warrior's duty and have found a warrior's grave,

And I weep not for my sorrows,—sorrow marked me from my birth,—
Child of Earth I seek in suffering bosom of my mother Earth !

But I grieve for dear Kausalya, sonless mother, widowed queen,
How she reckons days and seasons in her anguish ever green.

How she waits with eager longing till her Rama's exile o'er,
He would soothe her lifelong sorrow, bless her agéd eyes once more,

Sita's love ! Ayodhya's monarch ! Queen Kausalya's dearest born !
Rama soul of truth and virtue sleeps the sleep that knows no morn ! "

Sorely wept the sorrowing Sita in her accents soft and low,
And the silent stars of midnight wept to witness Sita's woe,

But Trijata her companion,—though a Raksha woman she,—
Felt her soul subdued by sadness, spake to Sita tenderly :

" Weep not, sad and saintly Sita, shed not widow's tears in vain,
For thy lord is sorely wounded, but shall live to fight again,

Rama and the gallant Lakshman, fainting, not bereft of life,
They shall live to fight and conquer,—thou shalt be a happy wife,

Mark the Vanars' marshalled forces, listen to their warlike cries,
'Tis not thus the soldiers gather when a chief and hero dies,

'Tis not thus round lifeless leader muster warriors true and brave,
For when falls the dying helmsman, sinks the vessel in the wave !

Mark the ring of hopeful Vanars, how they watch o'er Rama's face,
How they guard the younger Lakshman beaming yet with living
    grace,

Trust me,sad and sorrowing Sita, marks of death these eyes can trace,
Shade of death's decaying fingers sweeps not o'er thy Rama's face !

Listen more, my gentle Sita, though a captive in our keep,
For thy woes and for thy anguish see a Raksha woman weep,

Though thy Rama armed in battle is our unrelenting foe,
For a true and stainless warrior see a Raksha filled with woe !

Fainting on the field of battle, blood-ensanguined in their face,
They shall live to fight and conquer, worthy of their gallant race,

Cold nor rigid are their features, darkness dwells not on their brow,
Weep not thus, my gentle Sita,—hasten we to Lanka now."

And Trijata spake no falsehood, by the winged Garuda's skill,
Rama and the valiant Lakshman lived to fight their foemen still !

III

RAVAN's FIRST BATTLE—THE JAVELIN-STROKE

'Gainst the God-assisted Rama, Ravan's efforts all were vain,
Leaguered Lanka vainly struggled in her adamantine chain,

Wrathful Rakshas with their forces vainly issued through the gate,
Chiefs and serried ranks of warriors met the same resistless fate !

Dark-eyed chief Dhumraksha sallied with the fierce tornado's shock,
Hanuman of peerless prowess slayed him with a rolling rock,

Iron-toothéd Vajra-danshtra dashed through countless Vanars slain,
But the young and gallant Angad laid him lifeless on the plain,

Akampan unshaken warrior issued out of Lanka's wall,
Hanuman was true and watchful, speedy was the Raksha's fall,

Then the mighty-armed Prahasta strove to break the hostile line,
But the gallant Nila felled him as the woodman fells the pine !

Bravest chiefs and countless soldiers sallied forth to face the fight,
Broke not Rama's iron circle, 'scaped not Rama's wondrous might,

Ravan could no longer tarry, for his mightiest chiefs were slain,
Foremost leaders, dearest kinsmen, lying on the gory plain !

" Lofty scorn of foes unworthy spared them from my flaming ire,
But the blood of slaughtered kinsmen claims from me a vengeance
    dire,"

Speaking thus the wrathful Ravan mounted on his thundering car,
Flame-resplendent was the chariot drawn by matchless steeds of war!

Beat of drum and voice of *sankha* and the Raksha's battle cry,
Song of triumph, chanted *mantra*, smote the echoing vault of sky,

And the troops like cloudy masses with their eyes of lightning fire
Girt their monarch, as his legions girdle RUDRA in his ire !

Rolled the car with peal of thunder through the city's lofty gate,
And each fierce and fiery Raksha charged with warrior's deathless
    hate,

And the vigour of the onset cleft the stunned and scattered foe,
As a strong bark cleaves the billows riding on the ocean's brow !

Brave Sugriva king of Vanars met the foeman fierce and strong,
And a rock with mighty effort on the startled Ravan flung,

Vain the toil, disdainful Ravan dashed aside the flying rock,
Brave Sugriva pierced by arrows fainted neath the furious shock.

Next Susena chief and elder, Nala and Gavaksha bold,
Hurled them on the path of Ravan speeding in his car of gold,

Vainly heaved the rock and missile, vainly did with trees assail,
Onward sped the conquering Ravan, pierced the fainting Vanars fell.

Hanuman the son of MARUT next against the Raksha came,
Fierce and strong as stormy MARUT, warrior of unrivalled fame,

But the Raksha's mighty onset gods nor mortals might sustain,
Hanuman in red blood welt'ring rolled upon the gory plain.

Onward rolled the car of Ravan, where the dauntless Nila stood,
Armed with rock and tree and missile, thirsting for the Raksha's
    blood,

Vainly fought the valiant Nila, pierced by Ravan's pointed dart,
On the gory field of battle poured the red blood of his heart.

Onward through the scattered forces Ravan's conquering chariot
came,
Where in pride and dauntless valour Lakshman stood of warlike
fame,

Calm and proud the gallant Lakshman marked the all-resistless foe,
Boldly challenged Lanka's monarch as he held aloft his bow :

" Welcome, mighty Lord of Lanka ! wage with me an equal strife,
Wherefore with thy royal prowess seek the humble Vanars' life ! "

" Hath thy fate," so answered Ravan, " brought thee to thy deadly
foe,
Welcome, valiant son of Raghu ! Ravan longs to lay thee low ! "

Then they closed in dubious battle, Lanka's Lord his weapon bent,
Seven bright arrows, keen and whistling, on the gallant Lakshman
sent,

Vain the toil, for watchful Lakshman stout of heart and true of aim,
With his darts like shooting sunbeams cleft each arrow as it came.

Bleeding from the darts of Lakshman, pale with anger, wounded sore,
Ravan drew at last his *Sakti*, gift of Gods in days of yore,

Javelin of flaming splendour, deadly like the shaft of Fate,
Ravan hurled on dauntless Lakshman in his fierce and furious hate.

Vain were Lakshman's human weapons aimed with skill directed well,
Pierced by *Sakti*, gallant Lakshman in his red blood fainting fell,

Wrathful Rama saw the combat and arose in godlike might,
Bleeding Ravan turned to Lanka, sought his safety in his flight.

IV

FALL OF KUMBHA-KARNA

Once more healed and strong and valiant, Lakshman in his arms
arose,
Safe behind the gates of Lanka humbled Ravan shunned his foes,

Till the stalwart Kumbha-karna from his wonted slumbers woke,
Mightiest he of all the Rakshas ;—Ravan thus unto him spoke :

" Thou alone, O Kumbha-karna, can the Raksha's honour save,
Strongest of the Raksha warriors, stoutest-hearted midst the brave,

Speed thee like the Dread Destroyer to the dark and dubious fray,
Cleave through Rama's girdling forces, chase the scattered foe
    away ! "

Like a mountain's beetling turret Kumbha-karna stout and tall,
Passed the city's lofty portals and the city's girdling wall,

And he raised his voice in battle, sent his cry from shore to shore,
Solid mountains shook and trembled and the sea returned the roar !

INDRA nor the great VARUNA equalled Kumbha-karna's might,
Vanars trembled at the warrior, sought their safety in their flight,

But the prince of fair Kishkindha, Angad chief of warlike fame,
Marked his panic-stricken forces with a princely warrior's shame.

" Whither fly, ye trembling Vanars ? " thus the angry chieftain cried,
" All forgetful of your duty, of your worth and warlike pride,

Deem not stalwart Kumbha-karna is our match in open fight,
Forward let us meet in battle, let us crush his giant might ! "

Rallied thus, the broken army stone and tree and massive rock,
Hurled upon the giant Raksha speeding with the lightning's shock,

Vain each flying rock and missile, vain each stout and sturdy stroke,
On the Raksha's limbs of iron stone and tree in splinters broke.

Dashing through the scattered forces Kumbha-karna fearless stood,
As a forest conflagration feasts upon the parchéd wood,

Far as confines of the ocean, to the causeway they had made,
To the woods or caves or billows, Vanars in their terror fled !

Hanuman of dauntless valour turned not in his fear nor fled,
Heaved a rock with mighty effort on the Raksha's towering head,

With his spear-head Kumbha-karna dashed the flying rock aside,
By the Raksha's weapon stricken Hanuman fell in his pride.

Next Rishabha and brave Nila and the bold Sarabha came,
Gavaksha and Gandha-madan, chieftains of a deathless fame,

But the spear of Kumbha-karna hurled to earth his feeble foes,
Dreadful was the field of carnage, loud the cry of battle rose !

Angad prince of fair Kishkindha, filled with anger and with shame,
Tore a rock with wrathful prowess, to the fatal combat came,

Short the combat, soon the Raksha caught and turned his foe around
Hurled him in his deadly fury, bleeding, senseless on the ground !

Last, Sugriva king of Vanars with a vengeful anger woke,
Tore a rock from bed of mountain and in proud defiance spoke,

Vain Sugriva's toil and struggle, Kumbha-karna hurled a rock,
Fell Sugriva crushed and senseless 'neath the missile's mighty shock !

Piercing through the Vanar forces, like a flame through forest wood,
Came the Raksha where in glory Lakshman calm and fearless stood,

Short their contest,—Kumbha-karna sought a greater, mightier foe,
To the young and dauntless Lakshman spake in accents soft and low :

" Dauntless prince and matchless warrior, fair Sumitra's gallant son,
Thou hast proved unrivalled prowess and unending glory won,

But I seek a mightier foeman, to thy elder let me go,
I would fight the royal Rama, or to die or slay my foe ! "

" *Victor proud!*" *said gallant Lakshman,* " *peerless in thy giant might,*
Conqueror of great Immortals, Lakshman owns thy skill in fight,

Mightier foe than bright Immortals thou shalt meet in fatal war,
Death for thee in guise of Rama tarries yonder, not afar ! "

Ill it fared with Kumbha-karna when he strove with Rama's might,
Men on earth nor Gods immortal conquered Rama in the fight,

Deadly arrows keen and flaming from the hero's weapon broke,
Kumbha-karna faint and bleeding felt his death at every stroke,

Last, an arrow pierced his armour, from his shoulders smote his head,
Kumbha-karna, lifeless, headless, rolled upon the gory bed,

Hurled unto the heaving ocean Kumbha-karna's body fell,
And as shaken by a tempest, mighty was the ocean's swell !

V

INDRAJIT'S SACRIFICE AND SECOND BATTLE

Still around beleaguered Lanka girdled Rama's living chain,
Raksha chieftain after chieftain strove to break the line in vain,

Sons of Ravan,—brave Narantak was by valiant Angad slain,
Trisiras and fierce Devantak, Hanuman slew on the plain,

Atikaya, tall of stature, was by gallant Lakshman killed,
Ravan wept for slaughtered princes, brave in war in weapons skilled.

" Shed no tears of sorrow, father ! " Indrajit exclaimed in pride,
" While thy eldest son surviveth triumph dwells on Ravan's side,

Rama and that stripling Lakshman, I had left them in their gore,
Once again I seek their lifeblood,—they shall live to fight no more.

Hear my vow, O Lord of Rakshas ! ere descends yon radiant sun,
Rama's days and gallant Lakshman's on this wide earth shall be done,

Witness INDRA and VIVASWAT, VISHNU great and RUDRA dire,
Witness Sun and Moon and Sadhyas, and the living God of Fire ! "

Opened wide the gates of Lanka ; in the spacious field of war,
Indrajit arranged his army, foot and horse and battle car,

Then with gifts and sacred *mantras* bent before the God of Fire,
And invoked celestial succour in the battle dread and dire.

With his offerings and his garlands, Indrajit with spices rare,
Worshipped holy VAISWA-NARA on the altar bright and fair,

Spear and mace were ranged in order, dart and bow and shining blade
Sacred fuel, blood-red garments, fragrant flowers were duly laid,

Head of goat as black as midnight offered then the warrior brave,
And the shooting tongue of red fire omens of a conquest gave,

Curling to the right and smokeless, red and bright as molten gold,
Tongue of flame received the offering of the hero true and bold !

Victory the sign betokens ! Bow and dart and shining blade,
Sanctified by holy *mantras*, by the Fire the warrior laid,

Then with weapons consecrated, hid in mists as once before,
Indrajit on helpless foemen did his fatal arrows pour !

Fled the countless Vanar forces, panic-stricken, crushed and slain,
And the dead and dying warriors strewed the gory battle plain,

Then on Rama, and on Lakshman, from his dark and misty shroud,
Indrajit discharged his arrows bright as sunbeams through a cloud.

Scanning earth and bright sky vainly for his dark and hidden foe,
Rama to his brother Lakshman spake in grief and spake in woe :

" Once again that wily Raksha, slaying all our Vanar train,
From his dark and shadowy shelter doth on us his arrows rain,

By the grace of great SWAYAMBHU, Indrajit is lost to sight,
Useless is our human weapon 'gainst his gift of magic might,

If SWAYAMBHU wills it, Lakshman, we shall face these fatal darts,
We shall stand with dauntless patience, we shall die with dauntless
hearts ! "

Weaponless but calm and valiant, from the foeman's dart and spell
Patiently the princes suffered, fearlessly the heroes fell !

VI

INDRAJIT'S THIRD BATTLE AND FALL

Healing herbs from distant mountains Hanuman in safety brought,
Rama rose and gallant Lakshman, once again their foemen sought.

And when night its sable mantle o'er the earth and ocean drew,
Forcing through the gates of Lanka to the frightened city flew !

Gallant sons of Kumbha-karna vainly fought to stem the tide,
Hanuman and brave Sugriva slew the brothers in their pride,

Makaraksha, shark-eyed warrior, vainly struggled with the foe,
Rama laid him pierced and lifeless by an arrow from his bow.

Indrajit arose in anger for his gallant kinsmen slayed,
In his arts and deep devices Sita's beauteous image made,

And he placed the form of beauty on his speeding battle car,
With his sword he smote the image in the gory field of war !

Rama heard the fatal message which his faithful Vanars gave,
And a deathlike trance and tremor fell upon the warrior brave,

But Bibhishan deep in wisdom to the anguished Rama came,
With his words of consolation spake of Rama's righteous dame :

" Trust me, Rama, trust thy comrade,—for I know our wily house,—
Indrajit slays not the woman whom his father seeks as spouse,

'Tis for Sita, impious Ravan meets thee on the battle-field,
Stakes his life and throne and empire, but thy Sita will not yield,

Deem not that the king of Rakshas will permit her blood be shed,
Indrajit slays not the woman whom his father seeks to wed !

'Twas an image of thy Sita, Indrajit hath cleft in twain,
While our army wails and sorrows,—he performs his rites again,

To the holy Nikumbhila, Indrajit in secret hies,
For the rights which yield him prowess, hide him in the cloudy skies.

Let young Lakshman seek the foeman ere his magic rites be done,—
Once the sacrifice completed, none can combat Ravan's son,—

Let young Lakshman speed through Lanka till his wily foe is found,
Slay the secret sacrificer on the sacrificial ground ! "

Unto holy Nikumbhila, Lakshman with Bibhishan went
Bravest, choicest of the army, Rama with his brother sent,

Magic rites and sacrifices Indrajit had scarce begun,
When surprised by arméd foemen rose in anger Ravan's son !

" Art thou he," thus to Bibhishan, Indrajit in anger spake,
" Brother of my royal father, stealing thus my life to take,

Raksha born of Raksha parents, dost thou glory in this deed,
Traitor to thy king and kinsmen, false to us in direst need ?

Scorn and pity fill my bosom thus to see thee leave thy kin,
Serving as a slave of foemen, stooping to a deed of sin,

For the slave who leaves his kindred, basely seeks the foeman's grace,
Meets destruction from the foeman after he destroys his race ! "

" Untaught child of impure passions," thus Bibhishan answer made,
" Of my righteous worth unconscious bitter accents hast thou said,

Know, proud youth, that Truth and Virtue in my heart precedence
take,
And we shun the impious kinsman as we shun the pois'nous snake !

Listen, youth ! this earth no longer bears thy father's sin and strife,
Plunder of the righteous neighbour, passion for the neighbour's wife,

Earth and skies have doomed thy father for his sin-polluted reign,
Unto Gods his proud defiance and his wrongs to sons of men !

Listen more ! this fated Lanka groans beneath her load of crime,
And shall perish in her folly by the ruthless hand of Time,

Thou shalt perish and thy father and this proud presumptuous state,
Lakshman meets thee, impious Raksha, by the stern decree of Fate ! "

" Hast thou too forgot the lesson," Indrajit to Lakshman said,
" Twice in field of war unconscious thee with Rama have I laid,

Dost thou stealing like a serpent brave my yet unconquered might,
Perish, boy, in thy presumption, in this last and fatal fight ! "

Spake the hero : " Like a coward hid beneath a mantling cloud,
Thou hast battled like a caitiff safe behind thy sheltering shroud,

Now I seek an open combat, time is none to prate or speak,
Boastful word is coward's weapon, weapons and thy arrows seek ! "

Soon they mixed in dubious combat, fury fired each foeman's heart,
Either warrior felt his rival worthy of his bow and dart,

Lakshman with his hurtling arrows pierced the Raksha's golden mail,
Shattered by the Raksha's weapons Lakshman's useless armour fell,

Red with gore and dim in eyesight still the chiefs in fury fought,
Neither quailed before his foeman, pause nor grace nor mercy sought,

Till with more than human valour Lakshman drew his bow amain,
Slayed the Raksha's steeds and driver, severed too his bow in twain.

" If the great and godlike Rama is in faith and duty true,
Gods assist the cause of virtue ! "—Lakshman uttered as he drew,

Fatal was the dart unerring,—Gods assist the true and bold,—
On the field of Nikumbhila, Lakshman's foeman headless rolled !

VII

RAVAN'S LAMENT

" Quenched the light of Rakshas' valour ! " so the message-bearer
    said,
" Lakshman with the deep Bibhishan hath thy son in battle slayed,

Fallen is our prince and hero and his day on earth is done,
In a brighter world, O monarch, lives thy brave, thy gallant son ! "

Anguish filled the father's bosom and his fleeting senses failed,
Till to deeper sorrow wakened Lanka's monarch wept and wailed :

" Greatest of my gallant warriors, dearest to thy father's heart,
Victor over bright Immortals,— art thou slain by Lakshman's dart,

Noble prince whose peerless arrows could the peaks of Mandar stain,
And could daunt the Dread Destroyer,—art thou by a mortal slain ?

But thy valour lends a radiance to elysium's sunny clime,
And thy bright name adds a lustre to the glorious rolls of time,

In the skies the bright Immortals lisp thy name with terror pale,
On the earth our maids and matrons mourn thy fall with piercing
    wail !

Hark ! the voice of lamentation waking in the palace halls,
Like the voice of woe in forests when the forest monarch falls,

Hark ! the wailing widowed princess, mother weeping for her son,
Leaving them in tears and anguish, Indrajit, where art thou gone ?

Full of years,—so oft I pondered,—when the monarch Ravan dies,
Indrajit shall watch his bedside, Indrajit shall close his eyes,

But the course of nature changes, and the father weeps the son,
Youth is fallen, and the aged lives to fight the foe alone ! "

Tears of sorrow, slow and silent, fell upon the monarch's breast,
Then a swelling rage and passion woke within his heaving chest,

Like the sun of scorching summer glowed his face in wrathful shame,
From his brow and rolling eyeballs issued sparks of living flame !

" Perish she ! " exclaimed the monarch, " she-wolf Sita dies to-day,
Indrajit but cleft her image, Ravan will the woman slay ! "

Followed by his trembling courtiers, regal robes and garments rent,
Ravan shaking in his passion to *Asoka's* garden went,

Maddened by his wrath and anguish, with his drawn and flaming
    sword,
Sought the shades where soft-eyed Sita silent sorrowed for her lord.

Woman's blood the royal sabre on that fatal day had stained,
But his true and faithful courtiers Ravan's wrathful hand restrained..

And the watchful Raksha females girdled round the sorrowing dame,
Flung them on the path of Ravan to withstand a deed of shame.

" Not against a woman, Ravan, mighty warriors raise their hand,
In the battle," spake the courtiers, " duty bids thee use thy brand,

Versed in *Vedas* and in learning, court not thus a caitiff's fate,
Woman's blood pollutes our valour, closes heaven's eternal gate !

Leave the woman in her sorrow, mount upon thy battle car,
Faithful to our king and leader we will wake the voice of war,

'Tis the fourteenth day auspicious of the dark and waning moon,
Glory waiteth thee in battle and thy vengeance cometh soon,

All-resistless in the contest slay thy foeman in his pride,
Seek as victor of the combat widowed Sita as thy bride ! "

Slow and sullen, dark and silent, Ravan then his wrath restrained,
Vengeance on his son's destroyer deep within his bosom reigned !

VIII

Ravan's Second Battle and Vengeance

Voice of woe and lamentation and the cry of woman's wail,
Issuing from the homes of Lanka did the monarch's ears assail,

And a mighty thought of vengeance waked within the monarch's heart,
And he heaved a sigh of anguish as he grasped his bow and dart :

" Arm each chief and gallant Raksha ! be our sacred duty done,
Ravan seeks a fitting vengeance for his brave and noble son,

Mahodar and Virupaksha, Mahaparshwa warrior tall,
Arm ! this fated day will witness Lakshman's or your monarch's fall !

Call to mind each slaughtered hero,—Khara, Dushan, slain in fight,
Kumbha-karna giant warrior, Indrajit of magic might,

Earth nor sky shall hide my foemen nor the ocean's heaving swell,
Scattered ranks of Rama's forces shall my speedy vengeance tell,

Be the red-earth strewn and covered with our countless foemen slain,
Hungry wolves and blood-beaked vultures feed upon the ghastly plain,

For his great and gallant brother, for his brave and beauteous son,
Ravan seeks a fitting vengeance, Rakshas be your duty done ! "

House to house, in Lanka's city, Ravan's royal hest was heard,
Street and lane poured forth their warriors by a mighty passion stirred,

With the javelin and sabre, mace and club and axe and pike,
Sataghni and *bhindipala*, quoit and discus quick to strike.

And they formed the line of tuskers and the line of battle car,
Mule and camel fit for burden and the fiery steed of war,

Serried ranks of arméd soldiers shook the earth beneath their tread,
Horsemen that on wings of lightning o'er the field of battle spread.

Drum and conch and sounding trumpet waked the echoes of the sky,
Pataha and loud *mridanga* and the people's maddening cry,

Thundering through the gates of Lanka, Ravan's lofty chariot passed
Destined by his fortune, Ravan ne'er again those portals crost !

And the sun was dim and clouded and a sudden darkness fell,
Birds gave forth their boding voices and the earth confessed a spell,

Gouts of blood in rain descended, startled coursers turned to fly,
Vultures swooped upon the banner, jackals yelled their doleful cry,

Omens of a dark disaster mantled o'er the vale and rock,
And the ocean heaved in billows, nations felt the earthquake shock !

Darkly closed the fatal battle, sturdy Vanars fell in fight,
Warlike leaders of the Rakshas perished neath the foeman's might,

Mahodhar and Virupaksha were by bold Sugriva slain,
Crushed by Angad, Mahaparshwa slumbered lifeless on the plain.

But with more than mortal valour Ravan swept the ranks of war,
Warriors fell beneath his prowess, fled before his mighty car,

Cleaving through the Vanar forces, filled with vengeance deep and
        dire,
Ravan marked the gallant Lakshman flaming like a crimson fire !

Like the tempest cloud of summer Ravan's wingéd courses flew,
But Bibhishan in his prowess soon the gallant charges slew,

Dashing from his useless chariot Ravan leaped upon the ground,
And his false and traitor brother by his dearest foeman found !

Wrathful Ravan marked Bibhishan battling by the foeman's side,
And he hurled his pond'rous weapon for to slay him in his pride,

Lakshman marked the mighty jav'lin as it winged its whizzing flight,
Cleft it in its onward passage, saved Bibhishan by his might !

Grimly smiled the angry Ravan gloating in his vengeful wrath,
Spake to young and dauntless Lakshman daring thus to cross
        his path :

" Welcome, Lakshman ! thee I battle for thy deed of darkness done,
Face the anger of a father, cruel slayer of the son,

By thy skill and by thy valour, false Bibhishan thou hast saved,
Save thyself ! Deep in this bosom is a cruel grief engraved ! "

Father's grief and sad remembrance urged the lightning-wingéd dart,
Ravan's *Sakti* fell resistless on the senseless Lakshman's heart,

Wrathful Rama saw the combat and arose in godlike might,
Carless, steedless, wounded Ravan sought his safety in his flight.

IX

RAMA'S LAMENT

" Art thou fallen," sorrowed Rama, " weary of this endless strife,
Lakshman, if thy days are ended, Rama recks not for his life,

Gone is Rama's wonted valour, weapons leave his nerveless hand,
Drop his bow and shining arrows, useless hangs his sheathéd brand !

Art thou fallen, gallant Lakshman, death and faintness on me creep,
Weary of this fatal contest let me by my brother sleep,

Weary of the strife and triumph, since my faithful friend is gone,
Rama follows in his footsteps and his task on earth is done !

Thou hast from the far Ayodhya, followed me in deepest wood,
In the thickest of the battle thou hast by thy elder stood,

Love of woman, love of comrade, trite is love of kith and kind,
Love like thine, true-hearted brother, not on earth we often find !

When Sumitra seeks thee, Lakshman, ever weeping for thy sake,
When she asks me of her hero, what reply shall Rama make,

What reply, when Bharat questions,—Where is he who went to wood,
Where is true and faithful Lakshman who beside his elder stood ?

What great crime or fatal shadow darkens o'er my hapless life,
Victim to the sins of Rama sinless Lakshman falls in strife,

Best of brothers, best of warriors, wherefore thus unconscious lie,
Mother, wife, and brother wait thee, ope once more thy sleeping
    eye ! "

Tara's father, wise Susena, gentle consolation lent,
Hanuman from distant mountains herbs of healing virtue rent,

And by loving Rama tended, Lakshman in his strength arose,
Stirred by thoughts of fatal vengeance Rama sought the flying foes.

X

Celestial Arms and Chariot

Not in dastard terror Ravan sought his safety in his flight,
But to seek fresh steeds of battle ere he faced his foeman's might,

Harnessing his gallant coursers to a new and glorious car,
Sunlike in its radiant splendour, Ravan came once more to war.

Gods in wonder watched the contest of the more than mortal foes,
Ravan mighty in his vengeance, Rama lofty in his woes,

Gods in wonder marked the heroes, lion-like in jungle wood,
INDRA sent his arms and chariot where the human warrior stood !

"Speed, Matali," thus spake INDRA, *" speed thee with my heavenly car,
Where on foot the righteous Rama meets his mounted foe in war,*

*Speed, for Ravan's days are ended, and his moments brief and few,
Rama strives for right and virtue,—Gods assist the brave and true ! "*

Brave Matali drove the chariot drawn by steeds like solar ray,
Where the true and righteous Rama sought his foe in fatal fray,

Shining arms and heavenly weapons he to lofty Rama gave,—
When the righteous strive and struggle, Gods assist the true and
brave !

" Take this car," so said Matali, " which the helping Gods provide,
Rama, take these steeds celestial, INDRA's golden chariot ride,

Take this royal bow and quiver, wear this falchion dread and dire,
VISWA-KARMAN forged this armour in the flames of heavenly fire,

I shall be thy chariot driver and shall speed the thund'ring car,
Slay the sin-polluted Ravan in this last and fatal war ! "

Rama mounted on the chariot clad in arms of heavenly sheen,
And he mingled in a contest mortal eyes have never seen !

XI

RAVAN'S THIRD BATTLE AND FALL

Gods and mortals watched the contest and the heroes of the war,
Ravan speeding on his chariot, Rama on the heavenly car,

And a fiercer form the warriors in their fiery frenzy wore,
And a deeper weight of hatred on their anguished bosoms bore,

Clouds of dread and deathful arrows hid the radiant face of sky,
Darker grew the day of combat, fiercer grew the contest high !

Pierced by Ravan's pointed weapons bleeding Rama owned no pain,
Rama's arrows keen and piercing sought his foeman's life in vain,

Long and dubious battle lasted, and with fury wilder fraught,
Wounded, faint, and still unyielding, blind with wrath the rivals
fought,

Pike and club and mace and trident scaped from Ravan's vengeful
    hand,
Spear and arrows Rama wielded, and his bright and flaming brand !

Long and dubious battle lasted, shook the ocean, hill and dale,
Winds were hushed in voiceless terror and the livid sun was pale,

Still the dubious battle lasted, until Rama in his ire
Wielded BRAHMA's deathful weapon flaming with celestial fire !

Weapon which the Saint Agastya had unto the hero given,
Winged as lightning dart of INDRA, fatal as the bolt of heaven,

Wrapped in smoke and flaming flashes, speeding from the circled bow,
Pierced the iron heart of Ravan, lain the lifeless hero low,

And a cry of pain and terror from the Raksha ranks arose,
And a shout from joying Vanars as they smote their fleeing foes !

Heavenly flowers in rain descended on the red and gory plain,
And from unseen harps and timbrels rose a soft celestial strain,

And the ocean heaved in gladness, brighter shone the sunlit sky,
Soft and cool the gentle zephyrs through the forest murmured by,

Sweetest scent and fragrant odours wafted from celestial trees,
Fell upon the earth and ocean, rode upon the laden breeze !

Voice of blessing from the bright sky fell on Raghu's valiant son,—
" Champion of the true and righteous ! now thy noble task is done ! "

XII

MANDODARI'S LAMENT AND THE FUNERALS

" Hast thou fallen," wept in anguish Ravan's first and eldest bride,
Mandodari, slender-waisted, Queen of Lanka's state and pride,

" Hast thou fallen, king and consort, more than Gods in warlike
    might,
Slain by man, whom bright Immortals feared to face in dubious fight?

Not a man !—the Dark Destroyer came to thee in mortal form,
Or the heaven-traversing VISHNU, INDRA ruler of the storm,

Gods of sky in shape of Vanars helped the dark and cruel deed,
Girdling round the Discus-Wielder in the battle's direst need !

Well I knew,—when Khara, Dushan, were by Rama's prowess slain,
Rama was no earthly mortal, he who crossed the mighty main,

Well I knew,—when with his army he invested Lanka's gate,
Rama was no earthly mortal but the messenger of Fate,

And I prayed,—the faithful Sita might unto her consort go,
For 'tis writ that nations perish for a righteous woman's woe,

But for impious lust of woman,—all forgetful of thy wife,
Thou hast lost thy crown and kingdom, thou hast lost thy fated life !

Woe to me ! the sad remembrance haunts my tortured bosom still,
Of our days on famed Kailasa or on Meru's golden hill,

Gone the days of joy and gladness, Mandodari's days are done,
Since her lord and king and husband from her dear embrace is gone!"

Sorely wept the Queen of Lanka ; Rama, tender, tearful, true,
Bade the funeral rites and honours to a fallen foeman due,

And they heaped the wood of *Chandan* and the fragrant garland laid,
On the pyre they lifted Ravan in the richest robes arrayed,

Weeping queens and sorrowing Rakshas round their fallen leader
    stood,
Brahmans with their chaunted *mantras* piled the dry and scented
    wood,

Oil and cords and sacred offerings were upon the altar laid,
And a goat of inky darkness as a sacrifice was slayed.

Piously the good Bibhishan lighted Ravan's funeral pyre,
And the zephyrs gently blowing fanned the bright and blazing fire,

Slow and sad with due ablutions mourners left the funeral site,
Rama then unstrung his weapon, laid aside his arms of might.

BOOK XI

RAJYA-ABHISHEKA

(*Rama's Return and Consecration*)

THE real Epic ends with the war, and with Rama's happy return to Ayodhya. Sita proves her stainless virtue by an Ordeal of Fire, and returns with her lord and with Lakshman in an aërial car, which Ravan had won from the Gods, and which Bibhishan made over to Rama. Indian poets are never tired of descriptions of nature, and the poet of the Ramayana takes advantage of Rama's journey from Ceylon to Oudh to give us a bird's-eye view of the whole continent of India, as well as to recapitulate the principal incidents of his great Epic.

The gathering of men at Ayodhya, the greetings to Rama, and his consecration by the Vedic bard Vasishtha, are among the most pleasing passages in the whole poem. And the happiness enjoyed by men during the reign of Rama—described in the last few couplets of this Book—is an article of belief and a living tradition in India to this day.

The portions translated in this Book form the whole or portions of Sections cxviii., cxx., cxxv., cxxix., and cxxx. of Book vi. of the original text.

I

ORDEAL BY FIRE

For she dwelt in Ravan's dwelling,—rumour clouds a woman's fame—
Righteous Rama's brow was clouded, saintly Sita spake in shame :

" Wherefore spake ye not, my Rama, if your bosom doubts my faith,
Dearer than a dark suspicion to a woman were her death !

Wherefore, Rama, with your token came your vassal o'er the wave,
To assist a fallen woman and a tainted wife to save,

Wherefore with your mighty forces crossed the ocean in your pride,
Risked your life in endless combats for a sin-polluted bride ?

Hast thou, Rama, all forgotten ?—Saintly Janak saw my birth,
Child of harvest-bearing furrow, Sita sprang from Mother Earth,

As a maiden true and stainless unto thee I gave my hand,
As a consort fond and faithful roved with thee from land to land !

But a woman pleadeth vainly when suspicion clouds her name,
Lakshman, if thou lov'st thy sister, light for me the funeral flame,

When the shadow of dishonour darkens o'er a woman's life,
Death alone is friend and refuge of a true and trustful wife,

When a righteous lord and husband turns his cold averted eyes,
Funeral flame dispels suspicion, honour lives when woman dies ! "

Dark was Rama's gloomy visage and his lips were firmly sealed,
And his eye betrayed no weakness, word disclosed no thought
concealed,

Silent heaved his heart in anguish, silent drooped his tortured head,
Lakshman with a throbbing bosom funeral pyre for Sita made,

And Videha's sinless daughter prayed unto the Gods above,
On her lord and wedded consort cast her dying looks of love !

" *If in act and thought,*" she uttered, " *I am true unto my name,*
Witness of our sins and virtues, may this Fire protect my fame !

If a false and lying scandal brings a faithful woman shame,
Witness of our sins and virtues, may this Fire protect my fame !

If in lifelong loving duty I am free from sin and blame,
Witness of our sins and virtues, may this Fire protect my fame ! "

Fearless in her faith and valour Sita stepped upon the pyre,
And her form of beauty vanished circled by the clasping fire,

And an anguish shook the people like the ocean tempest-tost,
Old and young and maid and matron wept for Sita true and lost,

For bedecked in golden splendour and in gems and rich attire,
Sita vanished in the red fire of the newly lighted pyre !

Rishis and the great *Gandharvas*, Gods who know each secret deed,
Witnessed Sita's high devotion and a woman's lofty creed,

And the earth by ocean girdled with its wealth of teeming life,
Witnessed deed of dauntless duty of a true and stainless wife !

II

WOMAN'S TRUTH VINDICATED

Slow the red flames rolled asunder, God of Fire incarnate came,
Holding in his radiant bosom fair Videha's sinless dame,

Not a curl upon her tresses, not a blossom on her brow,
Not a fibre of her mantle did with tarnished lustre glow !

Witness of our sins and virtues, God of Fire incarnate spake,
Bade the sorrow-stricken Rama back his sinless wife to take :

" Ravan in his impious folly forced from thee thy faithful dame,
Guarded by her changeless virtue, Sita still remains the same,

Tempted oft by female Rakshas in the dark and dismal wood,
In her woe and in her sadness true to thee hath Sita stood,

Courted oft by royal Ravan in the forest far and lone,
True to wedded troth and virtue Sita thought of thee alone,

Pure is she in thought and action, pure and stainless, true and meek,
I, the witness of all actions, thus my sacred mandate speak ! "

Rama's forehead was unclouded and a radiance lit his eye,
And his bosom heaved in gladness as he spake in accents high :

" Never from the time I saw her in her maiden days of youth,
Have I doubted Sita's virtue, Sita's fixed and changeless truth,

I have known her ever sinless,—let the world her virtue know,
For the God of Fire is witness to her truth and changeless vow !

Ravan in his pride and passion conquered not a woman's love,
For the virtuous like the bright fire in their native radiance move,

Ravan in his rage and folly conquered not a faithful wife,
For like ray of sun unsullied is a righteous woman's life,

Be the wide world now a witness,—pure and stainless is my dame,
Rama shall not leave his consort till he leaves his righteous fame ! "

In his tears the contrite Rama clasped her in a soft embrace,
And the fond forgiving Sita in his bosom hid her face !

III

Return Home by the Aërial Car

" Mark my love," so Rama uttered, as on flying Pushpa car,
Borne by swans, the home-returning exiles left the field of war,

" Lanka's proud and castled city on Trikuta's triple crest,
As on peaks of bold Kailasa mansions of Immortals rest !

Mark the gory fields surrounding where the Vanars in their might,
Faced and fought the charging Rakshas in the long and deathful
fight,

Indrajit and Kumbha-karna, Ravan and his chieftains slain,
Fell upon the field of battle and their red blood soaks the plain.

Mark where dark-eyed Mandodari, Ravan's slender-waisted wife,
Wept her widow's tears of anguish when her monarch lost his life,

She hath dried her tears of sorrow and bestowed her heart and hand,
On Bibhishan good and faithful, crownéd king of Lanka's land.

See my love, round Ceylon's island how the ocean billows roar,
Hiding pearls in caves of corals, strewing shells upon the shore,

And the causeway far-extending,—monument of Rama's fame,—
' Rama's Bridge ' to distant ages shall our deathless deeds proclaim !

See the rockbound fair Kishkindha and her mountain-girdled town,
Where I slayed the warrior Bali, placed Sugriva on the throne,

And the hill of Rishyamuka where Sugriva first I met,
Gave him word,—he would be monarch ere the evening's sun had set.

See the sacred lake of Pampa by whose wild and echoing shore,
Rama poured his lamentations when he saw his wife no more,

And the woods of Janasthana where Jatayu fought and bled,
When the deep deceitful Ravan with my trusting Sita fled.

Dost thou mark, my soft-eyed Sita, cottage on the river's shore,
Where in righteous peace and penance Sita lived in days of yore,

And by gloomy Godavari, Saint Agastya's home of love,
Holy men by holy duties sanctify the sacred grove !

Dost thou, o'er the Dandak forest, view the Chitrakuta hill,
Deathless bard the Saint Valmiki haunts its shade and crystal rill,

Thither came the righteous Bharat and my loving mother came,
Longing in their hearts to take us to Ayodhya's town of fame,

Dost thou, dear devoted Sita, see the Jumna in her might,
Where in Bharad-waja's *asram* passed we, love, a happy night,

And the broad and ruddy Ganga sweeping in her regal pride,
Forest-dweller faithful Guha crossed us to the southern side.

Joy ! joy ! my gentle Sita ! Fair Ayodhya looms above,
Ancient seat of Raghu's empire, nest of Rama's hope and love,

Bow, bow, to bright Ayodhya ! Darksome did the exiles roam,
Now their weary toil is ended in their father's ancient home ! "

IV

GREETINGS

Message from returning Rama, Vanars to Ayodhya brought,
Righteous Bharat gave his mandate with a holy joy distraught :

" Let our city shrines and *chaityas* with a lofty music shake,
And our priests to bright Immortals grateful gifts and offerings make,

Bards, reciters of *Puranas*, minstrels versed in ancient song,
Women with their tuneful voices lays of sacred love prolong,

Let our queens and stately courtiers step in splendour and in state,
Chieftains with their marshalled forces range along the city gate,

And our white-robed holy Brahmans hymns and sacred *mantras* sing,
Offer greetings to our brother, render homage to our king ! "

Brave Satrughna heard his elder and his mandate duly kept :
" Be our great and sacred city levelled, cleansed, and duly swept,

And the grateful earth be sprinkled with the water from the well,
Strewn with parchéd rice and offering and with flower of sweetest
        smell,

On each turret, tower, and temple let our flags and colours wave,
On the gates of proud Ayodhya plant Ayodhya's banners brave,

Gay festoons of flowering creeper home and street and dwelling line,
And in gold and glittering garment let the gladdened city shine ! "

Elephants in golden trappings thousand chiefs and nobles bore,
Chariots, cars, and gallant chargers speeding by Sarayu's shore,

And the serried troops of battle marched with colours rich and brave,
Proudly o'er the gay procession did Ayodhya's banners wave.

In their stately gilded litters royal dames and damsels came,
Queen Kausalya first and foremost, Queen Sumitra rich in fame,

Pious priest and learned Brahman, chief of guild from near and far,
Noble chief and stately courtier with the wreath and water jar.

Girt by minstrel, bard, and herald chanting glorious deeds of yore,
Bharat came,—his elder's sandals still the faithful younger bore,—

Silver-white his proud umbrella, silver-white his garland brave,
Silver-white the fan of *chowri* which his faithful henchmen wave.

Stately march of gallant chargers and the roll of battle car,
Heavy tread of royal tuskers and the beat of drum of war,

Dundubhi and echoing *sankha*, voice of nations gathered nigh,
Shook the city's tower and temple and the pealing vault of sky !

Sailing o'er the cloudless ether Rama's Pushpa chariot came,
And ten thousand jocund voices shouted Rama's joyous name,

Women with their loving greetings, children with their joyous cry,
Tottering age and lisping infant hailed the righteous chief and high.

Bharat lifted up his glances unto Rama from afar,
Unto Sita, unto Lakshman, seated on the Pushpa car,

And he wafted high his greetings and he poured his pious lay,
As one wafts the chaunted *mantra* to the rising God of Day !

Silver swans by Rama's bidding soft descended from the air,
And on earth the chariot lighted,—car of flowers divinely fair,—

Bharat mounting on the chariot, sought his long-lost elder's grace,
Rama held his faithful younger in a brother's dear embrace.

With his greetings unto Lakshman, unto Rama's faithful dame,
To Bibhishan and Sugriva and each chief who thither came,

Bharat took the jewelled sandals with the rarest gems inlaid,
Placed them at the feet of Rama and in humble accents said :

" Tokens of thy rule and empire, *these* have filled thy royal throne,
Faithful to his trust and duty Bharat renders back thine own,

Bharat's life is joy and gladness, for returned from distant shore,
Thou shalt rule thy spacious kingdom and thy loyal men once more,

Thou shalt hold thy rightful empire and assume thy royal crown,
Faithful to his trust and duty,—Bharat renders back thine own ! "

V

THE CONSECRATION

Joy ! joy ! in bright Ayodhya gladness filled the hearts of all,
Joy ! joy ! a lofty music sounded in the royal hall,

Fourteen years of woe were ended, Rama now assumed his own,
And they placed the weary wand'rer on his father's ancient throne,

And they brought the sacred water from each distant stream and hill,
From the vast and boundless ocean, from each far and sacred rill.

Vasishtha the Bard of *Vedas* with auspicious rites and meet
Placed the monarch and his consort on the gemmed and jewelled seat,

Gautama and Katyayana, Vamadeva priest of yore,
Jabali and wise Vijaya versed in holy ancient lore,

Poured the fresh and fragrant water on the consecrated king,
As the Gods anointed INDRA from the pure ethereal spring !

Vedic priests with sacred *mantra*, dark-eyed virgins with their song,
Warriors girt in arms and weapons round the crownéd monarch
    throng,

Juices from each fragrant creeper on his royal brow they place,
And his father's crown and jewels Rama's ample forehead grace,

And as Manu, first of monarchs, was enthroned in days of yore,
So was Rama consecrated by the priests of Vedic lore !

Brave Satrughna on his brother cast the white umbrella's shade
Bold Sugriva and Bibhishan waved the *chowri* gem-inlaid,

VAYU, God of gentle zephyrs, gift of golden garland lent,
INDRA, God of rain and sunshine, wreath of pearls to Rama sent,

Gay *Gandharvas* raised the music, fair *Apsaras* formed the ring,
Men in nations hailed their Rama as their lord and righteous king !

And 'tis told by ancient sages, during Rama's happy reign,
Death untimely, dire diseases, came not to his subject men,

Widows wept not in their sorrow for their lords untimely lost,
Mothers wailed not in their anguish for their babes by YAMA *crost,*

Robbers, cheats, and gay deceivers tempted not with lying word,
Neighbour loved his righteous neighbour and the people loved their lord !

Trees their ample produce yielded as returning seasons went,
And the earth in grateful gladness never failing harvest lent,

Rains descended in their season, never came the blighting gale,
Rich in crop and rich in pasture was each soft and smiling vale,

Loom and anvil gave their produce and the tilled and fertile soil,
And the nation lived rejoicing in their old ancestral toil.

BOOK XII

ASWA-MEDHA

(*Sacrifice of the Horse*)

THE real Epic ends with Rama's happy return to Ayodhya. An *Uttara-Kanda* or Supplement is added, describing the fate of Sita, and giving the poem a sad ending.

The dark cloud of suspicion still hung on the fame of Sita, and the people of Ayodhya made reflections on the conduct of their king, who had taken back into his house a woman who had lived in the palace of Ravan. Rama gave way to the opinion of his people, and he sent away his loving and faithful Sita to live in forests once more.

Sita found an asylum in the hermitage of Valmiki, the reputed author of this Epic, and there gave birth to twins, Lava and Kusa. Years passed on, and Lava and Kusa grew up as hermit boys, and as pupils of Valmiki.

After years had passed, Rama performed a great Horse-sacrifice. Kings and princes were invited from neighbouring countries, and a great feast was held. Valmiki came to the sacrifice, and his pupils, Lava and Kusa, chanted there the great Epic, the *Ramayana*, describing the deeds of Rama. In this interesting portion of the poem we find how songs and poetry were handed down in ancient India by memory. The boys had learnt the whole of the Epic by heart, and chanted portions of it, day after day, till the recital was completed. We are told that the poem consists of seven books, 500 cantos, and 24,000 couplets. Twenty cantos were recited each day, so that the recital of the whole poem must have taken twenty-five days. It was by such feats of memory and by such recitals that literature was preserved in ancient times in India.

Rama recognised his sons in the boy-minstrels, and his heart yearned once more for Sita, whom he had banished but never forgotten. He asked the Poet Valmiki to restore his wife to him, and he desired that Sita might once more prove her purity in the great assembly, so that he might take her back with the approval of his people.

Sita came. But her life had been darkened by an unjust suspicion, her heart was broken, and she invoked the Earth to take her back.

And the Earth, which had given Sita birth, yawned and took back her suffering child into her bosom.

In the ancient hymns of the *Rig Veda*, Sita is simply the goddess of the field-furrow which bears crops for men. We find how that simple conception is concealed in the *Ramayana*, where Sita the heroine of the Epic is still born of the field-furrow, and after all her adventures returns to the Earth. To the millions of men and women in India, however, Sita is not an allegory ; she lives in their hearts and affections as the model of womanly love, womanly devotion, and a wife's noble self-abnegation.

The portions translated in this Book form the whole or portions of Sections xcii., xciii., xciv., and xcvii. of Book vii. of the original text.

I

THE SACRIFICE

Years have passed ; the lonely Rama in his joyless palace reigned,
And for righteous duty yearning, *Aswa-medha* rite ordained,

And a steed of darkest sable with the valiant Lakshman sent,
And with troops and faithful courtiers to Naimisha's forest went.

Fair was far Naimisha's forest by the limpid Gumti's shore,
Monarchs came and warlike chieftains, Brahmans versed in sacred
    lore,

Bharat with each friend and kinsman served them with the choicest
    food,
Proud retainers by each chieftain and each crownéd monarch stood.

Palaces and stately mansions were for royal guests assigned,
Peaceful homes for learnéd Brahmans were with trees umbrageous
    lined,

Gifts were made unto the needy, cloth by skilful weavers wrought,
Ere the suppliants spake their wishes, ere they shaped their inmost
    thought !

Rice unto the helpless widow, to the orphan wealth and gold,
Gifts they gave to holy Brahmans, shelter to the weak and old,

Garments to the grateful people crowding by their monarch's door,
Food and drink unto the hungry, home unto the orphan poor.

Ancient *rishis* had not witnessed feast like this in any land,
Bright Immortals in their bounty blest not with a kinder hand,

Through the year and circling seasons lasted Rama's sacred feast,
And the untold wealth of Rama by his kindly gifts increased !

II

VALMIKI AND HIS PUPILS

Foremost midst the gathered Sages to the holy *yajna* came
Deathless Bard of Lay Immortal—Saint Valmiki rich in fame,

Midst the humble homes of *rishis*, on the confines of the wood,
Cottage of the Saint Valmiki in the shady garden stood.

Fruits and berries from the jungle, water from the crystal spring,
With a careful hand Valmiki did unto his cottage bring,

And he spake to gentle Lava, Kusa child of righteous fame,—
Sita's sons, as youthful hermits to the sacred feast they came :

" Lift your voices, righteous pupils, and your richest music lend,
Sing the Lay of *Ramayana* from the first unto the end,

Sing it to the holy Brahman, to the warrior fair and tall,
In the crowded street and pathway, in the monarch's palace hall,

Sing it by the door of Rama,—he ordains this mighty feast,
Sing it to the royal ladies,—they shall to the story list,

Sing from day to day unwearied, in this sacrificial site,
Chant to all the gathered nations Rama's deeds of matchless might,

And this store of fruits and berries will allay your thirst and toil,
Gentle children of the forest, unknown strangers in this soil !

Twenty cantos of the Epic, morn to night, recite each day,
Till from end to end is chanted *Ramayana's* deathless Lay,

Ask no alms, receive no riches, nor of your misfortunes tell,
Useless unto us is bounty who in darksome forests dwell,

Children of the wood and mountain, cruel fortune clouds your birth,
Stainless virtue be your shelter, virtue be your wealth on earth !

If the royal Rama questions and your lineage seeks to know,
Say,—Valmiki is our Teacher and our Sire on earth below,

Wake your harps to notes of rapture and your softest accents lend,
With the music of the poet music of your voices blend,

Bow unto the mighty monarch, bow to Rama fair and tall,
He is father of his subjects, he is lord of creatures all ! "

III

RECITAL OF THE RAMAYANA

When the silent night was ended, and their pure ablutions done,
Joyous went the minstrel brothers, and their lofty lay begun,

Rama to the hermit minstrels lent a monarch's willing ear,
Blended with the simple music dulcet was the lay to hear,

And so sweet the chanted accents, Rama's inmost soul was stirred,
With his royal guests and courtiers still the deathless lay he heard !

Heralds versed in old *Puranas*, Brahmans skilled in pious rite,
Minstrels deep in lore of music, poets fired by heavenly might,

Watchers of the constellations, min'sters of the festive day,
Men of science and of logic, bards who sang the ancient lay,

Painters skilled and merry dancers who the festive joy prolong,
Hushed and silent in their wonder listed to the wondrous song !

And as poured the flood of music through the bright and livelong day,
Eyes and ears and hearts insatiate drank the nectar of the lay,

And the eager people whispered : " See the boys, how like our king
As two drops of limpid water from the parent bubble spring !

Were the boys no hermit-children, in the hermit's garments clad,
We would deem them Rama's image,—Rama as a youthful lad ! "

Twenty cantos of the Epic thus the youthful minstrels sung,
And the voice of stringéd music through the Epic rolled along,

Out spake Rama in his wonder : " Scarce I know who these may be,
Eighteen thousand golden pieces be the children-minstrels' fee ! "

" Not so," answered thus the children, " we in darksome forests
    dwell,
Gold and silver, bounteous monarch, forest life beseem not well! "

" Noble children ! " uttered Rama, " dear to me the words you say,
Tell me who composed this Epic,—Father of this deathless Lay ? "

"Saint Valmiki," spake the minstrels, "framed the great immortal song
Four and twenty thousand verses to this noble Lay belong,

Untold tales of deathless virtue sanctify his sacred line,
And five hundred glorious cantos in this glorious Epic shine,

In six Books of mighty splendour was the poet's task begun,
With a seventh Book, supplemental is the poet's labour done,

All thy matchless deeds, O monarch, in this Lay will brighter shine,
List to us from first to ending if thy royal heart incline ! "

" Be it so," thus Rama answered, but the hours of day were o'er,
And Valmiki's youthful pupils to their cottage came once more.

Rama with his guests and courtiers slowly left the royal hall,
Eager was his heart to listen, eager were the monarchs all,

And the voice of song and music thus was lifted day to day,
And from day to day they listened to Valmiki's deathless Lay !

IV

LAVA AND KUSA RECOGNISED

Flashed upon the contrite Rama glimpses of the dawning truth,
And with tears of love paternal Rama clasped each minstrel youth,

Yearned his sorrow-stricken bosom for his pure and peerless dame,
Sita banished to the forest, stainless in her righteous fame !

In his tears repentant Rama to Valmiki message sent,
That his heart with eager longing sought her from her banishment :

" Pure in soul ! before these monarchs may she yet her virtue prove,
Grace once more my throne and kingdom, share my unforgotten love,

Pure in soul ! before my subjects may her truth and virtue shine,
Queen of Rama's heart and empire may she once again be mine ! "

V

SITA LOST

Morning dawned ; and with Valmiki, Sita to the gathering came,
Banished wife and weeping mother, sorrow-stricken, suffering dame,

Pure in thought and deed, Valmiki gave his troth and plighted word,—
Faithful still the banished Sita in her bosom held her lord !

" Mighty Saint," so Rama answered as he bowed his humble head,
" Listening world will hear thy mandate and the word that thou hast said,

Never in his bosom Rama questioned Sita's faithful love,
And the God of Fire incarnate did her stainless virtue prove !

Pardon, if the voice of rumour drove me to a deed of shame,
Bowing to my people's wishes I disowned my sinless dame,

Pardon, if to please my subjects I have bade my Sita roam,
Tore her from my throne and empire, tore her from my heart and
home !

In the dark and dreary forest was my Sita left to mourn,
In the lone and gloomy jungle were my royal children born,

Help me, Gods, to wipe this error and this deed of sinful pride,
May my Sita prove her virtue, be again my loving bride ! "

Gods and Spirits, bright Immortals to that royal *Yajna* came,
Men of every race and nation, kings and chiefs of righteous fame,

Softly through the halls of splendour cool and scented breezes blew,
Fragrance of celestial blossoms o'er the royal chambers flew.

Sita saw the bright Celestials, monarchs gathered from afar,
Saw her royal lord and husband bright as heaven-ascending star,

Saw her sons as hermit-minstrels beaming with a radiance high,
Milk of love suffused her bosom, tear of sorrow filled her eye !

Rama's queen and Janak's daughter, will she stoop her cause to
plead,
Witness of her truth and virtue can a loving woman need ?

Oh ! her woman's heart is bursting, and her day on earth is done,
And she pressed her heaving bosom, slow and sadly thus begun :

" *If unstained in thought and action I have lived from day of birth,*
Spare a daughter's shame and anguish and receive her, Mother Earth !

If in duty and devotion I have laboured undefiled,
Mother Earth ! who bore this woman, once again receive thy child !

If in truth unto my husband I have proved a faithful wife,
Mother Earth ! relieve thy Sita from the burden of this life ! "

Then the earth was rent and parted, and a golden throne arose,
Held aloft by jewelled *Nagas* as the leaves enfold the rose,

And the Mother in embraces held her spotless sinless Child,
Saintly Janak's saintly daughter, pure and true and undefiled,

Gods and men proclaim her virtue !   But fair Sita is no more,
Lone is Rama's loveless bosom and his days of bliss are o'er!

CONCLUSION

IN the concluding portion of the *Uttara* or Supplemental Book, the descendants of Rama and his brothers are described as the founders of the great cities and kingdoms which flourished in Western India in the fourth and fifth centuries before the Christian Era.

Bharat had two sons, Taksha and Pushkala. The former founded Taksha-sila, to the east of the Indus, and known to Alexander and the Greeks as Taxila. The latter founded Pushkala-vati, to the west of the Indus, and known to Alexander and the Greeks as Peukelaotis. Thus the sons of Bharat are said to have founded kingdoms which flourished on either side of the Indus river in the fourth century before Christ.

Lakshman had two sons, Angada and Chandraketu. The former founded the kingdom of Karupada, and the latter founded the city of Chandrakanti in the Malwa country.

Satrughna had two sons, Suvahu and Satrughati. The former became king of Mathura, and the latter ruled in Vidisha.

Rama had two sons, Lava and Kusa. The former ruled in Sravasti, which was the capital of Oudh at the time of the Buddha in the fifth and sixth centuries before Christ. The latter founded Kusavati at the foot of the Vindhya mountains.

The death of Rama and his brothers was in accordance with Hindu ideas of the death of the righteous. Lakshman died under somewhat peculiar circumstances. A messenger from heaven sought a secret conference with Rama, and Rama placed Lakshman at the gate, with strict injunctions that whoever intruded on the private conference should be slain. Lakshman himself had to disturb the conference by the solicitation of the celestial *rishi* Durvasa, who always appears on earth to create mischief. And true to the orders passed by Rama, he surrendered his life by penances, and went to heaven.

In the fulness of time, Rama and his other brothers left Ayodhya, crossed the Sarayu, surrendered their mortal life, and entered heaven.

EPILOGUE TO THE *RAMAYANA*

By the Translator

ANCIENT India, like ancient Greece, boasts of two great Epics. The *Ramayana*, describing the adventures of a prince, banished from his country and wandering for long years in the wilderness of Southern India, has something in common with the Odyssey. The *Maha-bharata*, based on the legends and traditions of a great historical war in which all the warlike races of Northern India took a share, is the Iliad of India. The two together comprise the whole of the Epic literature of the ancient Hindus; and the two together present us with the most graphic and lifelike picture that exists of the civilisation and culture, the political and social life, the religion and thought of ancient India.

The *Ramayana*, like the *Maha-bharata*, is a growth of centuries, but the main story is more distinctly the creation of one mind. Among the many cultured races that flourished in Northern India about a thousand years before Christ, the Kosalas of Oudh and the Videhas of North Behar were perhaps the most cultured. Their monarchs were famed for their learning as well as for their prowess. Their priests distinguished themselves by founding schools of learning which were known all over India. Their sacrifices and gifts to the learned drew together the most renowned men of the age from distant regions. Their celebrated Universities (Parishads) were frequented by students from surrounding countries. Their compilations of the old *Vedic Hymns* were used in various parts of India. Their elaborate *Brahmanas* or Commentaries on the Vedas were handed down from generation to generation by priestly families. Their researches into the mysteries of the Soul, and into the nature of the One Universal Soul which pervades the creation, are still preserved in the ancient *Upanishads*, and are among the most valuable heritages which have been left to us by the ancients. And their researches and discoveries in science and philosophy gave them the foremost place among the gifted races of ancient India.

It would appear that the flourishing period of the Kosalas and the Videhas had already passed away, and the traditions of their prowess and learning had become a revered memory in India, when the poet composed the great Epic which perpetuates their fame. Distance of time lent a higher lustre to the achievements of these gifted races, and the age in which they flourished appeared to their descendants as the Golden Age of India. To the imagination of the poet, the age of the Kosalas and Videhas was associated with all that is great and glorious, all that is righteous and true. His description of Ayodhya, the capital town of the Kosalas, is a description of an ideal seat of righteousness. Dasa-ratha the king of the Kosalas is an ideal king, labouring for the good of a loyal people. Rama, the eldest son of Dasa-ratha and the hero of the Epic, is an ideal prince, brave and accomplished, devoted to his duty, unfaltering in his truth. The king of the Videhas, Janak (or rather Janaka, but I have omitted the final *a* of some names in this translation), is a monarch and a saint. Sita, the daughter of Janak and the heroine of the Epic, is the ideal of a faithful woman and a devoted wife. A pious reverence for the past pervades the great Epic ; a lofty admiration of what is true and ennobling in the human character sanctifies the work ; and delineations of the domestic life and the domestic virtues of the ancient Hindus, rich in tenderness and pathos, endear the picture to the hearts of the people of India to the present day.

It is probable that the first connected narrative of this Epic was composed within a few centuries after the glorious age of the Kosalas and the Videhas. But the work became so popular that it grew with age. It grew,—not like the *Maha-bharata* by the incorporation of new episodes, tales, and traditions,—but by fresh descriptions of the same scenes and incidents. Generations of poets were never tired of adding to the description of scenes which were dear to the Hindu, and patient Hindu listeners were never tired of listening to such repetitions. The virtues of Rama and the faithfulness of Sita were described again and again in added lines and cantos. The grief of the old monarch at the banishment of the prince, and the sorrows of the mother at parting from her son, were depicted by succeeding versifiers in fresh verses. The loving devotion of Rama's brothers, the sanctity of saints, and the peacefulness of the hermitages visited by Rama, were described with endless reiteration. The long account of the grief of Rama at the loss of his wife, and stories of unending battles waged for her recovery, occupied generations of busy interpolators.

The *Sloka* verse in which much of the *Ramayana* is composed is the easiest of Sanscrit metres, and afforded a fatal facility to poets ;

and often we have the same scene, fully and amply described in one canto, repeated again in the two or three succeeding cantos. The unity of the composition is lost by these additions, and the effect of the narrative is considerably weakened by such endless repetition.

It would appear that the original work ended with the sixth Book, which describes the return of the hero to his country and to his loving subjects. The seventh Book is called *Uttara* or Supplemental, and in it we are told something of the dimensions of the poem, apparently after the fatal process of additions and interpolations had gone on for centuries. We are informed that the poem consists of six Books and a Supplemental Book; and that it comprises 500 cantos and 24,000 couplets. And we are also told in this Supplemental Book that the descendants of Rama and his brothers founded some of the great towns and states which, we know from other sources, flourished in the fifth and fourth centuries before Christ. It is probable therefore that the Epic, commenced after 1000 B.C., had assumed something like its present shape a few centuries before the Christian Era.

The foregoing account of the genesis and growth of the *Rama-yana* will indicate in what respects it resembles the *Maha-bharata*, and in what respects the two Indian Epics differ from each other. The *Maha-bharata* grew out of the legends and traditions of a great historical war between the Kurus and the Panchalas; the *Ramayana* grew out of the recollections of the golden age of the Kosalas and the Videhas. The characters of the *Maha-bharata* are characters of flesh and blood, with the virtues and crimes of great actors in the historic world; the characters of the *Rama-yana* are more often the ideals of manly devotion to truth, and of womanly faithfulness and love in domestic life. The poet of the *Maha-bharata* relies on the real or supposed incidents of a war handed down from generation to generation in songs and ballads, and weaves them into an immortal work of art; the poet of the *Ramayana* conjures up the memories of a golden age, constructs lofty ideals of piety and faith, and describes with infinite pathos domestic scenes and domestic affections which endear the work to modern Hindus. As an heroic poem the *Maha-bharata* stands on a higher level; as a poem delineating the softer emotions of our everyday life the *Ramayana* sends its roots deeper into the hearts and minds of the million in India.

These remarks will be probably made clearer by a comparison of what may be considered parallel passages in the two great Epics

In heroic description, the bridal of Sita is poor and commonplace, compared with the bridal of Draupadi with all the bustle and tumult of a real contest among warlike suitors. The rivalry between Rama and Ravan, between Lakshman and Indrajit, is feeble in comparison with the lifelong jealousy and hatred which animated Arjun and Karna, Bhima and Duryodhan. Sita's protest and defiance, spoken to Ravan when he carried her away, lack the fire and the spirit of Draupadi's appeal on the occasion when she was insulted in court. The Council of War held by Ravan is a poor affair in comparison with the Council of War held by Yudhisthir in the Matsya kingdom. And Bibhishan's final appeal for peace and Ravan's scornful reply will scarcely compare with the sublime eloquence with which Krishna implored the old monarch of the Kurus not to plunge into a disastrous war, and the deep determination with which Duryodhan replied :—

" Town nor village, mart nor hamlet, help us righteous Gods in heaven,
    Spot that needle's point can cover shall not unto them be given ! "

In the whole of the *Ramayana* there is no character with the fiery determination and the deep-seated hatred for the foe which inspire Karna or Arjun, Bhima or Duryodhan. And in the unending battles waged by Rama and his allies there is no incident so stirring, so animated, so thrilling, as the fall of Abhimanyu, the vengeance of Arjun, the final contest between Arjun and Karna, or the final contest between Bhima and Duryodhan. The whole tenor of the *Ramayana* is subdued and calm, pacific and pious ; the whole tenor of the *Maha-bharata* is warlike and spirited.

And yet, without rivalling the heroic grandeur of the *Maha-bharata*, the *Ramayana* is immeasurably superior in its delineation of those softer and perhaps deeper emotions which enter into our everyday life and hold the world together. And these descriptions, essentially of Hindu life, are yet so true to nature that they apply to all races and nations.

There is something indescribably touching and tender in the description of the love of Rama for his subjects and the loyalty of his people towards Rama,—that loyalty which has ever been a part of the Hindu character in every age—

" As a father to his children to his loving men he came,
    Blessed our homes and maids and matrons till our infants lisped his name,

For our humble woes and troubles Rama hath the ready tear,
    To our humble tales of suffering Rama lends his willing ear ! "

Deeper than this was Rama's duty towards his father and his father's fondness for Rama ; and the portion of the Epic which narrates the dark scheme by which the prince was at last torn from the heart and home of his dying father is one of the most powerful and pathetic passages in Indian literature. The stepmother of Rama, won by the virtues and the kindliness of the prince, regards his proposed coronation with pride and pleasure, but her old nurse creeps into her confidence like a creeping serpent, and envenoms her heart with the poison of her own wickedness. She arouses the slumbering jealousy of a woman and awakens the alarms of a mother, till—

> " Like a slow but deadly poison worked the ancient nurse's tears,
> And a wife's undying impulse mingled with a mother's fears ! "

The nurse's dark insinuations work on the mind of the queen till she becomes a desperate woman, resolved to maintain her own influence on her husband, and to see her own son on the throne. The determination of the young queen tells with terrible effect on the weakness and vacillation of the feeble old monarch, and Rama is banished at last. And the scene closes with a pathetic story in which the monarch recounts his misdeed of past years, accepts his present suffering as the fruit of that misdeed, and dies in agony for his banished son. The inner workings of the human heart and of human motives, the dark intrigue of a scheming dependant, the awakening jealousy and alarm of a wife and a mother, the determination of a woman and an imperious queen, and the feebleness and despair and death of a fond old father and husband, have never been more vividly described. Shakespeare himself has not depicted the workings of stormy passions in the human heart more graphically or more vividly, with greater truth or with more terrible power.

It is truth and power in the depicting of such scenes, and not in the delineation of warriors and warlike incidents, that the *Ramayana* excels. It is in the delineation of domestic incidents, domestic affections, and domestic jealousies, which are appreciated by the prince and the peasant alike, that the *Ramayana* bases its appeal to the hearts of the million in India. And beyond all this, the righteous devotion of Rama, and the faithfulness and womanly love of Sita, run like two threads of gold through the whole fabric of the Epic, and ennoble and sanctify the work in the eyes of Hindus.

Rama and Sita are the Hindu ideals of a Perfect Man and a Perfect Woman ; their truth under trials and temptations, their endurance under privations, and their devotion to duty under all vicissitudes of fortune, form the Hindu ideal of a Perfect Life. In this respect the *Ramayana* gives us a true picture of Hindu faith and righteous life as Dante's " Divine Comedy " gives us a picture of the faith and belief of the Middle Ages in Europe. Our own ideals in the present day may not be the ideals of the tenth century before Christ or the fourteenth century after Christ ; but mankind will not willingly let die those great creations of the past which shadow forth the ideals and beliefs of interesting periods in the progress of human civilisation.

Sorrow and suffering, trial and endurance, are a part of the Hindu ideal of a Perfect Life of righteousness. Rama suffers for fourteen years in exile, and is chastened by privations and misfortunes, before he ascends the throne of his father. In a humble way this course of training was passed through by every pious Hindu of the ancient times. Every Aryan boy in India was taken away from his parents at an early age, and lived the hard life of an anchorite under his teacher for twelve or twenty-four or thirty-six years, before he entered the married life and settled down as a householder. Every Aryan boy assumed the rough garment and the staff and girdle of a student, lived as a mendicant and begged his food from door to door, attended on his preceptor as a menial, and thus trained himself in endurance and suffering as well as in the traditional learning of the age, before he became a householder. The pious Hindu saw in Rama's life the ideal of a true Hindu life, the success and the triumph which follow upon endurance and faith and devotion to duty. It is the truth and endurance of Rama under sufferings and privations which impart the deepest lessons to the Hindu character, and is the highest ideal of a Hindu righteous life. The ancient ideal may seem to us far-fetched in these days, but we can never fully comprehend the great moral Epic of the Hindus unless we endeavour to study fully and clearly its relations of old Hindu ideas and old Hindu life.

And if trial and endurance are a part of a Hindu's ideal of a man's life, devotion and self-abnegation are still more essentially a part of his ideal of a woman's life. Sita holds a place in the hearts of women in India which no other creation of a poet's imagination holds among any other nation on earth. There is not a Hindu woman whose earliest and tenderest recollections do not cling round the story of Sita's sufferings and Sita's faithfulness, told in the nursery, taught in the family circle, remembered and cherished through life. Sita's adventures in a desolate forest and in a hostile prison only represent in an exaggerated form the humbler trials of a woman's life ; and Sita's endurance and faithfulness teach her devotion to duty in all trials and troubles of life. " For," said Sita :

> " For my mother often taught me and my father often spake,
> That her home the wedded woman doth beside her husband make,
> As the shadow to the substance, to her lord is faithful wife,
> And she parts not from her consort till she parts with fleeting life !
> Therefore bid me seek the jungle and in pathless forests roam,
> Where the wild deer freely ranges and the tiger makes his home,
> Happier than in father's mansions in the woods will Sita rove,
> Waste no thought on home or kindred, nestling in her husband's love ! "

The ideal of life was joy and beauty and gladness in ancient Greece ; the ideal of life was piety and endurance and devotion in ancient India. The tale of Helen was a tale of womanly beauty and loveliness which charmed the western world. The tale of Sita was a tale of womanly faith and self-abnegation which charmed and fascinated the Hindu world. Repeated trials bring out in brighter relief the unfaltering truth of Sita's character ; she goes to a second banishment in the woods with the same trust and devotion to her lord as before, and she returns once more, and sinks into the bosom of her Mother Earth, true in death as she had been true in life. The creative imagination of the Hindus has conceived no loftier and holier character than Sita ; the literature of the world has not produced a higher ideal of womanly love, womanly truth, and womanly devotion.

The modern reader will now comprehend why India produced, and has preserved for well-nigh three thousand years, two Epics instead of one national Epic. No work of the imagination abides long unless it is animated by some sparks of imperishable truth, unless it truly embodies some portion of our human feelings, human faith, and human life. The *Maha-bharata* depicts the political life of ancient India, with all its valour and heroism, ambition and lofty chivalry. The *Ramayana* embodies the domestic and religious life of ancient India, with all its tenderness and sweetness, its endurance and devotion. The one picture without the other were incomplete ; and we should know but little of the ancient Hindus if we did not comprehend their inner life and faith as well as their political life and their warlike virtues. The two together give us a true and graphic picture of ancient Indian life and civilisation ; and no nation on earth has preserved a more faithful picture of its glorious past.

In condensing the *Ramayana* with its more than 24,000 Sanscrit couplets into 2,000 English couplets I have followed the same plan which was adopted in my translation of the *Maha-bharata*. I have selected those sections or cantos which tell the leading incidents of the Epic, and have translated the whole or main portions of them, and these selected passages are linked together by short notes. The plan, as was explained before, has this advantage, that the story is told not by the translator in his own way, but by the poet himself ; the passages placed before the reader are not the translator's abridgment of a long poem, but selected passages from the poem itself. It is the ancient poet of India, and not the translator, who narrates the old story ; but he narrates only such portions of it as describe the leading incidents. We are told that the sons of Rama recited the whole poem of 24,000 verses, divided into 500 cantos or sections, in twenty-five days. The modern reader has not the patience of the Hindu listener of the old school ; but a selection of the leading portions of that immortal song, arranged in 2,000 verses and in 84 short sections, may possibly receive a hearing, even from the much-distracted modern reader.

While speaking of my own translation I must not fail to make some mention of my predecessors in this work. The magnificent edition of the *Ramayana* (Bengal recension), published with an Italian translation by Gorresio, at the expense of Charles Albert King of Sardinia in 1843–67, first introduced this great Epic to the European public ; and it was not long before M. Hippolyte Fauche presented the European world with a French translation of this edition. The Benares recension of the *Ramayana* has since been lithographed in Bombay, and a printed edition of the same recension with Ramanuja's commentary was brought out by the venerable Hem Chandra Vidyaratna in Calcutta in 1869–85. The talented and indefatigable Mr. Ralph Griffith, C.I.E., who has devoted a lifetime to translating Indian poetry into English, has produced an almost complete translation of the first six Books in more than 24,000 English couplets, and has given an abstract of the seventh Book in prose. And a complete translation of the *Ramayana* into English prose has since appeared in Calcutta.

The object of the present work is very different from that of these meritorious editions and translations. The purpose of this work, as explained above, is not to attempt a complete translation of a voluminous Epic, but to place before the general reader the leading story of that Epic by translating a number of selected passages and connecting them together by short notes. The purpose of this volume is not to repeat the long poem which Rama's sons are supposed to have recited in 24,000 Sanscrit couplets, but only to narrate the main incidents of that poem within the reasonable limit of 2,000 verses. And the general reader who seeks for a practical acquaintance with the great Indian poem within a reasonable compass will, it is hoped, find in this book a handy and not unacceptable translation of the leading story of the Epic.

I have stated before that in India the *Ramayana* is still a living tradition and a living faith. It forms the basis of the moral instruction of a nation, and it is a part of the lives of two hundred millions of people. It is necessary to add that when the modern languages of India were first formed out of the ancient Sanscrit and Prakrits, in the ninth and tenth centuries after Christ, the *Ramayana* had the greatest influence in inspiring our modern poets and forming our modern tongues. Southern India took the lead, and a translation of the *Ramayana* in the Tamil language appeared as early as A.D. 1100. Northern India and Bengal and Bombay followed the example ; Tulasi Das's *Ramayana* is the great classic of the Hindi language, Krittibas's *Ramayana* is a classic in the Bengali language, and Sridhar's *Ramayana* is a classic in the Mahratta language. Generations of Hindus in all parts of India have studied the ancient story in these modern translations ; they have heard it recited in the houses of the rich ; and they have seen it acted on the stage at religious festivals in every great town and every populous village through the length and breadth of India.

More than this, the story of Rama has inspired our religious reformers, and purified the popular faith of our modern times. Rama, the true and dutiful, was accepted as the Spirit of God descended on earth, as an incarnation of Vishnu the Preserver of the World. The great teacher Ramanuja proclaimed the monotheism of Vishnu in Southern India in the twelfth century ; the reformer Ramananda proclaimed the same faith in Northern India in the thirteenth or fourteenth century ; and his follower the gifted Kabir conceived the bold idea of uniting Hindus and Mahomedans in the worship of One God. " The God of the Hindus," he said, " is the God of the Mahomedans, be he invoked as *Rama* or *Ali*." " The city of the Hindu God is Benares, and the city of the

Mahomedan God is Mecca ; but search your hearts, and there you will find the God both of Hindus and Mahomedans." "If the Creator dwells in tabernacles, whose dwelling is the universe ? "

The reformer Chaitanya preached the same sublime monotheism in Bengal, and the reformer Nanak in the Punjab, in the sixteenth century. And down to the present day the popular mind in India, led away by the worship of many images in many temples, nevertheless holds fast to the cardinal idea of One God, and believes the heroes of the ancient Epics—*Krishna* and *Rama*—to be the incarnations of that God. The various sects of the Hindus, specially the sects of Vishnu and of Siva who form the great majority of the people, quarrel about a name as they often did in Europe in the Middle Ages, and each sect gives to the Deity the special name by which the sect is known. In the teeming villages of Bengal, in the ancient shrines of Northern India, and far away in the towns and hamlets of Southern India, the prevailing faith of the million is a popular monotheism underlying the various ceremonials in honour of various images and forms—and that popular monotheism generally recognises the heroes of the two ancient Epics,—*Krishna* and *Rama*, as the earthly incarnations of the great God who pervades and rules the universe.

To know the Indian Epics is to understand the Indian people better. And to trace the influence of the Indian Epics on the life and civilisation of the nation, and on the development of their modern languages, literatures, and religious reforms, is to comprehend the real history of the people during three thousand years.

ROMESH DUTT.

MAHA-BHARATA
EPIC OF THE BHARATAS

THE EPIC OF THE BHARATAS

BOOK I

ASTRA DARSANA

(*The Tournament*)

THE scene of the Epic is the ancient kingdom of the Kurus which flourished along the upper course of the Ganges ; and the historical fact on which the Epic is based is a great war which took place between the Kurus and a neighbouring tribe, the Panchalas, in the thirteenth or fourteenth century before Christ.

According to the Epic, Pandu and Dhrita-rashtra, who was born blind, were brothers. Pandu died early, and Dhrita-rashtra became king of the Kurus, and brought up the five sons of Pandu along with his hundred sons.

Yudhishthir, the eldest son of Pandu, was a man of truth and piety ; Bhima, the second, was a stalwart fighter ; and Arjun, the third son, distinguished himself above all the other princes in arms. The two youngest brothers, Nakula and Sahadeva, were twins. Duryodhan was the eldest son of Dhrita-rashtra and was jealous of his cousins, the sons of Pandu. A tournament was held, and in the course of the day a warrior named Karna, of unknown origin, appeared on the scene and proved himself a worthy rival of Arjun. The rivalry between Arjun and Karna is the leading thought of the Epic, as the rivalry between Achilles and Hector is the leading thought of the Iliad.

It is only necessary to add that the sons of Pandu, as well as Karna, were, like the heroes of Homer, god-born chiefs. Some god inspired the birth of each. Yudhishthir was the son of Dharma or Virtue, Bhima of Vayu or Wind, Arjun of Indra or Rain-god, the twin youngest were the sons of the Aswin twins, and Karna was the son of Surya the Sun, but was believed by himself and by all others to be the son of a simple chariot-driver.

The portion translated in this Book forms Sections cxxxiv. to cxxxvii. of Book i. of the original Epic in Sanscrit (Calcutta edition of 1834).

I

The Gathering

Wrathful sons of Dhrita-rashtra, born of Kuru's royal race,
Righteous sons of noble Pandu, god-born men of godlike grace,

Skill in arms attained these princes from a Brahman warrior bold,
Drona, priest and proud preceptor, peerless chief of days of old !

Out spake Drona to the monarch in Hastina's royal hall,
Spake to Bhishma and to Kripa, spake to lords and courtiers all :

" Mark the gallant princes, monarch, trained in arms and warlike art,
Let them prove their skill and valour, rein the steed and throw the
    dart."

Answered then the ancient monarch, joyful was his royal heart,
" Best of Brahmans and of warriors, nobly hast thou done thy part,

Name the place and fix the moment, hold a royal tournament,
Publish wide the laws of combat, publish far thy king's consent.

Sightless roll these orbs of vision, dark to me is noonday light,
Happier men will mark the tourney and the peerless princes' fight,

Let the good and wise Vidura serve thy mandate and behest,
Let a father's pride and gladness fill this old and cheerless breast."

Forthwith went the wise Vidura to his sacred duties bound,
Drona, blessed with skill and wisdom, measured out the tourney
    ground,

Clear of jungle was the meadow, by a crystal fountain graced,
Drona on the lighted altar holy gifts and offerings placed,

Holy was the star auspicious, and the hour was calm and bright,
Men from distant town and hamlet came to view the sacred rite.

Then arose white stately mansions, built by architects of fame,
Decked with arms for Kuru's monarch and for every royal dame,

And the people built their stages circling round the listed green,
And the nobles with their white tents graced the fair and festive
    scene.

Brightly dawned the festal morning, and the monarch left his hall,
Bhishma and the pious Kripa with the lords and courtiers all,

And they came unto the mansions, gay and glittering, gold-encased,
Decked with gems and rich *baidurya*, and with strings of pearls
be-laced.

Fair Gandhari, queen of Kuru, Pritha, Pandu's widowed dame,
Ladies in their gorgeous garments, maids of beauty and of fame,

Mounted on their glittering mansions where the tints harmonious
blend,
As, on Meru's golden mountain, queens of heavenly gods ascend !

And the people of the city, Brahmans, Vaisyas, Kshatras bold,
Men from stall and loom and anvil gathered thick, the young and old,

And arose the sound of trumpet and the surging people's cry,
Like the voice of angry ocean, tempest-lashed, sublime and high !

Came the saintly white-robed Drona, white his sacrificial thread,
White his sandal-mark and garlands, white the locks that crowned
his head,

With his son renowned for valour walked forth Drona, radiant, high,
So the Moon with Mars conjoinéd walks upon the cloudless sky !

Offerings to the gods immortal then the priestly warrior made,
Brahmans with their chanted *mantra* worship and obeisance paid,

And the festive note of *sankha* mingled with the trumpet's sound,
Throngs of warriors, various-arméd, came unto the listed ground.

II

THE PRINCES

Gauntleted and jewel-girdled, now the warlike princes came,
With their stately bows and quivers, and their swords like wreaths
of flame,

Each behind his elder stepping, good Yudhishthir first of all,
Each his wondrous skill displaying held the silent crowds in thrall.

And the men in admiration marked them with a joyful eye,
Or by sudden panic stricken stooped to let the arrow fly !

Mounted on their rapid coursers oft the princes proved their aim,
Racing, hit the targe with arrows lettered with their royal name,

With their glinting sunlit weapons shone the youths sublime and high,
More than mortals seemed the princes, bright *Gandharvas* of the sky !

Shouts of joy the people uttered as by sudden impulse driven,
Mingled voice of tens of thousands struck the pealing vault of heaven.

Still the princes shook their weapons, drove the deep resounding car,
Or on steed or tusker mounted waged the glorious mimic war !

Mighty sword and ample buckler, ponderous mace the princes wield,
Brightly gleam their lightning rapiers as they range the listed field,

Brave and fearless is their action, and their movement quick and light
Skilled and true the thrust and parry of their weapons flaming bright !

III

BHIMA AND DURYODHAN

Bhima came and proud Duryodhan with their maces lifted high,
Like two cliffs with lofty turrets cleaving through the azure sky,

In their warlike arms accoutred with their girded loins they stood,
Like two untamed jungle tuskers in the deep and echoing wood !

And as tuskers range the forest, so they range the spacious field,
Right to left and back they wander and their ponderous maces wield.

Unto Kuru's sightless monarch wise Vidura drew the scene,
Pritha proudly of the princes spake unto the Kuru queen.

While the stalwart Bhima battled with Duryodhan brave and strong,
Fierce in wrath, for one or other, shouted forth the maddened throng,

" Hail to Kuru prince Duryodhan ! " " Hail to Bhima hero proud ! "
Sounds like these from surging myriads rose in tumult deep and loud.

And with troubled vision Drona marked the heaving restless plain.
Marked the crowd by anger shaken, like the tempest-shaken main,

To his son he softly whispered quick the tumult to appease,
Part the armed and angry wrestlers, bid the deadly combat cease,

With their lifted clubs the princes slow retired on signal given,
Like the parting of the billows, mighty-heaving, tempest-driven !

Came forth then the ancient Drona on the open battle-ground,
Stopped the drum and lofty trumpet, spake in voice like thunder's
    sound :

" Bid him come, the gallant Arjun ! pious prince and warrior skilled,
Arjun, born of mighty INDRA, and with VUSHNU'S prowess filled."

IV

THE ADVENT OF ARJUN

Gauntleted and jewel-girdled, with his bow of ample height,
Archer Arjun pious-hearted to the gods performed a rite,

Then he stepped forth proud and stately in his golden mail encased,
Like the sunlit cloud of evening with the golden rainbow graced,

And a gladness stirred the people all around the listed plain,
Voice of drum and blare of trumpet rose with *sankha's* festive strain !

" Mark ! the gallant son of Pandu, whom the happy Pritha bore,
Mark ! the heir of INDRA'S valour, matchless in his arms and lore,

Mark ! the warrior young and valiant, peerless in his skill of arms,
Mark ! the prince of stainless virtue, decked with grace and varied
    charms ! "

Pritha heard such grateful voices borne aloft unto the sky,
Milk of love suffused her bosom, tear of joy was in her eye !

And where rested Kuru's monarch, joyous accents struck his ear,
And he turned to wise Vidura seeking for the cause to hear :

" Wherefore like the voice of ocean, when the tempest winds prevail,
Rise the voices of the people and the spacious skies assail ? "

Answered him the wise Vidura, " It is Pritha's gallant boy,
Godlike moves in golden armour, and the people shout for joy ! "

" Pleased am I," so spake the monarch, " and I bless my happy fate,
Pritha's sons like fires of *yajna* sanctify this mighty State ! "

Now the voices of the people died away and all was still,
Arjun to his proud preceptor showed his might and matchless skill.

Towering high or lowly bending, on the turf or on his car,
With his bow and glist'ning arrows Arjun waged the mimic war.

Targets on the wide arena, mighty tough or wondrous small,
With his arrows still unfailing, Arjun pierced them one and all !

Wild-boar shaped in plates of iron coursed the wide-extending field,
In its jaws five glist'ning arrows sent the archer wondrous-skilled,

Cow-horn by a thread suspended was by winds unceasing swayed,
One and twenty well-aimed arrows on this moving mark he laid,

And with equal skill his rapier did the godlike Arjun wield,
Whirling round the mace of battle ranged the spacious tourney field !

V

The Advent of Karna

Now the feats of arms are ended, and the closing hour draws nigh,
Music's voice is hushed in silence, and dispersing crowds pass by,

Hark ! Like welkin-shaking thunder wakes a deep and deadly sound,
Clank and din of warlike weapons burst upon the tented ground !

Are the solid mountains splitting, is it bursting of the earth,
Is it tempest's pealing accent whence the lightning takes its birth ?

Thoughts like these alarm the people for the sound is dread and high,
To the gaze of the arena turns the crowd with anxious eye !

Gathered round preceptor Drona, Pandu's sons in armour bright,
Like the five-starred constellation round the radiant Queen of Night,

Gathered round the proud Duryodhan, dreaded for his exploits done,
All his brave and warlike brothers and preceptor Drona's son,

So the gods encircled INDRA, thunder-wielding, fierce and bold,
When he scattered Danu's children in the misty days of old !

Pale, before the unknown warrior, gathered nations part in twain,
Conqueror of hostile cities, lofty Karna treads the plain,

In his golden mail accoutred and his rings of yellow gold,
Like a moving cliff in stature, arméd comes the chieftain bold,

Pritha, yet unwedded, bore him, peerless archer on the earth,
Portion of the solar radiance, for the Sun inspired his birth !

Like a tusker in his fury, like a lion in his ire,
Like the sun in noontide radiance, like the all-consuming fire,

Lion-like in build and muscle, stately as a golden palm,
Blessed with every manly virtue, peerless, dauntless, proud and calm!

With his looks serene and lofty field of war the chief surveyed,
Scarce to Kripa or to Drona honour and obeisance made,

Still the panic-stricken people viewed him with unmoving gaze,
Who may be this unknown warrior, questioned they in hushed amaze!

Then in voice of pealing thunder spake fair Pritha's eldest son
Unto Arjun, Pritha's youngest, each, alas! to each unknown:

" All thy feats of weapons, Arjun, done with vain and needless boast,
These and greater I accomplish—witness be this mighty host ! "

Thus spake proud and peerless Karna in his accents deep and loud,
And as moved by sudden impulse joyous rose the listening crowd,

And a gleam of mighty transport glows in proud Duryodhan's heart,
Flames of wrath and jealous anger from the eyes of Arjun start,

Drona gave the word, and Karna, Pritha's war-beloving son,
With his sword and with his arrows did the feats by Arjun done !

VI

The Rival Warriors

Joyful was the proud Duryodhan, gladness gleamed upon his face,
And he spake to gallant Karna with a loving fond embrace :

" Welcome, mighty arméd chieftain! thou hast victor's honours won,
Thine is all my wealth and kingdom, name thy wish and it is done ! "

Answered Karna to Duryodhan, " Prince ! thy word is good as deed,
But I seek to combat Arjun and to win the victor's meed,"

" Noble is the boon thou seekest," answered Kuru's prince of fame,
" Be a joy unto your comrades, let the foeman dread thy name ! "

Anger flamed in Arjun's bosom, and he spake in accents rude
Unto Karna who in triumph calm and proud and fearless stood :

" Chief ! who comest uninvited, pratest in thy lying boast,
Thou shalt die the death of braggarts—witness be this mighty host!"

Karna answered calm and proudly, " Free this listed field to all,
Warriors enter by their prowess, wait not, Arjun, for thy call,

Warlike chieftains take their places by their strength of arm and
    might,
And their warrant is their falchion, valour sanctifies their right,

Angry word is coward's weapon, Arjun, speak with arrows keen,
Till I lay thee, witness Drona, low upon the listed green ! "

Drona gave the word impartial, wrathful Arjun, dread of foes,
Parted from his loving brothers, in his glist'ning arms arose,

Karna clasped the Kuru's princes, parted from them one and all,
With his bow and ample quiver proudly stepped the warrior tall.

Now the clouds with lurid flashes gathered darkling, thick and high,
Lines of cranes like gleams of laughter sailed across the gloomy sky,

Rain-god INDRA over Arjun watched with father's partial love,
Sun-god SURYA over Karna shed his light from far above,

Arjun stood in darkening shadow by the inky clouds concealed,
Bold and bright in open sunshine radiant Karna stood revealed !

Proud Duryodhan and his brothers stood by Karna calm and bold,
Drona stood by gallant Arjun, and brave Bhishma warrior old,

Women too with partial glances viewed the one or other chief,
But by equal love divided silent Pritha swooned in grief !

Wise Vidura, true to duty, with an anxious hurry came,
Sandal-drops and sprinkled waters roused the woe-distracted dame,

And she saw her sons in combat, words of woe she uttered none,
Speechless wept, for none must fathom Karna was her eldest son !

VII

THE ANOINTMENT OF KARNA

Crested Karna, helméd Arjun, proudly trod the spacious green,
Kripa, skilled in herald's duties, spake upon the dreadful scene :

" *This is helmet-wearing Arjun, sprung of Kuru's mighty race,*
Pandu's son and borne by Pritha, prince of worth and warlike grace,

Long-armed Chief ! declare thy lineage, and the race thou dost adorn,
Name thy mother and thy father, and the house that saw thee born,

By the rules of war Prince Arjun claims his rival chief to know,
Princes may not draw their weapon 'gainst a base and nameless foe ! "

Karna silent heard this mandate, rank nor lineage could he claim,
Like a raindrop-pelted lotus bent his humble head in shame !

" Prince we reckon," cried Duryodhan, " not the man of birth alone,
Warlike leader of his forces as a prince and chief we own,

Karna by his warlike valour is of crownéd kings the peer,
Karna shall be crownéd monarch, nations shall his mandate hear ! "

Forth they brought the corn and treasure, golden coin and water jar,
On the throne they seated Karna famed in many a deathful war,

Brahmans chanted sacred *mantra* which the holy books ordain,
And anointed crownéd Karna king of Anga's fair domain,

And they raised the red umbrella, and they waved the *chowri* fan,
" Blessings on the crownéd monarch ! honour to the bravest man ! "

Now the holy rites accomplished, in his kingly robes arrayed
Karna unto prince Duryodhan thus in grateful accents prayed :

" Gift of kingdom, good Duryodhan, speaketh well thy noble heart,
What return can grateful Karna humbly render on his part ? "

" Grant thy friendship," cried Duryodhan, " for no other boon I
    crave,
Be Duryodhan's dearest comrade, be his helper true and brave,"

" Be it so ! " responded Karna, with a proud and noble grace,
And he sealed his loyal friendship in a loving fond embrace !

VIII

The Chariot-driver

Dewed with drops of toil and languor, lo ! a chariot-driver came,
Loosely hung his scanty garments, and a staff upheld his frame.

Karna, now a crownéd monarch, to the humble Suta sped,
As a son unto a father, reverently bent his head !

With his scanty cloth the driver sought his dusty feet to hide,
And he hailed him as a father hails his offspring in his pride,

And he clasped unto his bosom crownéd Karna's noble head,
And on Karna's dripping forehead, fresh and loving tear-drops shed !

Is he son of chariot-driver ? Doubts arose in Bhima's mind,
And he sought to humble Karna with reproachful words unkind

" Wilt thou, high-descended hero, with a Kuru cross thy brand ?
But the goad of cattle-drivers better suits, my friend, thy hand !

Wilt thou as a crownéd monarch rule a mighty nation's weal ?
As the jackals of the jungle sacrificial offerings steal ! "

Quivered Karna's lips in anger, word of answer spake he none,
But a deep sigh shook his bosom, and he gazed upon the sun !

IX

CLOSE OF THE DAY

Like a lordly tusker rising from a beauteous lotus lake,
Rose Duryodhan from his brothers, proudly thus to Bhima spake :

" With such insults seek not, Bhima, thus to cause a warrior grief,
Bitter taunts but ill befit thee, warlike tiger-waisted chief,

Proudest chief may fight the humblest, for like river's noble course,
Noble deeds proclaim the warrior, and we question not their source !

Teacher Drona, priest and warrior, owns a poor and humble birth,
Kripa, noblest of Gautamas, springeth from the lowly earth,

Known to me thy lineage Bhima, thine and of thy brothers four,
Amorous gods your birth imparted, so they say, in days of yore !

Mark the great and gallant Karna decked in rings and weapons fair
She-deer breeds not lordly tigers in her poor and lowly lair,

Karna comes to rule the wide earth, not fair Anga's realms alone,
By his valour and his virtue, by the homage which I own,

And if prince or arméd chieftain doth my word or deed gainsay,
Let him take his bow and quiver, meet me in a deadly fray ! "

Loud applauses greet the challenge and the people's joyful cry,
But the thickening shades of darkness fill the earth and evening sky

And the red lamp's fitful lustre shone upon the field around,
Slowly with the peerless Karna proud Duryodhan left the ground.

Pandu's sons with warlike Drona marked the darksome close of day
And with Kripa and with Bhishma homeward silent bent their way

" Arjun is the gallant victor ! " " Valiant Karna's won the day ! "
" Prince Duryodhan is the winner ! " Various thus the people say

By some secret sign appriséd Pritha knew her gallant boy,
Saw him crownéd king of Anga with a mother's secret joy,

And with greater joy Duryodhan fastened Karna to his side,
Feared no longer Arjun's prowess, Arjun's skill of arms and pride

E'en Yudhishthir reckoned Karna mightiest warrior on the earth,
Half misdoubted Arjun's prowess, Arjun's skill and warlike worth !

BOOK II

SWAYAMVARA

(*The Bride's Choice*)

THE mutual jealousies of the princes increased from day to day, and when Yudhishthir, the eldest of all the princes and the eldest son of the late Pandu, was recognised heir-apparent, the anger of Duryodhan and his brothers knew no bounds. And they formed a dark scheme to kill the sons of Pandu.

The sons of Pandu were induced with their mother to pay a visit to a distant town called Varanavata. A house had been built there for their residence, constructed of inflammable materials. At the appointed time fire was set to the house; but the five brothers and their mother escaped the conflagration through a subterranean passage, retired into forests, and lived in the disguise of Brahmans.

In course of time they heard of the approaching celebrations of the marriage of the princess of Panchala, an ancient kingdom in the vicinity of modern Kanouj. All the monarchs of Northern India were invited, and the bride would choose her husband from among the assembled kings according to the ancient *Swayamvara* custom. The five sons of Pandu decided to go and witness the ceremony.

The portion translated in this Book formed Sections clxxxiv. to cxxxix. of Book i. of the original text.

I

JOURNEY TO PANCHALA

Now the righteous sons of Pandu, wand'ring far from day to day,
Unto South Panchala's country glad and joyful held their way,

For when travelling with their mother, so it chanced by will of fate,
They were met by pious Brahmans bound for South Panchala's State,

And the pure and holy Brahmans hailed the youth of noble fame,
Asked them whither they would journey, from what distant land
they came,

" From the land of Ekachakra," good Yudhishthir answered so,
" With our ancient mother travelling unto distant lands we go."

" Heard ye not," the Brahmans questioned, " in Panchala's fair
domain,
Drupad, good and gracious monarch, doth a mighty feast ordain,

To that festive land we journey, Drupad's bounteous gifts to share,
And to see the *swayamvara* of Panchala's princess fair,—

Human mother never bore her, human bosom never fed,
From the Altar sprang the maiden who some noble prince will wed !

Soft her eyes like lotus-petal, sweet her tender jasmine form,
And a maiden's stainless honour doth her gentle soul inform,

And her brother, mailed and arméd with his bow and arrows dire,
Radiant as the blazing altar, sprang from Sacrificial Fire !

Fair the sister slender-waisted, dowered with beauty rich and rare,
And like fragrance of blue lotus, perfumes all the sweetened air,

She will choose from noble suitors gathered from the west and east,
Bright and fair shall be the wedding, rich and bounteous be the feast !

Kings will come from distant regions sacrificing wealth and gold,
Stainless monarchs versed in *sastra*, pious-hearted, mighty-souled,

Handsome youths and noble princes from each near and distant land,
Car-borne chieftains bold and skilful, brave of heart and stout of
hand !

And to win the peerless princess they will scatter presents rare,
Food and milch-kine, wealth and jewels, gold and gifts and garments
fair,

Noble gifts we take as Brahmans, bless the rite with gladsome heart,
Share the feast so rich and bounteous, then with joyful minds depart.

Actors, mimes, and tuneful minstrels fair Panchala's court will throng,
Famed reciters of *puranas*, dancers skilled and wrestlers strong,

Come with us, the wedding witness, share the banquet rich and rare,
Pleased with gifts and noble presents to your distant home repair.

Dowered ye are with princely beauty, like the radiant gods above,
Even on you the partial princess may surrender heart and love,

And this youth so tall and stalwart, mighty-arméd, strong and bold,
He may win in feats of valour rich renown and wealth untold ! "

" Be it so," Yudhishthir answered, " to Panchala we repair,
View the wedding of the princess and the royal bounty share,"

And the righteous sons of Pandu with the Brahmans took their way,
Where in South Panchala's kingdom mighty Drupad held his sway.

Now it fell, the saintly *rishi*, deathless bard of deathless lay,
Herald of the holy Vedas, Vyasa stood before their way.

And the princes bowed unto him and received his blessings kind,
By his mandate to Panchala went with pleased and joyful mind !

Jungle woods and silver waters round their sylvan pathway lay,
Halting at each wayside station marched the princes day by day,

Stainless and intent on *sastra*, fair in speech and pure in heart,
Travelling slow they reached Panchala, saw its spacious town and
    mart,

Saw the fort, bazaar and city, saw the spire and shining dome,
In a potter's distant cottage made their humble unknown home,

And disguised as pious Brahmans sons of Pandu begged their food,
People knew not Kuru's princes in that dwelling poor and rude.

II

The Wedding Assembly

To the helméd son of Pandu, Arjun pride of Kuru's race,
Drupad longed to give his daughter peerless in her maiden grace,

And of massive wood unbending, Drupad made a stubborn bow,
Saving Arjun prince or chieftain might not bend the weapon low,

And he made a whirling discus, hung it 'neath the open sky,
And beyond the whirling discus placed a target far and high,

" Whoso strings this bow," said Drupad, " hits the target in his pride
Through the high and circling discus, wins Panchala's princely
    bride ! "

And they spake the monarch's mandate in the kingdoms near and far,
And from every town and country princes came and chiefs of war,

Came the pure and saintly *rishis* for to bless the holy rite,
Came the Kurus with brave Karna in their pride and matchless might,

Brahmans came from distant regions with their sacred learning blest,
Drupad with a royal welcome greeted every honoured guest.

Now the festal day approacheth ! Gathering men with ocean's voice,
Filled the wide and circling stages to behold the maiden's choice,

Royal guests and princely suitors came in pomp of wealth and pride,
Car-borne chiefs and mailéd warriors came to win the beauteous
    bride !

North-east of the festive city they enclosed a level ground,
Towering dome and stately palace cunning builders built around,

And by moat and wall surrounded, pierced by gate and archéd door,
By a canopy of splendour was the red field covered o'er !

Now the festal day approacheth ! Sacred censers fragrance lent,
Sprinkled *chandan* spread its coolness, wreaths were hung of
    sweetest scent,

All around were swan-white mansions, lofty domes and turrets high,
Like the peaks of white Kailasa cleaving through the azure sky !

Sparkling gems the chambers lighted, golden nets the windows laced,
Spacious stairs so wide and lofty were with beauteous carpets graced,

Rich festoons and graceful garlands gently waved like streamers gay,
And the swan-like silver mansions glinted in the light of day !

Now the festal day approacheth ! High the royal chambers lay,
With their lofty gilded turrets like the peaks of Himalay,

In these halls in pride and splendour dwelt each rich and royal guest,
Fired by mutual emulation, and in costly jewels drest,

Decked and perfumed sat these rulers, mighty-arméd, rich in fame,
Lion-monarchs, noble-destined, chiefs of pure and spotless name,

Pious to the mighty BRAHMA, and their subjects' hope and stay,
Loved of all for noble actions, kind and virtuous in their sway.

Now the festal day approacheth ! like the heaving of the main,
Surge the ranks of gathered nations o'er the wide and spacious
    plain,

Pandu's sons in guise of Brahmans mix with Brahmans versed in lore,
Mark proud Drupad's wealth and splendour, gazing, wondering
evermore,

Dancers charm the gathered people, singers sing and actors play,
Fifteen days of festive splendour greet the concourse rich and gay.

III

THE BRIDE

Sound the drum and voice the *sankha !* Brightly dawns the bridal day,
Fresh from morning's pure ablutions comes the bride in garments gay,

And her golden bridal garland, carrying on her graceful arm,
Softly, sweetly, steps Draupadi, queen of every winning charm !

Then a Brahman versed in *mantra*, ancient priest of lunar race,
Lights the Fire, with pious offerings seek its blessings and its grace,

Whispered words of benediction saints and holy men repeat,
Conch and trumpet's voice is silent, hushed the lofty war-drum's beat,

And there reigns a solemn silence, and in stately pomp and pride,
Drupad's son leads forth his sister, fair Panchala's beauteous bride !

In his loud and lofty accents like the distant thunder's sound,
Drupad's son his father's wishes thus proclaims to all around :

" *Mark this bow, assembled monarchs, and the target hung on high,*
Through yon whirling piercéd discus let five glist'ning arrows fly,

Whoso, born of noble lineage, hits the far suspended aim,
Let him stand and as his guerdon Drupad's beauteous maiden claim ! "

Then he turns unto Draupadi, tells each prince and suitor's name,
Tells his race and lofty lineage, and his warlike deeds of fame.

IV

THE SUITORS

" Brave Duryodhan and his brothers, princes of the Kuruland,
Karna proud and peerless archer, sister ! seek thy noble hand,

And Gandhara's warlike princes, Bhoja's monarch true and bold,
And the son of mighty Drona, all bedecked in gems and gold !

King and prince from Matsya kingdom grace this noble wedding-
feast,
Monarchs from more distant regions north and south and west and
east,

Tamralipta and Kalinga on the eastern ocean wave,
Pattan's port whose hardy children western ocean's dangers brave !

From the distant land of Madra car-borne monarch Salya came,
And from Dwarka's sea-girt regions Valadeva known to fame,

Valadeva and his brother Krishna sprung from Yadu's race,
Of the Vrishni clan descended, soul of truth and righteous grace !

This is mighty Jayadratha come from Sindhu's sounding shore,
Famed for warlike feats of valour, famed alike for sacred lore,

This is fair Kosala's monarch whose bright deeds our heralds sing,
From the sturdy soil of Chedi, this is Chedi's peerless king !

This is mighty Jarasandha, come from far Magadha's land,
These are other princely suitors, sister ! eager for thy hand,

All the wide earth's warlike rulers seek to shoot the distant aim,
Princess, whoso hits the target, choose as thine that prince of fame !"

Decked with jewels, young and valiant, all aflame with soft desire,
Conscious of their worth and valour, all the suitors rose in ire,

Nobly born, of lofty presence, full of young unyielding pride,
Like the tuskers wild and lordly on Himalay's wooded side !

Each his rival marks as foeman as in field of deadly strife,
Each regards the fair Draupadi as his own his queenly wife,

On the gorgeous field they gather by a maddening passion fired,
And they strive as strove the bright gods, when by Uma's love
inspired !

And the gods in cloud-borne chariots came to view the scene so fair,
Bright ADITYAS in their splendour, MARUTS in the moving air,

Winged *Suparnas*, scaly *Nagas*, saints celestial pure and high,
For their music famed, *Gandharvas*, fair *Apsaras* of the sky !

Valadeva armed with ploughshare, Krishna chief of righteous fame,
With the other Yadu chieftains to that wondrous bridal came,

Krishna marked the sons of Pandu eager for the maiden queen,
Like wild tuskers for a lotus, like the fire that lurks unseen,

And he knew the warlike brothers in their holy Brahman guise,
Pointed them to Valadeva, gazing with a glad surprise !

But the other chiefs and monarchs with their eyes upon the bride,
Marked nor knew the sons of Pandu sitting speechless by their side,

And the long-armed sons of Pandu smitten by KANDARPA'S dart,
Looked on her with longing languor and with love-impassioned heart!

Bright Immortals gaily crowding viewed the scene surpassing fair,
Heavenly blossoms soft descending with a perfume filled the air,

Bright celestial cars in concourse sailed upon the cloudless sky,
Drum and flute and harp and tabor sounded deep and sounded high !

V

TRIAL OF SKILL

Uprose one by one the suitors, marking still the distant aim,
Mighty monarchs, gallant princes, chiefs of proud and warlike fame,

Decked in golden crown and necklace, and inflamed by pride and
    love,
Stoutly strove the eager suitors viewing well the targe above,

Strove to string the weapon vainly, tough unbending was the bow,
Slightly bent, rebounding quickly, laid the gallant princes low !

Strove the handsome suitors vainly, decked in gem and burnished
    gold,
Reft of diadem and necklace, fell each chief and warrior bold,

Reft of golden crown and garland, shamed and humbled in their pride,
Groaned the suitors in their anguish, sought no more Panchala's
    bride !

Uprose Karna, peerless archer, proudest of the archers he,
And he went and strung the weapon, fixed the arrows gallantly,

Stood like SURYA in his splendour and like AGNI in his flame,—
Pandu's sons in terror whispered, Karna sure must hit the aim !

But in proud and queenly accents Drupad's queenly daughter said :
" Monarch's daughter, born a Kshatra, Suta's son I will not wed,"

Karna heard with crimsoned forehead, left the emprise almost done,
Left the bow already circled, silent gazed upon the Sun !

Uprose Chedi's haughty monarch, mightiest of the monarchs he,
Other kings had failed inglorious, Sisupala stood forth free,

Firm in heart and fixed in purpose, bent the tough unbending bow,
Vainly ! for the bow rebounding laid the haughty monarch low !

Uprose sturdy Jarasandha, far Magadha's mighty chief,
Held the bow and stood undaunted, tall and stately as a cliff,

But once more the bow rebounded, fell the monarch in his shame,
Left in haste Panchala's mansions for the region whence he came !

Uprose Salya, king of Madra, with his wondrous skill and might,
Faltering, on his knees descending, fell in sad inglorious plight,

Thus each monarch fell and faltered, merry whispers went around,
And the sound of stifled laughter circled round the festive ground !

VI

THE DISGUISED ARJUN

Hushed the merry sound of laughter, hushed each suitor in his shame,
Arjun, godlike son of Pritha, from the ranks of Brahmans came,

Guised as priest serene and holy, fair as INDRA's rainbow bright,
All the Brahmans shook their deerskins, cheered him in their
    hearts' delight !

Some there were with sad misgivings heard the sound of joyous cheer
And their minds were strangely anxious, whispered murmurs spake
    their fear :

" Wondrous bow which Sisupala, mighty Salya could not strain,
Jarasandha famed for prowess strove to bend the string in vain,

Can a Brahman weak by nature, and in warlike arms untrained,
Wield the bow which crownéd monarchs, long-armed chieftains
    have not strained ?

Sure the Brahman boy in folly dares a foolish thoughtless deed,
And amidst this throng of monarchs shame will be our only meed,

Youth in youthful pride or madness will a foolish emprise dare,
Sager men should stop his rashness and the Brahman's honour
    spare ! "

" Shame he will not bring unto us," other Brahmans made reply,
" Rather, in this throng of monarchs, rich renown and honour high,

Like a tusker strong and stately, like Himalay's towering crest,
Stands unmoved the youthful Brahman, ample-shouldered, deep in
    chest,

Lion-like his gait is agile, and determined is his air,
Trust me he can do an emprise who hath lofty will to dare !

He will do the feat of valour, will not bring disgrace and stain,
Nor is task in all this wide earth which a Brahman tries in vain,

Holy men subsist on wild fruits, in the strength of penance strong,
Spare in form, in spirit mightier than the mightiest warlike throng !

Ask not if 'tis right or foolish when a Brahman tries his fate,
If it leads to woe or glory, fatal fall or fortune great,

Son of *rishi* Jamadagni baffled kings and chieftains high,
And Agastya stainless *rishi* drained the boundless ocean dry,

Let this young and daring Brahman undertake the warlike deed,
Let him try and by his prowess win the victor's noble meed ! "

While the Brahmans deep revolving hopes and timid fears expressed,
By the bow the youthful Arjun stood unmoved like mountain crest,

Silent round the wondrous weapon thrice the mighty warrior went,
To the God of Gods, ISANA, in a silent prayer he bent,

Then the bow which gathered warriors vainly tried to bend and strain,
And the monarchs of the wide earth sought to string and wield in
    vain,

Godlike Arjun born of INDRA, filled with VISHNU's matchless might,
Bent the wondrous bow of Drupad, fixed the shining darts aright,

Through the disc the shining arrows fly with strange and hissing
    sound,
Hit and pierce the distant target, bring it thundering on the ground !

Shouts of joy and loud applauses did the mighty feat declare,
Heavenly blossoms soft descended, heavenly music thrilled the air,

And the Brahmans shook their deerskins, but each irritated chief
In a lowly muttered whisper spake his rising rage and grief,

Sankha's note and voice of trumpet Arjun's glorious deed prolong,
Bards and heralds chant his praises in a proud and deathless song !

Drupad in the Brahman's mantle knew the hero proud and brave,
'Gainst the rage of baffled suitors sought the gallant prince to save,

With his twin-born youngest brothers left Yudhishthir, peaceful,
    good,
Bhima marked the gathering tempest and by gallant Arjun stood !

Like a queen the beauteous maiden smiled upon the archer brave,
Flung on him the bridal garland and the bridal robe she gave,

Arjun by his skill and prowess won Panchala's princess-bride,
People's shouts and Brahmans' blessings sounded joyful far and
    wide !

VII

The Tumult

Spake the suitors, anger-shaken, like a forest tempest-torn,
As Panchala's courteous monarch came to greet a Brahman-born :

" Shall he like the grass of jungle trample us in haughty pride,
To a prating priest and Brahman wed the proud and peerless bride ?

To our hopes like nourished saplings shall he now the fruit deny,
Monarch proud who insults monarchs sure a traitor's death shall die,

Honour for his rank we know not, have no mercy for his age,
Perish foe of crownéd monarchs, victim to our righteous rage !

Hath he asked us to his palace, favoured us with royal grace,
Feasted us with princely bounty, but to compass our disgrace,

In this concourse of great monarchs, glorious like a heavenly band,
Doth he find no likely suitor for his beauteous daughter's hand ?

And this rite of *swayamvara*, so our sacred laws ordain,
Is for warlike Kshatras only, priests that custom shall not stain,

If this maiden on a Brahman casts her eye, devoid of shame,
Let her expiate her folly in a pyre of blazing flame !

Leave the priestling in his folly sinning through a Brahman's greed,
For we wage no war with Brahmans and forgive a foolish deed,

Much we owe to holy Brahmans for our realm and wealth and life,
Blood of priest or wise preceptor shall not stain our noble strife,

In the blood of sinful Drupad we the righteous laws maintain,
Such disgrace in future ages monarchs shall not meet again ! "

Spake the suitors, tiger-hearted, iron-handed, bold and strong,
Fiercely bent on blood and vengeance blindly rose the maddened
    throng,

On they came, the angry monarchs, armed for cruel vengeful strife,
Drupad midst the holy Brahmans trembling fled for fear of life,

Like wild elephants of jungle rushed the kings upon their foes,
Calm and stately, stalwart Bhima and the gallant Arjun rose !

With a wilder rage the monarchs viewed these brothers cross their
    path,
Rushed upon the daring warriors for to slay them in their wrath,

Weaponless was noble Bhima, but in strength like lightning's brand,
Tore a tree with peerless prowess, shook it as a mighty wand !

And the foe-compelling warrior held that mace of living wood,
Strong as death with deadly weapon, facing all his foes he stood,

Arjun too with godlike valour stood unmoved, his bow in hand,
Side by side the dauntless brothers faced the fierce and fiery band !

VIII

Krishna to the Rescue

Krishna knew the sons of Pandu though in robes of Brahmans dressed,
To his elder, Valadeva, thus his inner thoughts expressed :

" Mark that youth with bow and arrow and with lion's lordly gait,
He is helmet-wearing Arjun ! greatest warrior midst the great,

Mark his mate, with tree uprooted how he meets the suitor band,
Save the tiger-waisted Bhima none can claim such strength of hand !

And the youth with eyes like lotus, he who left the court erewhile,
He is pious-souled Yudhishthir, man without a sin or guile,

And the others by Yudhishthir, Pandu's twin-born sons are they,
With these sons the righteous Pritha 'scaped where death and
    danger lay,

For the jealous, fierce Duryodhan darkly schemed their death by fire,
But the righteous sons of Pandu 'scaped his unrelenting ire ! ''

Krishna rose amidst the monarchs, strove the tumult to appease,
And unto the angry suitors spake in words of righteous peace,

Monarchs bowed to Krishna's mandate, left Panchala's festive land,
Arjun took the beauteous princess, gently led her by the hand.

BOOK III

RAJASUYA

(*The Imperial Sacrifice*)

A CURIOUS incident followed the bridal of Draupadi. The five sons of Pandu returned with her to the potter's house, where they were living on alms according to the custom of Brahmans, and the brothers reported to their mother that they had received a great gift on that day. " Enjoy ye the gift in common," replied their mother, not knowing what it was. And as a mother's mandate cannot be disregarded, Draupadi became the common wife of the five brothers.

The real significance of this strange legend is unknown. The custom of brothers marrying a common wife prevails to this day in Thibet and among the hill-tribes of the Himalayas, but it never prevailed among the Aryan Hindus of India. It is distinctly prohibited in their laws and institutes, and finds no sanction in their literature, ancient or modern. The legend in the *Maha-bharata*, of brothers marrying a wife in common, stands alone and without a parallel in Hindu traditions and literature.

Judging from the main incidents of the Epic, Draupadi might rather be regarded as the wife of the eldest brother Yudhishthir. Bhima had already mated himself to a female in a forest, by whom he had a son, Ghatotkacha, who distinguished himself in war later on. Arjun too married the sister of Krishna, shortly after Draupadi's bridal, and had by her a son, Abhimanyu, who was one of the heroes of the war. On the other hand, Yudhishthir took to himself no wife save Draupadi, and she was crowned with Yudhishthir in the Rajasuya or Imperial Sacrifice. Notwithstanding the legend, therefore, Draupadi might be regarded as wedded to Yudhishthir, though won by the skill of Arjun, and this assumption would be in keeping with Hindu customs and laws, ancient and modern.

The jealous Duryodhan heard that his contrivance to kill his cousins at Varanavata had failed. He also heard that they had found a powerful friend in Drupad, and had formed an alliance with him. It was no longer possible to keep them from their rightful inheritance. The Kuru kingdom was accordingly parcelled ; Duryodhan retained the eastern and richer portion with

its ancient capital *Hastina-pura* on the Ganges ; and the sons of
Pandu were given the western portion on the Jumna, which was
then a forest and a wilderness.   The sons of Pandu cleared the
forest and built a new capital *Indra-prastha*, the supposed ruins of
which, near modern Delhi, are still pointed out to the curious
traveller.

Yudhishthir, the eldest of the five sons of Pandu, and now king
of Indra-prastha, resolved to perform the Rajasuya sacrifice, which
was a formal assumption of the Imperial title over all the kings of
ancient India.   His brothers went out with troops in all directions
to proclaim his supremacy over all surrounding kings.   Jarasandha,
the powerful and semi-civilised king of Magadha or South Behar,
opposed and was killed ; but other monarchs recognised the supremacy of Yudhishthir and came to the sacrifice with tributes.   King
Dhrita-rashtra and his sons, now reigning at Hastina-pura, were
politely invited to take a share in the performance of the sacrifice.

The portion translated in this Book forms Sections **xxxiii.** to
xxxvi. and Section xliv. of Book ii. of the original.

I

THE ASSEMBLAGE OF KINGS

Ancient halls of proud Hastina mirrored bright on Ganga's wave !
Thither came the son of Pandu, young Nakula true and brave,

Came to ask Hastina's monarch, chief of Kuru's royal race,
To partake Yudhishthir's banquet and his sacrifice to grace.

Dhrita-rashtra came in gladness unto Indra-prastha's town,
Marked its new-built tower and turret on the azure Jumna frown,

With him came preceptor Kripa, and the ancient Bhishma came,
Elders of the race of Kuru, chiefs and Brahmans known to fame.

Monarchs came from distant regions to partake the holy rite,
Warlike chiefs from court and castle in their arms accoutred bright,

Kshatras came with ample tribute for the holy sacrifice,
Precious gems and costly jewels, gold and gifts of untold price.

Proud Duryodhan and his brothers came in fair and friendly guise,
With the ancient Kuru monarch and Vidura good and wise,

With his son came brave Suvala from Gandhara's distant land,
Car-borne Salya, peerless Karna, came with bow and spear and brand.

Came the priest and proud preceptor Drona skilled in arms and lore,
Jayadratha famed for valour came from Sindhu's sounding shore,

Drupad came with gallant princes from Panchala's land of fame,
Salwa lord of outer nations to the mighty gathering came.

Bhagadatta came in chariot from the land of nations brave,
Prag-jyotisha, where the red sun wakes on Brahma-putra's wave,

With him came untutored *Mlechchas* who beside the ocean dwell,
Uncouth chiefs of dusky nations from the lands where mountains
swell.

Came Virata, Matsya's monarch, and his warlike sons and bold,
Sisupala, king of Chedi, with his son bedecked in gold.

Came the warlike chiefs of Vrishni from the shores of Western Sea,
And the lords of Madhya-desa, ever warlike ever free !

II

Feast and Sacrifice

Jumna's dark and limpid waters laved Yudhishthir's palace walls
And to hail him *Dharma-raja*, monarchs thronged his royal halls,

He to honoured kings and chieftains with a royal grace assigned
Palaces with sparkling waters and with trees umbrageous lined,

Honoured thus, the mighty monarchs lived in mansions milky white,
Like the peaks of famed Kailasa lifting proud their snowy height !

Graceful walls that swept the meadows circled round the royal halls,
Nets of gold belaced the casements, gems bedecked the shining walls,

Flights of steps led up to chambers many-tinted-carpet-graced,
And festooning fragrant garlands were harmonious interlaced !

Far below from spacious gateways rose the people's gathering cry,
And from far the swan-white mansions caught the ravished gazer's
eye,

Richly graced with precious metals shone the turrets bright and gay,
Like the rich-ored shining turrets of the lofty Himalay,

And the scene bedecked by *rishis* and by priests and kings of might,
Shone like azure sky in splendour graced by deathless Sons of Light !

Spake Yudhishthir unto Bhishma, elder of the Kuru race,
Unto Drona proud preceptor, rich in lore and warlike grace,

Spake to wise preceptor Kripa, versed in sacred rites of old,
To Duryodhan and his brothers, honoured guests and kinsmen bold :

" Friends and kinsmen, grant your favour and your sweet affection
    lend,
May your kindness ever helpful poor Yudhishthir's rite attend,

As your own, command my treasure, costly gifts and wealth untold,.
To the poor and to the worthy scatter free my gems and gold ! "

Speaking thus he made his *diksha*, and to holy work inclined,
To his friends and to his kinsmen all their various tasks assigned :

Proud Duhsasan in his bounty spread the rich and sumptuous feast,
Drona's son with due devotion greeted saint and holy priest,

Sanjay with a regal honour welcomed king and chief of might,
Bhishma and the pious Drona watched the sacrificial rite,

Kripa guarded wealth and treasure, gold and gems of untold price,
And with presents unto Brahmans sanctified the sacrifice,

Dhrita-rashtra, old and sightless, through the scene of gladness
    strayed,
With a careful hand Vidura all the mighty cost defrayed,

Proud Duryodhan took the tribute which the chiefs and monarchs
    paid,
Pious Krishna unto Brahmans honour and obeisance made.

'Twas a gathering fair and wondrous on fair Jumna's sacred shore,
Tributes in a thousand *nishkas* every willing monarch bore,

Costly gifts proclaimed the homage of each prince of warlike might,
Chieftains vied with rival chieftains to assist the holy rite.

Bright Immortals, robed in sunlight, sailed across the liquid sky,
And their gleaming cloud-borne chariots rested on the turrets high,

Hero-monarchs, holy Brahmans, filled the halls bedecked in gold,
White-robed priests adept in *mantra* mingled with the chieftains
    bold.

And amidst this scene of splendour, pious-hearted, pure and good,
Like the sinless god VARUNA, gentle-souled Yudhishthir stood,

Six bright fires Yudhishthir lighted, offerings made to gods above,
Gifts unto the poor and lowly spake the monarch's boundless love.

Hungry men were fed and feasted with an ample feast of rice,
Costly gifts to holy Brahmans graced the noble sacrifice,

Ida, ajya, homa offerings, pleased the " Shining Ones " on high,
Brahmans pleased with costly presents with their blessings filled
the sky!

.

III

GLIMPSES OF THE TRUTH

Dawned the day of *abhisheka*, proud anointment, sacred bath,
Crownéd kings and learnéd Brahmans crowded on Yudhishthir's
path,

And as gods and heavenly *rishis* throng in BRAHMA'S mansions
bright,
Holy priests and noble monarchs graced the inner sacred site !

Measureless their fame and virtue, great their penance and their
power,
And in converse deep and learned Brahmans passed the radiant hour,

And on subjects great and sacred, oft divided in their thought,
Various sages in their wisdom various diverse maxims taught,

Weaker reasons seemed the stronger, faultless reasons often failed,
Keen disputants like the falcon fell on views their rivals held !

Some were versed in Laws of Duty, some the Holy Vows professed,
Some with gloss and varied comment still his learned rival pressed,

Bright the concourse of the Brahmans unto sacred learning given,
Like the concourse of the bright stars in the glorious vault of heaven,

None of impure caste and conduct trespassed on the holy site,
None of impure life and manners stained Yudhishthir's sacred rite !

Deva-rishi, saintly Narad, marked the sacrificial rite,
Sanctifying by its lustre good Yudhishthir's royal might,

And a ray of heavenly wisdom lit the *rishi's* inner eye,
As he saw the gathered monarchs in the concourse proud and high !

He had heard from lips celestial in the heavenly mansions bright,
All these kings were god incarnate, portions of Celestial Light,

And he saw in them embodied beings of the upper sky,
And in lotus-eyéd Krishna saw the Highest of the High !

Saw the ancient World's Preserver, great Creation's Primal Cause,
Who had sent the gods as monarchs to uphold his righteous laws,

Battle for the cause of virtue, perish in a deadly war,
Then to seek their upper mansions in the radiant realms afar !

" NARAYANA, World's Preserver, sent immortal gods on earth,
He himself in race of Yadu hath assumed his mortal birth,

Like the moon among the planets born in Vrishni's noble clan,—
He whom bright gods render worship,—NARAYANA, Son of Man,

Primal Cause and Self-created ! when is done his purpose high,
NARAYANA leads Immortals to their dwelling in the sky."

Such bright glimpses of the Secret flashed upon his inner sight,
As in lofty contemplation Narad gazed upon the rite.

IV

THE ARGHYA

Outspake Bhishma to Yudhishthir : " Monarch of this wide domain,
Honour due to crownéd monarchs doth our sacred law ordain,

Arghya to the wise Preceptor, to the Kinsman and to Priest,
To the Friend and to the Scholar, to the King as lord of feast,

Unto these is due the *arghya*, so our holy writs have said,
Therefore to these kings assembled be the highest honour paid,

Noble are these crownéd monarchs, radiant like the noonday sun,
To the noblest, first in virtue, be the foremost honour done ! "

" Who is noblest," quoth Yudhishthir, " in this galaxy of fame,
Who of chiefs and crownéd monarchs doth our foremost honour
    claim ? "

Pond'ring spake the ancient Bhishma in his accents deep and clear :
" Greatest midst the great is Krishna ! chief of men without a peer !

Midst these monarchs pure in lustre, purest-hearted and most high
Like the radiant sun is Krishna midst the planets of the sky,

Sunless climes are warmed to verdure by the sun's returning ray,
Windless wastes are waked to gladness when reviving breezes play,

Even so this *rajasuya*, this thy sacrificial rite,
Owes its sanctity and splendour unto Krishna's holy might ! "

Bhishma spake and Sahadeva served his mandate quick as thought,
And the *arghya* duly flavoured unto peerless Krishna brought,

Krishna trained in rules of virtue then the offered *arghya* took,
Darkened Sisupala's forehead and his frame in tremor shook,

To Yudhishthir and to Bhishma turns the chief his flaming eyes,
To the great and honoured Krishna, Sisupala wrathful cries.

V

SISUPALA'S PRIDE

" Not to Vrishni's uncrowned hero should this reverence be paid,
Midst these mighty crownéd monarchs in their kingly pomp arrayed,

Ill beseems the good Yudhishthir, royal Pandu's righteous son,
Homage to an uncrowned chieftain, to the lowly honour done !

Pandu's sons are yet untutored, and with knowledge yet unblessed,
Knowing Bhishma blessed with wisdom hath the rules of courts
　　transgressed,

Learnéd in the Laws of Duty he hath sinned from partial love,
Conscious breach of rules of honour doth our deeper hatred move !

In this throng of crownéd monarchs, ruling kings of righteous fame,
Can this uncrowned Vrishni chieftain foremost rank and honour
　　claim ?

Doth he as a sage and elder claim the homage to him done ?
Sure his father Vasudeva hath his claims before his son !

Doth he as Yudhishthir's kinsman count as foremost and the best ?
Royal Drupad by alliance surely might the claim contest !

Doth he as a wise preceptor claim the highest, foremost place,
When the great preceptor Drona doth his royal mansion grace ?

Unto Krishna as a *rishi* should the foremost rank be given ?
Saintly Vyasa claims the honour, Vedic bard inspired by Heaven !

Unto Krishna should we render honour for his warlike fame ?
Thou, O Bhishma ! Death's Subduer, surely might precedence
claim !

Unto Krishna for his knowledge should the noble prize we yield ?
Drona's son unmatched in learning surely might contest the field !

Great Duryodhan midst the princes stands alone without a peer,
Kripa priest of royal Kurus, holiest of all priests is here !

Archer Karna—braver archer none there is of mortal birth—
Learnt his arms from Par'su Rama, he who slew the kings of earth !

Wherefore then to unknown Krishna render we this homage free !
Saintly priest, nor wise preceptor, king nor foremost chief is he ! "

VI

Sisupala's Fall

Tiger-hearted Sisupala spake in anger stern and high,
Calm unto him Krishna answered, but a light was in his eye :

" List, O chiefs and righteous monarchs ! from a daughter of our race
Evil-destined Sisupala doth his noble lineage trace,

Spite of wrong and frequent outrage, spite of insult often flung,
Never in his heart hath Krishna sought to do his kinsman wrong !

Once I went to eastern regions, Sisupala like a foe
Burnt my far-famed seaport Dwarka, laid the mart and temple low,

Once on Bhoja's trusting monarch faithless Sisupala fell,
Slew his men and threw him captive in his castle's dungeon cell,

Once for holy *aswamedha* Vasudeva sent his steed,
Sisupala stole the charger, sought to stop the righteous deed,

Once on saintly Babhru's consort, pious-hearted, pure and just,
Sisupala fell in madness, forced the lady to his lust,

Once Visala's beauteous princess went to seek her husband's side,
In her husband's garb disguiséd Sisupala clasped the bride,

This and more hath Krishna suffered, for his mother is our kin,
But the sickening tale appalleth, and he addeth sin to sin !

One more tale of sin I mention : by his impious passion fired,
To my saintly wife, Rukmini, Sisupala hath aspired,

As the low-born seeks the *Veda*, soiling it with impure breath,
Sisupala sought my consort, and his righteous doom is Death ! "

Krishna spake ; the rising red blood speaks each angry hero's shame,
Shame for Chedi's impious actions, grief for Sisupala's fame !

Loudly laughed proud Sisupala, spake with bitter taunt and jeer,
Answered Krishna's lofty menace with disdain and cruel sneer :

" Wherefore in this vast assembly thus proclaim thy tale of shame,
If thy wedded wife and consort did inspire my youthful flame ?

Doth a man of sense and honour, blest with wisdom and with pride,
Thus proclaim his wedded consort was another's loving bride ?

Do thy worst !   Or if by anger or by weak forbearance led,
Sisupala seeks no mercy, nor doth Krishna's anger dread ! "

Lowered Krishna's eye and forehead, and unto his hands there came
Fatal disc, the dread of sinners, disc that never missed its aim,

" Monarchs in this hall assembled ! " Krishna in his anger cried,
" Oft hath Chedi's impious monarch Krishna's noble rage defied,

For unto his pious mother plighted word and troth was given,
Sisupala's hundred follies would by Krishna be forgiven,

I have kept the plighted promise, but his crimes exceed the tale,
And beneath this vengeful weapon Sisupala now shall quail ! "

Then the bright and whirling discus, as this mandate Krishna said,
Fell on impious Sisupala, from his body smote his head,

Fell the mighty-arméd monarch like a thunder-riven rock,
Severed from the parent mountain by the bolt's resistless shock !

And his soul be-cleansed of passions came forth from its mortal shroud,
Like the radiant sun in splendour from a dark and mantling cloud,

Unto Krishna good and gracious, like a lurid spark aflame,
Chastened of its sin and anger, Sisupala's spirit came !

Rain descends in copious torrents, quick the lurid lightnings fly,
And the wide earth feels a tremor, restless thunders shake the sky,

Various feelings sway the monarchs as they stand in hushed amaze,
Mutely in those speechless moments on the lifeless warrior gaze !

Some there are who seek their weapons, and their nervous fingers
      shake,
And their lips they bite in anger, and their frames in tremor quake,

Others in their inmost bosom welcome Krishna's righteous deed,
Look on death of Sisupala as a sinner's proper meed,

Rishis bless the deed of Krishna as they wend their various ways,
Brahmans pure and pious-hearted chant the righteous Krishna's
      praise !

Sad Yudhishthir, gentle-hearted, thus unto his brothers said :
" Funeral rites and regal honours be performed unto the dead,"

Duteously his faithful brothers then performed each pious rite,
Honours due to Chedi's monarch, to his rank and peerless might,

Sisupala's son they seated in his mighty father's place,
And with holy *abhisheka* hailed him king of Chedi's race !

VII

YUDHISHTHIR EMPEROR

Thus removed the hapless hindrance, now the holy sacrifice
Was performed with joy and splendour and with gifts of gold and rice,

Godlike Krishna watched benignly with his bow and disc and mace,
And Yudhishthir closed the feasting with his kindliness and grace.

Brahmans sprinkled holy water on the empire's righteous lord,
All the monarchs made obeisance, spake in sweet and graceful word :

" Born of race of Ajamidha ! thou hast spread thy father's fame,
Rising by thy native virtue thou hast won a mightier name,

And this rite unto thy station doth a holier grace instil,
And thy royal grace and kindness all our hope and wish fulfil,

Grant us, king of mighty monarchs, now unto our realms we go,
Emperor o'er earthly rulers, blessings and thy grace bestow ! "

Good Yudhishthir to the monarchs parting grace and honours paid,
And unto his duteous brothers thus in loving-kindness said :

" To our feast these noble monarchs came from loyal love they bear,
Far as confines of their kingdoms, with them let our friends repair."

And his brothers and his kinsmen duteously his hest obey,
With each parting guest and monarch journey on the homeward way,

Arjun wends with high-souled Drupad, famed for lofty warlike grace,
Dhrishta-dyumna with Virata, monarch of the Matsya race,

Bhima on the ancient Bhishma and on Kuru's king doth wait,
Sahadeva waits on Drona, great in arms, in virtue great,

With Gandhara's warlike monarch brave Nakula holds his way,
Other chiefs with other monarchs where their distant kingdoms lay.

Last of all Yudhishthir's kinsman, righteous Krishna fain would part,
And unto the good Yudhishthir opens thus his joyful heart :

" Done this glorious *rajasuya*, joy and pride of Kuru's race,
Grant, O friend ! to sea-girt Dwarka, Krishna now his steps must
     trace."

" By thy grace and by thy valour," sad Yudhishthir thus replies,
" By thy presence, noble Krishna, I performed this high emprise,

By thy all-subduing glory monarchs bore Yudhishthir's sway,
Came with gifts and costly presents, came their tributes rich to pay,

Must thou part ? my uttered accents may not bid thee, friend, to go,
In thy absence vain were empire, and this life were full of woe,

Yet thou partest, sinless Krishna, dearest, best belovéd friend,
And to Dwarka's sea-washed mansions Krishna must his footsteps
     bend ! ' "

Then unto Yudhishthir's mother, pious-hearted Krishna hies,
And in accents love-inspiring thus to ancient Pritha cries :

" Regal fame and righteous glory crown thy sons, reveréd dame,
Joy thee in their peerless prowess, in their holy spotless fame,

May thy sons' success and triumph cheer a widowed mother's heart,
Grant me leave, O noble lady ! for to Dwarka I depart."

From Yudhishthir's queen Draupadi parts the chief with many a tear,
And from Arjun's wife Sabhadra, Krishna's sister ever dear,

Then with rites and due ablutions to the gods are offerings made,
Priests repeat their benedictions, for the righteous Krishna said,

And his faithful chariot-driver brings his falcon-bannered car,
Like the clouds in massive splendour and resistless in the war,

Pious Krishna mounts the chariot, fondly greets his friends once more,
Leaves blue Jumna's sacred waters for his Dwarka's dear-loved shore.

Still Yudhishthir and his brothers, sad and sore and grieved at heart,
Followed Krishna's moving chariot, for they could not see him part,

Krishna stopped once more his chariot, and his parting blessing gave,
Thus the chief with eyes of lotus spake in accents calm and brave :

" *King of men ! with sleepless watching ever guard thy kingdom fair,*
Like a father tend thy subjects with a father's love and care,

Be unto them like the rain-drop nourishing the thirsty ground,
Be unto them tree of shelter shading them from heat around,

Like the blue sky ever bending be unto them ever kind,
Free from pride and free from passion rule them with a virtuous mind ! "

Spake and left the saintly Krishna, pure and pious-hearted chief,
Sad Yudhishthir wended homeward and his heart was filled with grief.

BOOK IV

DYUTA

(*The Fatal Dice*)

DURYODHAN came back from the Imperial Sacrifice filled with jealousy against Yudhishthir, and devised plans to effect his fall. Sakuni, prince of Gandhara, shared Duryodhan's hatred towards the sons of Pandu, and helped him in his dark scheme.

Yudhishthir with all his piety and righteousness had one weakness, the love of gambling, which was one of the besetting sins of the monarchs of the day. Sakuni was an expert at false dice, and challenged Yudhishthir, and Yudhishthir held it a point of honour not to decline such a challenge.

He came from his new capital, Indra-prastha, to Hastina-pura the capital of Duryodhan, with his mother and brothers and Draupadi. And as Yudhishthir lost game after game, he was stung with his losses, and with the recklessness of a gambler still went on with the fatal game. His wealth and hoarded gold and jewels, his steeds, elephants and cars, his slaves male and female, his empire and possessions, were all staked and lost !

The madness increased, and Yudhishthir staked his brothers, and then himself, and then the fair Draupadi, and lost ! And thus the Emperor of Indra-prastha and his family were deprived of every possession on earth, and became the bond-slaves of Duryodhan. The old king Dhrita-rashtra released them from actual slavery, but the five brothers retired to forests as homeless exiles.

Portions of Section lxv. and the whole of Sections lxix., lxxvi., and lxxvii. of Book ii. of the original text have been translated in this Book.

I

DRAUPADI IN THE COUNCIL HALL

Glassed on Ganga's limpid waters brightly shine Hastina's walls !
Queen Draupadi duly honoured lives within the palace halls,

But as steals a lowly jackal in a lordly lion's den,
Base Duryodhan's humble menial came to proud Draupadi's ken.

"Pardon, Empress," quoth the menial, "royal Pandu's righteous son,
Lost his game and lost his reason, Empress, thou art staked and won,

Prince Duryodhan claims thee, lady, and the victor bids me say,
Thou shalt serve him as his vassal, as his slave in palace stay ! "

" Have I heard thee, menial, rightly ? " questioned she in anguish
    keen,
" Doth a crownéd king and husband stake his wife and lose his queen,

Did my noble lord and monarch sense and reason lose at dice,
Other stake he did not wager, wedded wife to sacrifice ! "

" Other stakes were duly wagered," so he spake with bitter groan,
" Wealth and empire, every object which Yudhishthir called his own,

Lost himself and all his brothers, bondsmen are those princes brave,
Then he staked his wife and empress, thou art prince Duryodhan's
    slave ! "

Rose the queen in queenly anger, and with woman's pride she spake :
" Hie thee, menial, to thy master, Queen Draupadi's answer take,

If my lord, himself a bondsman, then hath staked his queen and wife,
False the stake, for owns a bondsman neither wealth nor other's life,

Slave can wager wife nor children, and such action is undone,
Take my word to prince Duryodhan, Queen Draupadi is unwon ! "

Wrathful was the proud Duryodhan when he heard the answer bold,
To his younger, wild Duhsasan, this his angry mandate told :

" Little-minded is the menial, and his heart in terror fails,
For the fear of wrathful Bhima, lo ! his coward-bosom quails,

Thou Duhsasan, bid the princess as our humble slave appear,
Pandu's sons are humble bondsmen, and thy heart it owns no fear ! "

Fierce Duhsasan heard the mandate, blood-shot was his flaming eye,
Forthwith to the inner chambers did with eager footsteps hie,

Proudly sat the fair Draupadi, monarch's daughter, monarch's wife,
Unto her the base Duhsasan spake the message, insult-rife :

" Lotus-eyed Panchala-princess ! fairly staked and won at game,
Come and meet thy lord Duryodhan, chase that mantling blush of
    shame,

Serve us as thy lords and masters, be our beauteous bright-eyed slave,
Come unto the Council Chamber, wait upon the young and brave ! "

Proud Draupadi shakes with tremor at Duhsasan's hateful sight,
And she shades her eye and forehead, and her bloodless cheeks are
    white,

At his words her chaste heart sickens, and with wild averted eye,
Unto rooms where dwelt the women, Queen Draupadi seeks to fly,

Vainly sped the trembling princess in her fear and in her shame,
By her streaming wavy tresses fierce Duhsasan held the dame !

Sacred locks ! with holy water dewed at *rajasuya* rite,
And by *mantra* consecrated, fragrant, flowing, raven-bright,

Base Duhsasan by those tresses held the faint and flying queen,
Feared no more the sons of Pandu, nor their vengeance fierce and keen,

Dragged her in her slipping garments by her long and trailing hair,
And like sapling tempest-shaken, wept and shook the trembling fair !

Stooping in her shame and anguish, pale with wrath and woman's
    fear,
Trembling and in stifled accents, thus she spake with streaming tear :

" Leave me, shameless prince Duhsasan ! elders, noble lords are here,
Can a modest wedded woman thus in loose attire appear ? "

Vain the words and soft entreaty which the weeping princess made,
Vainly to the gods and mortals she in bitter anguish prayed,

For with cruel words of insult still Duhsasan mocked her woe :
" Loosely clad or void of clothing,—to the council hall you go,

Slave-wench fairly staked and conquered, wait upon thy masters
    brave,
Live among our household menials, serve us as our willing slave ! "

II

DRAUPADI'S PLAINT

Loose-attired, with trailing tresses, came Draupadi weak and faint,
Stood within the Council Chamber, tearful made her piteous plaint :

" Elders ! versed in holy *sastra*, and in every holy rite,
Pardon if Draupadi cometh in this sad unseemly plight,

Stay thy sinful deed, Duhsasan, nameless wrongs and insults spare,
Touch me not with hands uncleanly, sacred is a woman's hair,

Honoured elders, righteous nobles, have on me protection given,
Tremble sinner, seek no mercy from the wrathful gods in heaven !

Here in glory, son of DHARMA, sits my noble righteous lord,
Sin nor shame nor human frailty stains Yudhishthir's deed or word,

Silent all ? and will no chieftain rise to save a woman's life,
Not a hand or voice is lifted to defend a virtuous wife ?

Lost is Kuru's righteous glory, lost is Bharat's ancient name,
Lost is Kshatra's kingly prowess, warlike worth and knightly fame,

Wherefore else do Kuru warriors tamely view this impious scene,
Wherefore gleam not righteous weapons to protect an outraged
    queen ?

Bhishma, hath he lost his virtue, Drona, hath he lost his might,
Hath the monarch of the Kurus ceased to battle for the right,

Wherefore are ye mute and voiceless, councillors of mighty fame,
Vacant eye and palsied right arm watch this deed of Kuru's shame ?"

III

INSULT AND VOW OF REVENGE

Spake Draupadi slender-waisted, and her words were stern and high,
Anger flamed within her bosom and the tear was in her eye,

And her sparkling speaking glances fell on Pandu's sons like fire,
Stirred in them a mighty passion and a thirst for vengeance dire,

Lost their empire wealth and fortune, little recked they for the fall,
But Draupadi's pleading glances like a poniard smote them all !

Darkly frowned the ancient Bhishma, wrathful Drona bit his tongue,
Pale Vidura marked with anger insults on Draupadi flung,

Fulsome word nor foul dishonour could their truthful utterance taint,
And they cursed Duhsasan's action, when they heard Draupadi's
    plaint.

But brave Karna, though a warrior,—Arjun's deadly foe was he,—
'Gainst the humbled sons of Pandu spake his scorn in scornful glee :

" 'Tis no fault of thine, fair princess, fallen to this servile state,
Wife and son rule not their actions, others rule their hapless fate,

Thy Yudhishthir sold his birthright, sold thee at the impious play,
And the wife falls with the husband, and her duty—to obey !

Live thou in this Kuru household, do the Kuru princes' will,
Serve them as thy lords and masters, with thy beauty please them
    still,

Fair One ! seek another husband who in foolish reckless game
Will not stake a loving woman, will not cast her forth in shame !

For they censure not a woman, when she is a menial slave,
If her woman's fancy wanders to the young and to the brave,

For thy lord is not thy husband, as a slave he hath no wife,
Thou art free with truer lover to enjoy a wedded life,

They whom at the *swayamvara*, thou had'st chose, Panchala's bride,
They have lost thee, sweet Draupadi, lost their empire and their
    pride ! "

Bhima heard, and quick and fiercely heaved his bosom in his shame,
And his red glance fell on Karna like a tongue of withering flame,

Bound by elder's plighted promise Bhima could not smite in ire,
Looked the painted form of Anger flaming with an anguish dire !

" King and elder ! " uttered Bhima, and his words were few and
    brave,
" Vain were wrath and righteous passion in the sold and bounden
    slave,

Would that son of chariot-driver fling on us this insult keen,
Hadst thou, noble king and elder, staked nor freedom nor our
    queen ? "

Sad Yudhishthir heard in anguish, bent in shame his lowly head,
Proud Duryodhan laughed in triumph, and in scornful accents said :

" Speak, Yudhishthir, for thy brothers own their elder's righteous
    sway,
Speak, for truth in thee abideth, virtue ever marks thy way,

Hast thou lost thy new-built empire, and thy brothers proud and
    brave,
Hast thou lost thy fair Draupadi, is thy wedded wife our slave ? "

Lip nor eye did move Yudhishthir, hateful truth might not deny,
Karna laughed, but saintly Bhishma wiped his old and manly eye.

Madness seized the proud Duryodhan, and inflamed by passion base,
Sought the prince to stain Draupadi with a deep and dire disgrace,

On the proud and peerless woman cast his wicked lustful eye,
Sought to hold the high-born princess as his slave upon his knee !

Bhima penned his wrath no longer, lightning-like his glance he flung,
And the ancient hall of Kurus with his thunder accents rung :

" *May I never reach those mansions where my fathers live on high,
May I never meet ancestors in the bright and happy sky,*

*If that knee, by which thou sinnest, Bhima breaks not in his ire,
In the battle's red arena with his weapon, deathful, dire !* "

Red fire flamed on Bhima's forehead, sparkled from his angry eye,
As from tough and gnarléd branches fast the crackling red sparks fly !

IV

DHRITA-RASHTRA'S KINDNESS

Hark ! within the sacred chamber, where the priests in white attire
With libations morn and evening feed the sacrificial fire,

And o'er sacred rights of *homa* Brahmans chant their *mantra* high,
There is heard the jackal's wailing and the raven's ominous cry !

Wise Vidura knew that omen, and the Queen Gandhari knew,
Bhishma muttered " *svasti ! svasti !* " at this portent strange and
new,

Drona and preceptor Kripa uttered too that holy word,
Spake her fears the Queen Gandhari to her spouse and royal lord.

Dhrita-rashtra heard and trembled with a sudden holy fear,
And his feeble accents quavered, and his eyes were dimmed by tear :

" Son Duryodhan, ever luckless, godless, graceless, witless child,
Hast thou Drupad's virtuous daughter thus insulted and reviled,

Hast thou courted death and danger, for destruction clouds our path,
Can an old man's soft entreaties still avert this sign of wrath ? "

Slow and gently to Draupadi was the sightless monarch led,
And in kind and gentle accents unto her the old man said :

" Noblest empress, dearest daughter, good Yudhishthir's stainless
   wife,
Purest of the Kuru ladies, nearest to my heart and life,

Pardon wrong and cruel insult and avert the wrath of Heaven,
Voice thy wish and ask for blessing, be my son's misdeed forgiven ! "

Answered him the fair Draupadi : " Monarch of the Kuru's line,
For thy grace and for thy mercy every joy on earth be thine,

Since thou bid'st me name my wishes, this the boon I ask of thee,
That my gracious lord Yudhishthir once again be bondage-free !

I have borne a child unto him, noble boy and fair and brave,
Be he prince of royal station, not the son of bounden slave,

Let not light unthinking children point to him in utter scorn,
Call him slave and *dasaputra*, of a slave and bondsman born ! "

" Virtuous daughter, have thy wishes," thus the ancient monarch
   cried,
" Name a second boon and blessing, and it shall be gratified."

"Grant me then, O gracious father ! mighty Bhima, Arjun brave,
And the youngest twin-born brothers,—none of them may be a slave

With their arms and with their chariots let the noble princes part,
Freemen let them range the country, strong of hand and stout of
   heart ! "

" Be it so, high-destined princess ! " ancient Dhrita-rashtra cried,
" Name another boon and blessing, and it shall be gratified,

Foremost of my queenly daughters, dearest-cherished and the best,
Meeting thus thy gentle wishes now I feel my house is blest ! "

" Not so," answered him the princess, " other boon I may not seek,
Thou art bounteous, and a woman should be modest, wise and meek,

Twice I asked, and twice you granted, and a Kshatra asks no more,
Unto Brahmans it is given, asking favours evermore,

Now my lord and warlike brothers, from their hateful bondage freed,
Seek their fortune by their prowess and by brave and virtuous deed !"

V

THE BANISHMENT

Now Yudhishthir 'reft of empire, far from kinsmen, hearth and home,
With his wife and faithful brothers must as houseless exiles roam,

Parting blessings spake Yudhishthir, " Elder of the Kuru line,
Noble grandsire stainless Bhishma, may thy glories ever shine,

Drona priest and great preceptor, saintly Kripa true and brave,
Kuru's monarch Dhrita-rashtra, may the gods thy empire save,

Good Vidura true and faithful, may thy virtue serve thee well,
Warlike sons of Dhrita-rashtra, let me bid you all farewell ! "

So he spake unto his kinsmen, wishing good for evil done,
And in silent shame they listened, parting words they uttered none,

Pained at heart was good Vidura, and he asked in sore distress :
" Noble Pritha, will she wander in the pathless wilderness ?

Royal-born, unused to hardship, weak and long unused to roam,
Agéd is thy saintly mother, let fair Pritha stay at home,

And by all beloved, respected, in my house shall Pritha dwell,
Till your years of exile over, ye shall greet her safe and well."

Answered him the sons of Pandu : " Be it even as you say,
Unto us thou art a father, we thy sacred will obey,

Give us then thy holy blessings, friend and father, ere we part,
Blessings from the true and righteous brace the feeble, fainting heart."

Spake Vidura, pious-hearted : " Best of Bharat's ancient race,
Let me bless thee and thy brothers, souls of truth and righteous grace,

Fortune brings no weal to mortals who may win by wicked wile,
Sorrow brings no shame to mortals who are free from sin and guile !

Thou art trained in laws of duty, Arjun is unmatched in war,
And on Bhima in the battle kindly shines his faithful star,

And the Twins excel in wisdom, born to rule a mighty State,
Fair Draupadi, ever faithful, wins the smiles of fickle Fate !

Each with varied gifts encircled, each beloved of one and all,
Ye shall win a spacious empire, greater, mightier, after fall,

And your exile, good Yudhishthir, is ordained to serve your weal,
Is a trial and *samadhi*, for it chastens but to heal !

Meru taught thee righteous maxims where Himalay soars above,
And in Varnavata's forest Vyasa taught thee holy love,

Rama preached the laws of duty far on Bhrigu's lofty hill,
Sambhu showed the path of virtue by fair Drisad-vati's rill,

Fell from lips of saint Asita, words of wisdom deep and grave,
Bhrigu touched with fire thy bosom by the dark Kalmashi's wave !

Now once more the teaching cometh, purer, brighter, oftener taught,
Learn the truth from heavenly Narad, happy is thy mortal lot,

Greater than the son of Ila, than the kings of earth in might,
Holier than the holy *rishis*, be thou in thy virtue bright !

INDRA help thee in thy battles, proud subduer of mankind,
YAMA in the mightier duty, in the conquest of thy mind,

Good KUVERA teach thee kindness, hungry and the poor to feed,
King VARNUA quell thy passions, free thy heart from sin and greed,

Like the Moon in holy lustre, like the Earth in patience deep,
Like the Sun be full of radiance, strong like Wind's resistless sweep !

In thy sorrow, in affliction, ever deeper lessons learn,
Righteous be your life in exile, happy be your safe return,

May these eyes again behold thee in Hastina's ancient town,
Conqueror of earthly trials, crowned with virtue's heavenly crown ! "

Spake Vidura to the brothers, and they felt their might increase,
Bowed to him in salutation, filled with deeper, holier peace,

Bowed to Bhishma and to Drona, and to chiefs and elders all,
Exiles to the pathless jungle left their father's ancient hall !

VI

PRITHA'S LAMENT

In the inner palace chambers where the royal ladies dwell,
Unto Pritha came Draupadi, came to speak her sad farewell,

Monarch's daughter, monarch's consort, as an exile she must go,
Pritha wept and in the chambers rose the wailing voice of woe !

Heaving sobs convulsed her bosom as a silent prayer she prayed,
And in accents choked by anguish thus her parting words she said :

" Grieve not, child, if bitter fortune so ordains that we must part,
Virtue hath her consolations for the true and loving heart,

And I need not tell thee, daughter, duties of a faithful wife,
Drupad's and thy husband's mansions thou hast brightened by thy
    life !

Nobly from the sinning Kurus thou hast turned thy righteous wrath,
Safely, with a mother's blessing, tread the trackless jungle path,

Dangers bring no woe or sorrow to the true and faithful wife,
Sinless deed and holy conduct ever guard her charméd life,

Nurse thy lord with woman's kindness, and his brothers, where ye go,
Young in years in Sahadeva, gentle and unused to woe ! "

" May thy blessings help me, mother," so the fair Draupadi said,
" Safe in righteous truth and virtue, forest paths we fearless tread ! "

Wet her eyes and loose her tresses, fair Draupadi bowed and left,
Ancient Pritha weeping followed of all earthly joy bereft,

As she went, her duteous children now before their mother came,
Clad in garments of the deer-skin, and their heads were bent in shame !

Sorrow welling in her bosom choked her voice and filled her eye,
Till in broken stifled accents faintly thus did Pritha cry :

" Ever true to path of duty, noble children void of stain,
True to gods, to mortals faithful, why this undeservéd pain,

Wherefore hath untimely sorrow like a darksome cloud above,
Cast its pale and deathful shadow on the children of my love ?

Woe to me, your wretched mother, woe to her who gave you birth,
Stainless sons, for sins of Pritha have ye suffered on this earth,

Shall ye range the pathless forest dreary day and darksome night,
'Reft of all save native virtue, clad in native, inborn might ?

Woe to me, from rocky mountains where I dwelt by Pandu's side,
When I lost him, to Hastina wherefore came I in my pride,

Happy is your sainted father, dwells in regions of the sky,
Sees nor feels these earthly sorrows gathering on us thick and high,

Happy too is faithful Madri, for she trod the virtuous way,
Followed Pandu to the bright sky, and is now his joy and stay !

Ye alone are left to Pritha, dear unto her joyless heart,
Mother's hope and widow's treasure, and ye may not, shall not part,

Leave me not alone on wide earth, loving sons, your virtues prove,
Dear Draupadi, loving daughter, let a mother's tear-drops move,

Grant me mercy, kind Creator, and my days in mercy close,
End my sorrows, kind VIDHATA, end my life with all my woes !

Help me, pious-hearted Krishna, friend of friendless, wipe my pain,
All who suffer pray unto thee and they never pray in vain,

Help me, Bhishma, warlike Drona, Kripa ever good and wise,
Ye are friends of truth and virtue, righteous truth ye ever prize,

Help me from thy starry mansions, husband, wherefore dost thou
        wait,
Seest thou not thy godlike children exiled by a bitter fate !

Part not, leave me not, my children, seek ye not the trackless way,
Stay but one, if one child only, as your mother's hope and stay,

Youngest, gentlest Sahadeva, dearest to this widowed heart,
Wilt thou watch beside thy mother, while thy cruel brothers part ?"

Whispering words of consolation, Pritha's children wiped her tear,
Then unto the pathless jungle turned their footsteps lone and drear!

Kuru dames with fainting Pritha to Vidura's palace hie,
Kuru queens for weeping Pritha raise their voice in answering cry,

Kuru maids for fair Draupadi fortune's fitful will upbraid,
And their tear-dewed lotus-faces with their streaming fingers shade,

Dhrita-rashtra, ancient monarch, is by sad misgivings pained,
Questions oft with anxious bosom what the cruel fates ordained.

BOOK V

PATIVRATA-MAHATMYA

(*Woman's Love*)

TRUE to their word the sons of Pandu went with Draupadi into exile, and passed twelve years in the wilderness ; and many were the incidents which checkered their forest life. Krishna, who had stood by Yudhishthir in his prosperity, now came to visit him in his adversity ; he consoled Draupadi in her distress, and gave good advice to the brothers. Draupadi with a woman's pride and anger still thought of her wrongs and insults, and urged Yudhishthir to disregard the conditions of exile and recover his kingdom. Bhima too was of the same mind, but Yudhishthir would not be moved from his plighted word.

The great *rishi* Vyasa came to visit Yudhishthir, and advised Arjun, great archer as he was, to acquire celestial arms by penance and worship. Arjun followed the advice, met the god SIVA in the guise of a hunter, pleased him by his prowess in combat, and obtained his blessings and the *pasupata* weapon. Arjun then went to INDRA's heaven and obtained other celestial arms.

In the meanwhile Duryodhan, not content with sending his cousins to exile, wished to humiliate them still more by appearing before them in all his regal power and splendour. Matters however turned out differently from what he expected, and he became involved in a quarrel with some *gandharvas*, a class of aerial beings. Duryodhan was taken captive by them, and it was the Pandav brothers who released him from his captivity, and allowed him to return to his kingdom in peace. This act of generosity rankled in his bosom and deepened his hatred.

Jayadratha, king of the Sindhu or Indus country, and a friend and ally of Duryodhan, came to the woods, and in the absence of the Pandav brothers carried off Draupadi. The Pandavs however pursued the king, chastised him for his misconduct, and rescued Draupadi.

Still more interesting than these various incidents are the tales and legends with which this book is replete. Great saints came to see Yudhishthir in his exile, and narrated to him legends of ancient times and of former kings. One of these beautiful episodes, the tale of Nala and Damayanti, has been translated into graceful English verse by Dean Milman, and is known to many English readers.   The legend of Agastya who drained the ocean dry ; of Parasu-Rama a Brahman who killed the Kshatriyas of the earth ; of Bhagiratha who brought down the Ganges from the skies to the earth ; of Manu and the universal deluge ; of Vishnu and various other gods ; of Rama and his deeds which form the subject of the Epic *Ramayana ;*—these and various other legends have been interwoven in the account of the forest-life of the Pandavs, and make it a veritable storehouse of ancient Hindu tales and traditions.

Among these various legends and tales I have selected one which is singular and striking.   The great truth proclaimed under the thin guise of an eastern allegory is that a True Woman's Love is not conquered by Death.   The story is known by Hindu women high and low, rich and poor, in all parts of India ; and on a certain night in the year millions of Hindu women celebrate a rite in honour of the woman whose love was not conquered by death. Legends like these, though they take away from the unity and conciseness of the Epic, impart a moral instruction to the millions of India the value of which cannot be overestimated.

The portion translated in this Book forms Sections ccxcii. and ccxciii., a part of Section ccxciv. and Sections ccxcv. and ccxcvi. of Book iii. of the original text.

I

Forest Life

In the dark and pathless forest long the Pandav brothers strayed,
In the bosom of the jungle with the fair Draupadi stayed,

And they killed the forest red-deer, hewed the gnarléd forest wood,
From the stream she fetched the water, cooked the humble daily food,

In the morn she swept the cottage, lit the cheerful fire at eve,
But at night in lonesome silence oft her woman's heart would grieve,

Insults rankled in her bosom and her tresses were unbound,—
So she vowed,—till fitting vengeance had the base insulters found !

Oft when evening's shades descended, mantling o'er the wood and lea,
When Draupadi by the cottage cooked the food beneath the tree,

Rishis came to good Yudhishthir, sat beside his evening fires,
Many olden tales recited, legends of our ancient sires.

Markandeya, holy *rishi*, once unto Yudhishthir came,
When his heart was sorrow-laden with the memories of his shame,

" Pardon, father ! " said Yudhishthir, " if unbidden tears will start,
But the woes of fair Draupadi grieve a banished husband's heart,

By her tears the saintly woman broke my bondage worse than death,
By my sins she suffers exile and misfortune's freezing breath !

Dost thou, sage and saintly *rishi*, know of wife or woman born,
By such nameless sorrow smitten, by such strange misfortune torn,

Hast thou in thy ancient legends heard of true and faithful wife,
With a stronger wife's affection, with a sadder woman's life ? "

" Listen, monarch ! " said the *rishi*, " to a tale of ancient date,
How Savitri loved and suffered, how she strove and conquered Fate ! "

II

The Tale of Savitri

In the country of fair Madra lived a king in days of old,
Faithful to the holy BRAHMA, pure in heart and righteous-souled,

He was loved in town and country, in the court and hermit's den,
Sacrificer to the bright gods, helper to his brother men,

But the monarch, Aswapati, son or daughter had he none,
Old in years and sunk in anguish, and his days were almost done !

Vows he took and holy penance, and with pious rules conformed,
Spare in diet as *brahmachari* many sacred rites performed,

Sang the sacred hymn, *savitri*, to the gods oblations gave,
Through the lifelong day he fasted, uncomplaining, meek and brave !

Year by year he gathered virtue, rose in merit and in might,
Till the goddess of *savitri* smiled upon his sacred rite,

From the fire upon the altar which a holy radiance flung,
In the form of beauteous maiden, goddess of *savitri* sprung !

And she spake in gentle accents, blessed the monarch good and brave,
Blessed his rites and holy penance and a boon unto him gave :

" Penance and thy sacrifices can the Powers Immortal move,
And the pureness of thy conduct doth thy heart's affection prove,

Ask thy boon, king Aswapati, from creation's Ancient Sire,
True to virtue's sacred mandate speak thy inmost heart's desire."

" For an offspring brave and kingly," so the saintly king replied,
" Holy rites and sacrifices and this penance I have tried,

If these rites and sacrifices move thy favour and thy grace,
Grant me offspring, Prayer-Maiden, worthy of my noble race."

" Have thy object," spake the maiden, " Madra's pious-hearted king,
From SWAYMBHU, Self-created, blessings unto thee I bring,

For HE lists to mortal's prayer springing from a heart like thine,
And HE wills,—a noble daughter grace thy famed and royal line,

Aswapati, glad and grateful, take the blessing which I bring,
Part in joy and part in silence, bow unto Creation's King ! "

Vanished then the Prayer-Maiden, and the king of noble fame,
Aswapati, Lord of coursers, to his royal city came,

Days of hope and nights of gladness Madra's happy monarch passed,
Till his queen of noble offspring gladsome promise gave at last !

As the moon each night increaseth chasing darksome nightly gloom,
Grew the unborn babe in splendour in its happy mother's womb,

And in fulness of the season came a girl with lotus-eye,
Father's hope and joy of mother, gift of kindly gods on high !

And the king performed its birth-rites with a glad and grateful mind,
And the people blessed the dear one with their wishes good and kind,

As *Savitri*, Prayer-Maiden, had the beauteous offspring given,
Brahmans named the child *Savitri*, holy gift of bounteous Heaven !

Grew the child in brighter beauty like a goddess from above,
And each passing season added fresher sweetness, deeper love,

Came with youth its lovelier graces, as the buds their leaves unfold,
Slender waist and rounded bosom, image as of burnished gold,

Deva-Kanya ! born a goddess, so they said in all the land,
Princely suitors struck with splendour ventured not to seek her hand.

Once upon a time it happened on a bright and festive day,
Fresh from bath the beauteous maiden to the altar came to pray,

And with cakes and pure libations duly fed the Sacred Flame,
Then like SRI in heavenly radiance to her royal father came.

And she bowed to him in silence, sacred flowers beside him laid,
And her hands she folded meekly, sweetly her obeisance made,

With a father's pride, upon her gazed the ruler of the land,
But a strain of sadness lingered, for no suitor claimed her hand.

"Daughter," whispered Aswapati, "now, methinks, the time is come,
Thou shouldst choose a princely suitor, grace a royal husband's home,

Choose thyself a noble husband worthy of thy noble hand,
Choose a true and upright monarch, pride and glory of his land.

As thou choosest, gentle daughter, in thy loving heart's desire,
Blessing and his free permission will bestow thy happy sire.

For our sacred *sastras* sanction, holy Brahmans oft relate,
That the duty-loving father sees his girl in wedded state,

That the duty-loving husband watches o'er his consort's ways,
That the duty-loving offspring tends his mother's widowed days,

Therefore choose a loving husband, daughter of my house and love,
So thy father earn no censure or from men or gods above."

Fair Savitri bowed unto him and for parting blessings prayed,
Then she left her father's palace and in distant regions strayed,

With her guard and aged courtiers whom her watchful father sent,
Mounted on her golden chariot unto sylvan woodlands went.

Far in pleasant woods and jungle wandered she from day to day,
Unto *asrams*, hermitages, pious-hearted held her way,

Oft she stayed in holy *tirthas* washed by sacred limpid streams,
Food she gave unto the hungry, wealth beyond their fondest dreams.

Many days and months are over, and it once did so befall,
When the king and *rishi* Narad sat within the royal hall,

From her journeys near and distant and from places known to fame,
Fair Savitri with the courtiers to her father's palace came,

Came and saw her royal father, *rishi* Narad by his seat,
Bent her head in salutation, bowed unto their holy feet.

III

THE FATED BRIDEGROOM

"Whence comes she," so Narad questioned, "whither was Savitri led,
Wherefore to a happy husband hath Savitri not been wed ? "

"Nay, to choose her lord and husband," so the virtuous monarch said,
" Fair Savitri long hath wandered and in holy *tirthas* stayed,

Maiden ! speak unto the *rishi*, and thy choice and secret tell,"
Then a blush suffused her forehead, soft and slow her accents fell !

" Listen, father ! Salwa's monarch was of old a king of might,
Righteous-hearted Dyumat-sena, feeble now and void of sight,

Foemen robbed him of his kingdom when in age he lost his sight,
And from town and spacious empire was the monarch forced to flight.

With his queen and with his infant did the feeble monarch stray,
And the jungle was his palace, darksome was his weary way,

Holy vows assumed the monarch and in penance passed his life,
In the wild woods nursed his infant and with wild fruits fed his wife,

Years have gone in rigid penance, and that child is now a youth,
Him I choose my lord and husband, Satyavan, the Soul of Truth ! "

Thoughtful was the *rishi* Narad, doleful were the words he said :
" Sad disaster waits Savitri if this royal youth she wed,

Truth-beloving is his father, truthful is the royal dame,
Truth and virtue rule his actions, Satyavan his sacred name,

Steeds he loved in days of boyhood and to paint them was his joy,
Hence they called him young Chitraswa, art-beloving gallant boy,

But O pious-hearted monarch ! fair Savitri hath in sooth
Courted Fate and sad disaster in that noble gallant youth ! "

" Tell me," questioned Aswapati, " for I may not guess thy thought,
Wherefore is my daughter's action with a sad disaster fraught,

Is the youth of noble lustre, gifted in the gifts of art,
Blest with wisdom and with prowess, patient in his dauntless heart ? "

" SURYA'S lustre in him shineth," so the *rishi* Narad said,
" BRIHASPATI'S wisdom dwelleth in the youthful prince's head,

Like MAHENDRA in his prowess, and in patience like the Earth,
Yet O king ! a sad disaster marks the gentle youth from birth ! "

" Tell me, *rishi*, then thy reason," so the anxious monarch cried,
" Why to youth so great and gifted may this maid be not allied,

Is he princely in his bounty, gentle-hearted in his grace,
Duly versed in sacred knowledge, fair in mind and fair in face ? "

" Free in gifts like Rantideva," so the holy *rishi* said,
" Versed in lore like monarch Sivi who all ancient monarchs led,

Like Yayati open-hearted and like CHANDRA in his grace,
Like the handsome heavenly ASVINS fair and radiant in his face,

Meek and graced with patient virtue he controls his noble mind,
Modest in his kindly actions, true to friends and ever kind,

And the hermits of the forest praise him for his righteous truth,
Nathless, king, thy daughter may not wed this noble-hearted youth ! "

" Tell me, *rishi*," said the monarch, " for thy sense from me is hid,
Has this prince some fatal blemish, wherefore is this match forbid ? "

" Fatal fault ! " exclaimed the *rishi*, " fault that wipeth all his grace,
Fault that human power nor effort, rite nor penance can efface,

Fatal fault or destined sorrow ! for it is decreed on high,
On this day, a twelve-month later, this ill-fated prince will die ! "

Shook the startled king in terror and in fear and trembling cried :
" Unto short-lived, fated bridegroom ne'er my child shall be allied,

Come, Savitri, dear-loved maiden, choose another happier lord,
Rishi Narad speaketh wisdom, list unto his holy word !

Every grace and every virtue is effaced by cruel Fate,
On this day, a twelve-month later, leaves the prince his mortal state ! "

" Father ! " answered thus the maiden, soft and sad her accents fell,
" I have heard thy honoured mandate, holy Narad counsels well,

Pardon witless maiden's fancy, but beneath the eye of Heaven,
Only once a maiden chooseth, twice her troth may not be given,

Long his life or be it narrow, and his virtues great or none,
Satyavan is still my husband, he my heart and troth hath won,

What a maiden's heart hath chosen that a maiden's lips confess,
True to him thy poor Savitri goes into the wilderness ! "

" Monarch!" uttered then the *rishi*, " fixed is she in mind and heart,
From her troth the true Savitri never, never will depart,

More than mortal's share of virtue unto Satyavan is given,
Let the true maid wed her chosen, leave the rest to gracious Heaven!"

" *Rishi* and preceptor holy ! " so the weeping monarch prayed,
" Heaven avert all future evils, and thy mandate is obeyed ! "

Narad wished him joy and gladness, blessed the loving youth and
    maid,
Forest hermits on their wedding every fervent blessing laid.

IV

Overtaken by Fate

Twelve-month in the darksome forest by her true and chosen lord,
Sweet Savitri served his parents by her thought and deed and word,

Bark of tree supplied her garments draped upon her bosom fair,
Or the red cloth as in *asrams* holy women love to wear.

And the aged queen she tended with a fond and filial pride,
Served the old and sightless monarch like a daughter by his side,

And with love and gentle sweetness pleased her husband and her lord,
But in secret, night and morning, pondered still on Narad's word !

Nearer came the fatal morning by the holy Narad told,
Fair Savitri reckoned daily and her heart was still and cold,

Three short days remaining only ! and she took a vow severe
Of *triratra*, three nights' penance, holy fasts and vigils drear.

Of Savitri's rigid penance heard the king with anxious woe,
Spake to her in loving accents, so the vow she might forgo :

"Hard the penance, gentle daughter, and thy woman's limbs are frail,
After three nights' fasts and vigils sure thy tender health may fail,"

" Be not anxious, loving father," meekly this Savitri prayed,
" Penance I have undertaken, will unto the gods be made."

Much misdoubting then the monarch gave his sad and slow assent,
Pale with fast and unseen tear-drops, lonesome nights Savitri spent,

Nearer came the fatal morning, and to-morrow he shall die,
Dark, lone hours of nightly silence ! Tearless, sleepless is her eye !

"Dawns that dread and fated morning !" said Savitri, bloodless,
    brave,
Prayed her fervent prayers in silence, to the Fire oblations gave,

Bowed unto the forest Brahmans, to the parents kind and good,
Joined her hands in salutation and in reverent silence stood.

With the usual morning blessing, " *Widow may'st thou never be,*"
Anchorites and agéd Brahmans blessed Savitri fervently,

O ! that blessing fell upon her like the rain on thirsty air,
Struggling hope inspired her bosom as she drank those accents fair,

But returned the dark remembrance of the *rishi* Narad's word,
Pale she watched the creeping sunbeams, mused upon her fated lord !

" Daughter, now thy fast is over," so the loving parents said,
" Take thy diet after penance, for thy morning prayers are prayed,"

" Pardon, father," said Savitri, " let this other day be done,"
Unshed tear-drops filled her eyelids, glistened in the morning sun !

Satyavan, sedate and stately, ponderous axe on shoulder hung,
For the distant darksome jungle issued forth serene and strong,

But unto him came Savitri and in sweetest accents prayed,
As upon his manly bosom gently she her forehead laid :

" Long I wished to see the jungle where steals not the solar ray,
Take me to the darksome forest, husband, let me go to-day ! "

" Come not, love," he sweetly answered with a loving husband's care,
" Thou art all unused to labour, forest paths thou may'st not dare,

And with recent fasts and vigils pale and bloodless is thy face,
And thy steps are weak and feeble, jungle paths thou may'st not
    trace."

" Fasts and vigils make me stronger," said the wife with wifely pride,
" Toil I shall not feel nor languor when my lord is by my side,

For I feel a woman's longing with my lord to trace the way,
Grant me, husband ever gracious, with thee let me go to-day ! "

Answered then the loving husband, as his hands in hers he wove,
" Ask permission from my parents in the trackless woods to rove,"

Then Savitri to the monarch urged her longing strange request,
After duteous salutation thus her humble prayer addrest.

" To the jungle goes my husband, fuel and the fruit to seek,
I would follow if my mother and my loving father speak,

Twelve-month from this narrow *asram* hath Savitri stepped nor
    strayed,
In this cottage true and faithful ever hath Savitri stayed,

For the sacrificial fuel wends my lord his lonesome way,
Please my kind and loving parents, I would follow him to-day."

" Never since her wedding morning," so the loving king replied,
" Wish or thought Savitri whispered, for a boon or object sighed,

Daughter, thy request is granted, safely in the forest roam,
Safely with thy lord and husband seek again thy cottage home."

Bowing to her loving parents did the fair Savitri part,
Smile upon her pallid features, anguish in her inmost heart,

Round her sylvan greenwoods blossomed 'neath a cloudless Indian
    sky,
Flocks of pea-fowls gorgeous plumaged flew before her wondering
    eye,

Woodland rills and crystal nullahs gently roll'd o'er rocky bed,
Flower-decked hills in dewy brightness towering glittered overhead,

Birds of song and beauteous feather trilled a note in every grove,
Sweeter accents fell upon her, from her husband's lips of love !

Still with thoughtful eye Savitri watched her dear and fated lord,
Flail of grief was in her bosom but her pale lips shaped no word,

And she listened to her husband still on anxious thought intent,
Cleft in two her throbbing bosom as in silence still she went !

Gaily with the gathered wild-fruits did the prince his basket fill,
Hewed the interlacéd branches with his might and practised skill,

Till the drops stood on his forehead, weary was his aching head,
Faint he came unto Savitri and in faltering accents said :

" Cruel ache is on my forehead, fond and ever faithful wife,
And I feel a hundred needles pierce me and torment my life,

And my feeble footsteps falter and my senses seem to reel,
Fain would I beside thee linger for a sleep doth o'er me steal."

With a wild and speechless terror pale Savitri held her lord,
On her lap his head she rested as she laid him on the sward,

Narad's fatal words remembered as she watched her husband's head,
Burning lip and pallid forehead and the dark and creeping shade,

Clasped him in her beating bosom, kissed his lips with panting breath,
Darker grew the lonesome forest, and he slept the sleep of death !

V

TRIUMPH OVER FATE

In the bosom of the shadows rose a Vision dark and dread,
Shape of gloom in inky garment and a crown was on his head,

Gleaming Form of sable splendour, blood-red was his sparkling eye,
And a fatal noose he carried, grim and godlike, dark and high !

And he stood in solemn silence, looked in silence on the dead,
And Savitri on the greensward gently placed her husband's head,

And a tremor shook Savitri, but a woman's love is strong,
With her hands upon her bosom thus she spake with quivering
     tongue :

" More than mortal is thy glory ! If a radiant god thou be,
Tell me what bright name thou bearest, what thy message unto me."

" Know me," thus responded YAMA, " mighty monarch of the dead,
Mortals leaving earthly mansion to my darksome realms are led,

Since with woman's full affection thou hast loved thy husband dear,
Hence before thee, faithful woman, YAMA doth in form appear,

But his days and loves are ended, and he leaves his faithful wife,
In this noose I bind and carry spark of his immortal life,

Virtue graced his life and action, spotless was his princely heart,
Hence for him I came in person, princess, let thy husband part."

YAMA from the prince's body, pale and bloodless, cold and dumb,
Drew the vital spark, *purusha*, smaller than the human thumb,

In his noose the spark he fastened, silent went his darksome way,
Left the body shorn of lustre to its rigid cold decay,

Southward went the dark-hued YAMA with the youth's immortal life,
And, for woman's love abideth, followed still the faithful wife.

" Turn, Savitri," outspake YAMA, " for thy husband loved and lost,
Do the rites due unto mortals by their Fate predestined crost,

For thy wifely duty ceases, follow not in fruitless woe,
And no farther living creature may with monarch YAMA go ! "

" But I may not choose but follow where thou takest my husband's
      life,
For Eternal Law divides not loving man and faithful wife,

For a woman's true affection, for a woman's sacred woe,
Grant me in thy godlike mercy farther still with him I go !

Fourfold are our human duties : first to study holy lore,
Then to live as good householders, feed the hungry at our door,

Then to pass our days in penance, last to fix our thoughts above,
But the final goal of virtue, it is Truth and deathless Love ! "

" True and holy are thy precepts," listening YAMA made reply,
" And they fill my heart with gladness and with pious purpose high,

I would bless thee, fair Savitri, but the dead come not to life,
Ask for other boon and blessing, faithful, true and virtuous wife ! "

" Since you so permit me, YAMA," so the good Savitri said,
" For my husband's banished father let my dearest suit be made,

Sightless in the darksome forest dwells the monarch faint and weak,
Grant him sight and grant him vigour, YAMA, in thy mercy speak ! "

"Duteous daughter," YAMA answered, "be thy pious wishes given,
And his eyes shall be restoréd to the cheerful light of heaven,

Turn, Savitri, faint and weary, follow not in fruitless woe,
And no farther living creature may with monarch YAMA go!"

"Faint nor weary is Savitri," so the noble princess said,
"Since she waits upon her husband, gracious Monarch of the dead,

What befalls the wedded husband still befalls the faithful wife,
Where he leads she ever follows, be it death or be it life!

And our sacred writ ordaineth and our pious *rishis* sing,
Transient meeting with the holy doth its countless blessings bring,

Longer friendship with the holy purifies the mortal birth,
Lasting union with the holy is the bright sky on the earth,

Union with the pure and holy is immortal heavenly life,
For Eternal Law divides not loving man and faithful wife!"

"Blesséd are thy words," said YAMA, "blesséd is thy pious thought,
With a higher purer wisdom are thy holy lessons fraught,

I would bless thee, fair Savitri, but the dead come not to life,
Ask for other boon and blessing, faithful, true and virtuous wife!"

"Since you so permit me, YAMA," so the good Savitri said,
"Once more for my husband's father be my supplication made,

Lost his kingdom, in the forest dwells the monarch faint and weak,
Grant him back his wealth and kingdom, YAMA, in thy mercy speak!"

"Loving daughter," YAMA answered, "wealth and kingdom I
    bestow,
Turn, Savitri, living mortal may not with King YAMA go!"

Still Savitri, meek and faithful, followed her departed lord,
YAMA still with higher wisdom listened to her saintly word,

And the Sable King was vanquished, and he turned on her again,
And his words fell on Savitri like the cooling summer rain,

"Noble woman, speak thy wishes, name thy boon and purpose
    high,
What the pious mortal asketh gods in heaven may not deny!"

" Thou hast," so Savitri answered, " granted father's realm and
    might,
To his vain and sightless eyeballs hast restored their blesséd sight,

Grant him that the line of monarchs may not all untimely end,
Satyavan may see his kingdom to his royal sons descend ! "

" Have thy object," answered YAMA, " and thy lord shall live again,
He shall live to be a father, and his children too shall reign,

For a woman's troth abideth longer that the fleeting breath,
And a woman's love abideth higher than the doom of Death ! "

VI

RETURN HOME

Vanished then the Sable Monarch, and Savitri held her way
Where in dense and darksome forest still her husband lifeless lay,

And she sat upon the greensward by the cold unconscious dead,
On her lap with deeper kindness placed her consort's lifeless head,

And that touch of true affection thrilled him back to waking life,
As returned from distant regions gazed the prince upon his wife,

" Have I lain too long and slumbered, sweet Savitri, faithful spouse,
But I dreamt a Sable Person took me in a fatal noose ! "

" Pillowed on this lap," she answered, " long upon the earth you lay,
And the Sable Person, husband, he hath come and passed away,

Rise and leave this darksome forest if thou feelest light and strong,
For the night is on the jungle and our way is dark and long."

Rising as from happy slumber looked the young prince on all around,
Saw the wide-extending jungle mantling all the darksome ground,

" Yes," he said, " I now remember, ever loving faithful dame,
We in search of fruit and fuel to this lonesome forest came,

As I hewed the gnarléd branches, cruel anguish filled my brain,
And I laid me on the greensward with a throbbing piercing pain,

Pillowed on thy gentle bosom, solaced by thy gentle love,
I was soothed, and drowsy slumber fell on me from skies above.

All was dark and then I witnessed, was it but a fleeting dream,
God or Vision, dark and dreadful, in the deepening shadows gleam,

Was this dream my fair Savitri, dost thou of this Vision know,
Tell me, for before my eyesight still the Vision seems to glow ! "

" Darkness thickens," said Savitri, " and the evening waxeth late,
When the morrow's light returneth I shall all these scenes narrate,

Now arise, for darkness gathers, deeper grows the gloomy night,
And thy loving anxious parents trembling wait thy welcome sight,

Hark the rangers of the forest ! how their voices strike the ear,
Prowlers of the darksome jungle ! how they fill my breast with fear !

Forest-fire is raging yonder, for I see a distant gleam,
And the rising evening breezes help the red and radiant beam,

Let me fetch a burning faggot and prepare a friendly light,
With these fallen withered branches chase the shadows of the night,

And if feeble still thy footsteps,—long and weary is our way,—
By the fire repose, my husband, and return by light of day."

" For my parents, fondly anxious," Satyavan thus made reply,
" Pains my heart and yearns my bosom, let us to their cottage hie,

When I tarried in the jungle or by day or dewy eve,
Searching in the hermitages often did my parents grieve,

And with father's soft reproaches and with mother's loving fears,
Chid me for my tardy footsteps, dewed me with their gentle tears.

Think then of my father's sorrow, of my mother's woeful plight,
If afar in wood and jungle pass we now the livelong night,

Wife beloved, I may not fathom what mishap or load of care,
Unknown dangers, unseen sorrows, even now my parents share ! "

Gentle drops of filial sorrow trickled down his manly eye,
Fond Savitri sweetly speaking softly wiped the tear-drops dry :

" Trust me, husband, if Savitri hath been faithful in her love,
If she hath with pious offerings served the righteous gods above,

If she hath a sister's kindness unto brother men performed,
If she hath in speech and action unto holy truth conformed,

Unknown blessings, mighty gladness, trust thy ever faithful wife,
And not sorrows or disasters wait this eve our parents' life ! "

Then she rose and tied her tresses, gently helped her lord to rise,
Walked with him the pathless jungle, looked with love into his eyes,

On her neck his clasping left arm sweetly winds in soft embrace,
Round his waist Savitri's right arm doth as sweetly interlace,

Thus they walked the darksome jungle, silent stars looked from
      above,
And the hushed and throbbing midnight watched Savitri's deathless
      love.

BOOK VI
GO-HARANA

(*Cattle-Lifting*)

THE conditions of the banishment of the sons of Pandu were hard. They must pass twelve years in exile, and then they must remain a year in concealment. If they were discovered within this last year, they must go into exile for another twelve years.

Having passed the twelve years of exile in forests, the Pandav brothers disguised themselves and entered into the menial service of Virata, king of the Matsyas, to pass the year of concealment. Yudhishthir presented himself as a Brahman, skilled in dice, and became a courtier of the king. Bhima entered the king's service as cook. For Arjun, who was so well known, a stricter concealment was necessary. He wore conch bangles and earrings and braided his hair, like those unfortunate beings whom nature has debarred from the privileges of men and women, and he lived in the inner apartments of the king. He assumed the name of *Brihannala*, and taught the inmates of the royal household in music and dancing. Nakula became a keeper of the king's horses, and Sahadeva took charge of the king's cows. Draupadi too disguised herself as a waiting-woman, and served the princess of the Matsya house in that humble capacity.

In these disguises the Pandav brothers safely passed a year in concealment in spite of all search which Duryodhan made after them. At last an incident happened which led to their discovery when the year was out.

Cattle-lifting was a common practice with the kings of ancient India, as with the chiefs of ancient Greece. The king of the Trigartas and the king of the Kurus combined and fell on the king of the Matsyas in order to drive off the numerous herd of fine cattle for which his kingdom was famed. The Trigartas entered the Matsya kingdom from the south-east, and while Virata went out with his troops to meet the foe, Duryodhan with his Kuru forces fell on the kingdom from the north.

When news came that the Kurus had invaded the kingdom, there was no army in the capital to defend it. King Virata had gone out with most of his troops to face the Trigartas in the south-

east, and the prince Uttara had no inclination to face the Kurus in
the north. The disguised Arjun now came to the rescue in the
manner described in this Book. The description of the bows,
arrows, and swords of the Pandav brothers which they had concealed in a tree, wrapped like human corpses to frighten away in-
quisitive travellers, throws some light on the arts and manufactures
of ancient times. The portions translated in this Book form Sections xxxv., xxxvi., xl. to xliii., a portion of Section xliv., and
Sections liii. and lxxii. of Book iv. of the original text.

I

COMPLAINT OF THE COWHERD

Monarch of the mighty Matsyas, brave Virata known to fame,
Marched against Trigarta chieftains who from southward regions
    came,

From the north the proud Duryodhan, stealing onwards day by day,
Swooped on Matsya's fattened cattle like the hawk upon its prey !

Bhishma, Drona, peerless Karna, led the Kuru warriors brave,
Swept the kingdom of Virata like the ocean's surging wave,

Fell upon the trembling cowherds, chased them from the pasture-field,
Sixty thousand head of cattle was the Matsya country's yield !

And the wailing chief of cowherds fled forlorn, fatigued and spent,
Speeding on his rapid chariot to the royal city went,

Came inside the city portals, came within the palace gate,
Struck his forehead in his anguish and bewailed his luckless fate.

Meeting there the prince Uttara, youth of beauty and of fame,
Told him of the Kurus' outrage and lamented Matsya's shame :

" Sixty thousand head of cattle, bred of Matsya's finest breed,
To Hastina's distant empire do the Kuru chieftains lead,

Glory of the Matsya nation ! save thy father's valued kine,
Quick thy footsteps, strong thy valour, vengeance deep and dire be
    thine !

'Gainst the fierce Trigarta chieftains Matsya's warlike king is gone,
Thee we count our lord and saviour as our monarch's gallant son,

Rise, Uttara ! beat the Kurus, homeward lead the stolen kine,
Like an elephant of jungle, pierce the Kurus' shattered line !

As the *Vina* speaketh music, by musicians tuned aright,
Let thy sounding bow and arrows speak thy deeds of matchless might,

Harness quick thy milk-white coursers to thy sounding battle-car,
Hoist thy golden lion-banner, speed thee, prince, unto the war !

And as thunder-wielding INDRA smote *Asuras* fierce and bold,
Smite the Kurus with thy arrows winged with plumes of yellow gold

As the famed and warlike Arjun is the stay of Kuru's race,
Thou art refuge of the Matsyas and thy kingdom's pride and grace ! "

But the prince went not to battle from the foe to guard the State,
To the cowherd answered gaily, sheltered by the palace gate :

" Not unknown to me the usage of the bow and wingéd dart,
Not unknown the warrior's duty or the warrior's noble art,

I would win my father's cattle from the wily foeman's greed,
If a skilful chariot-driver could my fiery coursers lead.

For my ancient chariot-driver died on battle's gory plain,
Eight and twenty days we wrestled, many warlike chiefs were slain,

Bring me forth a skilful driver who can urge the battle-steed,
I will hoist my lion-banner, to the dubious battle speed.

Dashing through the foeman's horses, ranks of elephant and car,
I will win the stolen cattle rescued in the field of war,

And like thunder-wielding INDRA, smiting Danu's sons of old,
I will smite the Kuru chieftains, drive them to their distant hold !

Bhishma and the proud Duryodhan, archer Karna known to fame,
Drona too shall quail before me and retreat in bitter shame,

For those warriors in my absence Matsya's far-famed cattle steal,
But beneath my countless arrows Matsya's vengeance they shall feel,

Bring me forth a chariot-driver, let me speed my battle-car,
And in wonder they will question—Is this Arjun famed in war ? "

II

The Disguised Charioteer

Arjun, guised as Brihannala, heard the boast Uttara made,
And to try his skill and valour thus to fair Draupadi prayed:

" Say to him that Brihannala will his battle-chariot lead,
That as Arjun's chariot-driver he hath learned to urge the steed,

Say that faithful Brihannala many a dubious war hath seen,
And will win his father's cattle in this contest fierce and keen."

Fair Draupadi, guised as menial, Arjun's secret hest obeyed,
Humbly stepped before Uttara and in gentle accents prayed:

" Hear me, prince, yon Brihannala will thy battle-chariot lead,
He was Arjun's chariot-driver, skilled to urge the flying steed,

Trained in war by mighty Arjun, trained to drive the battle-car,
He hath followed helméd Arjun in the glorious field of war,

And when Arjun conquered Khandav, this, Uttara, I have seen,
Brihannala drove his chariot, for I served Yudhishthir's queen."

Heard Uttara hesitating, spake his faint and timid mind,
" I would trust thee, beauteous maiden, lotus-bosomed, ever kind,

But a poor and sexless creature, can he rein the warlike steed,
Can I ask him, worse than woman, in the battle's ranks to lead ? "

" Need is none," Draupadi answered, " Brihannala's grace to ask,
He is eager like the war-horse for this great and warlike task,

And he waits upon thy sister, she will bid the minion speed,
And he wins thy father's cattle, and the victor's glorious meed ! "

Matsya's princess spake to Arjun, Arjun led the battle-car,
Led the doubting prince Uttara to the dread and dubious war.

III

Arms and Weapons

Arjun drove the prince of Matsya to a darksome *sami* tree,
Spake unto the timid warrior in his accents bold and free:

" Prince, thy bow and shining arrows, pretty handsome toys are these,
Scarcely they beseem a warrior, and a warrior cannot please,

Thou shalt find upon this *sami*, mark my words which never fail,
Stately bows and wingéd arrows, banners, swords and coats of mail,

And a bow which strongest warriors scarce can in the battle bend,
And the limits of a kingdom widen when that bow is strained,

Tall and slender like a palm-tree, worthy of a warrior bold,
Smooth the wood of hardened fibre, and the ends are yellow gold ! "

Doubting still Uttara answered : " In this *sami's* gloomy shade
Corpses hang since many seasons in their wrappings duly laid,

Now I mark them all suspended, horrent, in the open air,
And to touch the unclean objects, friend, is more than I can dare ! "

" Fear not warrior," Arjun answered, " for the tree conceals no dead,
Warriors' weapons, cased like corpses, lurk within its gloomy shade,

And I ask thee, prince of Matsya, not to touch an unclean thing,
But unto a chief and warrior weapons and his arms to bring."

Prince Uttara gently lighted, climbed the dark and leafy tree,
Arjun from the prince's chariot bade him speed the arms to free,

And the young prince cut the wrappings ; lo ! the shining bows appear
Twisted, voiced like hissing serpents, like the bright stars glistening
    clear !

Seized with wonder prince Uttara silently the weapons eyed,
And unto his chariot-driver thus in trembling accents cried :

" Whose this bow so tall and stately, speak to me my gentle friend,
On the wood are golden bosses, tipped with gold is either end,

Whose this second ponderous weapon stout and massive in the hold,
On the staff are worked by artists elephants of burnished gold,

And what great and mighty monarch owns this other bow of might,
Set with golden glittering insects on its ebon back so bright,

Golden suns of wondrous brightness on this fourth their lustre lend,
Who may be the unknown archer who this stately bow can bend,

And the fifth is set with jewels, gems and stones of purest ray,
Golden fire-flies glint and sparkle in the yellow light of day !

Who doth own these shining arrows with their heads in gold encased,
Thousand arrows bright and feathered in the golden quivers placed,

Next are these with vulture-feather, golden-yellow in their hue,
Made of iron keen and whetted, whose may be these arrows true,

Next upon this sable quiver jungle tigers gleam in gold,
And these keen and boar-eared arrows speak some chieftain fierce
    and bold,

Fourth are these seven hundred arrows, crescent in their shining blade,
Thirsting for the blood of foemen and by cunning artists made,

And the fifth are golden-crested, made of tempered steel and bright,
Parrot feathers wing these arrows whetted and of wondrous might !

Mark again this wondrous sabre, shape of toad is on the hilt,
On the blade a toad is given and the scabbard nobly gilt,

Larger, stouter is this second in its sheath of tiger-skin,
Decked with bells and gold-surmounted and the blade is bright
    and keen,

Next this scimitar so curious by the skilled *Nishadas* made,
Scabbard made of wondrous cowhide sheathes the bright and
    polished blade,

Fourth, a long and beauteous weapon glittering sable in its hue,
With its sheath of softer goat-skin worked with gold on azure blue,

And the fifth is broad and massive over thirty fingers long,
Golden-sheathed and gold embosséd like a snake or fiery tongue ! "

Joyously responded Arjun : " Mark this bow embossed with gold.
'Tis the wondrous bow, *Gandiva*, worthy of a warrior bold,

Gift of heaven ! to archer Arjun kindly gods this weapon sent,
And the confines of a kingdom widen when the bow is bent,

Next, this mighty ponderous weapon worked with elephants of gold,
With this bow the stalwart Bhima hath the tide of conquests rolled,

And the third with golden insects by a cunning hand inlaid,
'Tis Yudhishthir's royal weapon by the noblest artists made,

Next the bow with solar lustre brave Nakula wields in fight,
And the fifth is Sahadeva's, decked with gems and jewels bright !

Mark again these thousand arrows, unto Arjun they belong,
And the darts whose blades are crescent unto Bhima brave and strong,

Boar-ear shafts are young Nakula's, in the tiger-quiver cased,
Sahadeva owns the arrows with the parrot's feather graced,

These three-knotted shining arrows, thick and yellow vulture-plumed,
They belong to King Yudhishthir, with their heads by gold illumed !

Listen more, if of these sabres, prince of Matsya, thou wouldst know,
Arjun's sword is toad-engraven, ever dreaded by the foe,

And the sword in tiger-scabbard, massive and of mighty strength,
None save tiger-waisted Bhima wields that sword of wondrous length,

Next the sabre golden-hilted, sable and with gold embossed,
Brave Yudhishthir kept that sabre when the king his kingdom lost,

Yonder sword with goat-skin scabbard brave Nakula wields in war,
In the cowhide Sahadeva keeps his shining scimitar ! "

" Strange thy accents," spake Uttara, " stranger are the weapons
    bright,
Are they arms of sons of Pandu famed on earth for matchless might,

Where are now those pious princes by a dire misfortune crossed,
Warlike Arjun, good Yudhishthir, by his subjects loved and lost,

Where is tiger-waisted Bhima, matchless fighter in the field,
And the brave and twin-born brothers skilled the arms of war to
    wield ?

O'er a game they lost their empire and we heard of them no more,
Or perchance they lonesome wander on some wild and distant shore,

And Draupadi noble princess, purest best of womankind,
Doth she wander with Yudhishthir, changeless in her heart and
    mind ? "

Proudly answered valiant Arjun, and a smile was on his face,
" Not in distant lands the brothers do their wandering footsteps trace.

In thy father's court disguiséd lives Yudhishthir just and good,
Bhima in thy father's palace as a cook prepares the food,

Brave Nakula guards the horses, Sahadeva tends the kine,
As thy sister's waiting-woman doth the fair Draupadi shine,

Pardon, prince, these rings and bangles, pardon strange unmanly guise,
'Tis no poor and sexless creature,—Arjun greets thy wondering eyes ! "

IV

RESCUE OF THE CATTLE

Arjun decked his mighty stature in the gleaming arms of war,
And with voice of distant thunder rolled the mighty battle-car,

And the Kurus marked with wonder Arjun's standard lifted proud,
Heard with dread the deep *Gandiva* sounding oft and sounding loud,

And they knew the wondrous bowman wheeling round the battle-car,
And with doubts and grave misgivings whispered Drona skilled in
war :

" That is Arjun's monkey-standard, how it greets my ancient eyes,
Well the Kurus know the standard like a comet in the skies,

Hear ye not the deep *Gandiva ?* How my ear its accents greet,
Mark ye not these pointed arrows falling prone before my feet,

By these darts his salutation to his teacher loved of old,
Years of exile now completed, Arjun sends with greetings bold !

How the gallant prince advances ! Now I mark his form and face,
Issuing from his dark concealment with a brighter, haughtier grace,

Well I know his bow and arrows and I know his standard well,
And the deep and echoing accents of his far-resounding shell,

In his shining arms accoutred, gleaming in his helmet dread,
Shines he like the flame of *homa* by libations duly fed ! "

Arjun marked the Kuru warriors arming for th' impending war,
Whispered thus to prince Uttara as he drove the battle-car :

" Stop thy steeds, O prince of Matsya ! for too close we may not go,
Stop thy chariot whence my arrows reach and slay the distant foe,

Seek we out the Kuru monarch, proud Duryodhan let us meet,
If he falls we win the battle, other chieftains will retreat.

There is Drona my preceptor, Drona's warlike son is there,
Kripa and the mighty Bhishma, archer Karna tall and fair,

Them I seek not in this battle, lead, O lead thy chariot far,
Midst the chiefs Duryodhan moves not, moves not in the ranks of war,

But to save the pilfered cattle speeds he onward in his fear,
While these warriors stay and tarry to defend their monarch's rear,

But I leave these car-borne warriors, other work to-day is mine,
Meet Duryodhan in the battle, win thy father's stolen kine ! "

Matsya's prince then turned the courses, left behind the war's array,
Where Duryodhan with the cattle quickly held his onward way,

Kripa marked the course of Arjun, guessed his inmost thought aright,
Thus he spake to brother warriors urging speed and instant fight :

" Mark ye, chieftains, gallant Arjun wheels his sounding battle-car,
'Gainst our prince and proud Duryodhan seeks to turn the tide of war,

Let us fall upon our foeman and our prince and leader save,
Few save INDRA, god of battles, conquers Arjun fierce and brave,

What were Matsya's fattened cattle, many thousands though they be,
If our monarch sinks in battle like a ship in stormy sea ! "

Vain were Kripa's words of wisdom, Arjun drove the chariot fair,
While his shafts like countless locusts whistled through the ambient
    air,

Kuru soldiers struck with panic neither stood and fought, nor fled,
Gazed upon the distant Arjun, gazed upon their comrades dead !

Arjun twanged his mighty weapon, blew his far-resounding shell,
Strangely spake his monkey-standard, Kuru warriors knew it well,

Sankha's voice, *Gandiva's* accents, and the chariot's booming sound,
Filled the air like distant thunder, shook the firm and solid ground.

Kuru soldiers fled in terror or they slumbered with the dead,
And the rescued lowing cattle with their tails uplifted fled !

V

WARRIOR'S GUERDON

Now with joy the king Virata to his royal city came,
Saw the rescued herds of cattle, saw Uttara prince of fame,

Marked the great and gallant Arjun, helmet-wearing, armour-cased,
Knew Yudhishthir and his brothers now as royal princes dressed,

And he greeted good Yudhishthir, truth-beloving brave and strong,
And to valiant Arjun offered Matsya's princess fair and young !

" Pardon, monarch," answered Arjun, " but I may not take as bride,
Matsya's young and beauteous princess whom I love with father's
    pride,

She hath often met me trusting in the inner palace hall,
As a daughter on a father waited on my loving call !

I have trained her *kokil* accents, taught her maiden steps in dance,
Watched her skill and varied graces all her native charms enhance,

Pure is she in thought and action, spotless as my hero boy,
Grant her to my son, O monarch, as his wedded wife and joy !

Abhimanyu trained in battle, handsome youth of godlike face,
Krishna's sister, fair Subhadra, bore the child of princely grace,

Worthy of thy youthful daughter, pure in heart and undefiled,
Grant it, sire, my Abhimanyu wed thy young and beauteous child ! "

Answered Matsya's noble monarch with a glad and grateful heart :
" Words like these befit thy virtue, nobly hast thou done thy part,

Be it as thou sayest, Arjun, unto Pandu's race allied,
Matsya's royal line is honoured, Matsya's king is gratified ! "

VI

The Wedding

Good Yudhishthir heard the tidings and he gave his free assent,
Unto distant chiefs and monarchs kindly invitations sent,

In the town of Upa-plavya, of fair Matsya's towns the best,
Made their home the pious brothers to receive each royal guest.

Came unto them Kasi's monarch and his arméd troopers came,
And the king of fair Panchala with his sons of warlike fame,

Came the sons of fair Draupadi early trained in art of war,
Other chiefs and sacrifices came from regions near and far.

Krishna decked in floral garlands with his elder brother came,
And his sister fair Subhadra, Arjun's loved and longing dame,

Arjun's son brave Abhimanyu came upon his flowery car,
With his elephants and chargers, troopers trained in art of war.

Vrishnis from the sea-girt Dwarka, brave Andhakas known to fame,
Bhojas from the mighty Chumbal with the righteous Krishna came,

He to gallant sons of Pandu made his presents rich and rare,
Gems and gold and costly garments, slaves and damsels passing fair.

With its quaint and festive greetings came at last the bridal day,
Matsya maids were merry-hearted, Pandu's sons were bright and gay,

Conch and cymbal, horn and trumpet spake forth music soft and
    sweet
In Virata's royal palace, in the peopled mart and street !

And they slay the jungle red-deer, and they spread the ample board,
And prepare the cooling palm-drink with the richest viands stored,

Mimes and actors please the people, bards recite the ancient song,
Glories of heroic houses minstrels by their lays prolong !

And deep-bosomed dames of Matsya, jasmine-form and lotus-face,
With their pearls and golden garlands joyously the bridal grace,

Circled by those royal ladies, though they all are bright and fair,
Brightest shines the fair Draupadi with a beauty rich and rare,

Stately dames and merry maidens lead the young and soft-eyed bride,
As the queens of gods encircle INDRA's daughter in her pride !

Arjun from the Matsya monarch takes the princess passing fair,
For his son by fair Subhadra, nursed by Krishna's loving care,

With a godlike grace Yudhishthir stands by faithful Arjun's side,
As a father takes a daughter, takes the young and beauteous bride.

Joins her hands to Abhimanyu's, and with cake and parchéd rice,
On the altar brightly blazing doth the holy sacrifice.

Matsya's monarch on the bridegroom rich and costly presents pressed,
Elephants he gave two hundred, steeds seven thousand of the best,

Poured libations on the altar, on the priests bestowed his gold,
Offered to the sons of Pandu rich domain and wealth untold.

With a pious hand Yudhishthir, true in heart and pure in mind,
Made his gifts in gold and garments, kine and wealth of every kind,

Costly chariots, beds of splendour, robes with thread of gold belaced,
Viands rich and sweet confection, drinks the richest and the best,

Lands he gave unto the Brahman, bullocks to the labouring swain,
Steeds he gave unto the warrior, to the people gifts and grain,

And the city of the Matsyas, teeming with a wealth untold,
Shone with festive joy and gladness and with flags and cloth of gold.

BOOK VII

UDYOGA

(*The Council of War*)

THE term of banishment having expired, Yudhishthir demanded
that the kingdom of Indra-prastha should be restored to him.
The old Dhrita-rashtra and his queen and the aged and virtuous
councillors advised the restoration, but the jealous Duryodhan hated
his cousins with a genuine hatred, and would not consent. All
negotiations were therefore futile, and preparations were made on
both sides for the most sanguinary and disastrous battle that had
ever been witnessed in Northern India.

The portions translated in this Book are from Sections i., ii.,
iii., xciv., cxxiv., and cxxvi. of Book v. of the original text.

I

KRISHNA'S SPEECH

Mirth and song and nuptial music waked the echoes of the night,
Youthful bosoms throbbed with pleasure, lovelit glances sparkled
bright,

But when young and white-robed USHAS ope'd the golden gates of day,
To Virata's council chamber chieftains thoughtful held their way,

Stones inlaid in arch and pillar glinted in the glittering dawn,
Gay festoons and graceful garlands o'er the golden cushions shone !

Matsya's king, Panchala's monarch, foremost seats of honour claim,
Krishna too and Valadeva, Dwarka's chiefs of righteous fame,

By them sate the bold Satyaki from the sea-girt western shore,
And the godlike sons of Pandu,—days of dark concealment o'er,

Youthful princes in their splendour graced Virata's royal hall,
Valiant sons of valiant fathers, brave in war, august and tall,

In their gem-bespangled garments came the warriors proud and high,
Till the council chamber glittered like the star-bespangled sky !

Kind the greetings, sweet the converse, soft the golden moments fly,
Till intent on graver questions all on Krishna turn their eye,

Krishna with his inner vision then the state of things surveyed,
And his thoughts before the monarchs thus in weighty accents laid :

" Known to all, ye mighty monarchs ! May your glory ever last,
True to plighted word Yudhishthir hath his weary exile passed.

Twelve long years with fair Draupadi in the pathless jungle strayed,
And a year in menial service in Virata's palace stayed,

He hath kept his plighted promise, braved affliction, woe, and shame,
And he begs, assembled monarchs, ye shall now his duty name.

For he swerveth not from duty kingdom of the sky to win,
Prizeth hamlet more than empire, so his course be free from sin,

Loss of realm and wealth and glory higher virtues in him prove,
Thoughts of peace and not of anger still the good Yudhishthir move !

Mark again the sleepless anger and the unrelenting hate
Harboured by the proud Duryodhan driven by his luckless fate,

From a child, by fire or poison, impious guile or trick of dice,
He hath compassed dark destruction by deceit and low device !

Ponder well, ye gracious monarchs, with a just and righteous mind,
Help Yudhishthir with your counsel, with your grace and blessings
    kind,

Should the noble son of Pandu seek his right by open war,
Seek the aid of righteous monarchs and of chieftains near and far ?

Should he smite his ancient foemen skilled in each deceitful art,
Unforgiving in their vengeance, unrelenting in their heart ?

Should he rather send a message to the proud unbending foe,
And Duryodhan's haughty purpose seek by messenger to know ?

Should he send a noble envoy, trained in virtue, true and wise,
With his greetings to Duryodhan in a meek and friendly guise ?

Ask him to restore the kingdom on the sacred Jumna's shore,
Either king may rule his empire as in happy days of yore ? "

Krishna uttered words of wisdom pregnant with his peaceful thought,
For in peace and not by bloodshed still Yudhishthir's right he
    sought.

II

VALADEVA'S SPEECH

Krishna's elder Valadeva, stalwart chief who bore the plough,
Rose and spake, the blood of Vrishnis mantled o'er his lofty brow :

" Ye have listened, pious monarchs, to my brother's gentle word,
Love he bears to good Yudhishthir and to proud Hastina's lord,

For his realm by dark blue Jumna good Yudhishthir held of yore,
Brave Duryodhan ruled his kingdom on the ruddy Ganga's shore,

And once more in love and friendship either prince may rule his share,
For the lands are broad and fertile, and each realm is rich and fair !

Speed the envoy to Hastina with our love and greetings kind,
Let him speak Yudhishthir's wishes, seek to know Duryodhan's
mind,

Make obeisance unto Bhishma and to Drona true and bold,
Unto Kripa, archer Karna, and to chieftains young and old,

To the sons of Dhrita-rashtra, rulers of the Kuru land,
Righteous in their kingly duties, stout of heart and strong of hand,

To the princes and to burghers gathered in the council hall,
Let him speak Yudhishthir's wishes, plead Yudhishthir's cause to all.

Speak he not in futile anger, for Duryodhan holds the power,
And Yudhishthir's wrath were folly in this sad and luckless hour,

By his dearest friends dissuaded, but by rage or madness driven,
He hath played and lost his empire, may his folly be forgiven !

Indra-prastha's spacious empire now Duryodhan deems his own,
By his tears and soft entreaty let Yudhishthir seek the throne,

Open war I do not counsel, humbly seek Duryodhan's grace,
War will not restore the empire nor the gambler's loss replace ! "

Thus with cold and cruel candour stalwart Valadeva cried,
Wrathful rose the brave Satyaki, fiercely thus to him replied.

III

SATYAKI'S SPEECH

" Shame unto the halting chieftain who thus pleads Duryodhan's part,
Timid counsel, Valadeva, speaks a woman's timid heart,

Oft from warlike stock ariseth weakling chief who bends the knee,
As a withered fruitless sapling springeth from a fruitful tree !

From a heart so faint and craven, faint and craven words must flow,
Monarchs in their pride and glory list not to such counsel low,

Couldst thou, impious Valadeva, midst these potentates of fame,
On Yudhishthir pious-hearted cast this undeservéd blame ?

Challenged by his wily foeman and by dark misfortune crost,
Trusting to their faith Yudhishthir played a righteous game and lost,

Challenge from a crownéd monarch can a crownéd king decline,
Can a Kshatra warrior fathom fraud in sons of royal line ?

Nathless he surrendered empire true to faith and plighted word,
Lived for years in pathless forests Indra-prastha's mighty lord,

Past his years of weary exile, now he claims his realm of old,
Claims it, not as humble suppliant, but as king and warrior bold,

Past his year of dark concealment, bold Yudhishthir claims his own,
Proud Duryodhan now must render Indra-prastha's jewelled throne !

Bhishma counsels, Drona urges, Kripa pleads for right in vain,
False Duryodhan will not render sinful conquest, fraudful gain,

Open war I therefore counsel, ruthless and relentless war,
Grace we seek not when we meet them speeding in our battle-
car !

And our weapons, not entreaties, shall our foemen force to yield,
Yield Yudhishthir's rightful kingdom or they perish on the field,

False Duryodhan and his forces fall beneath our battle's shock,
As beneath the bolt of thunder falls the crushed and riven rock !

Who shall meet the helméd Arjun in the gory field of war,
Krishna with his fiery discus mounted on his battle-car,

Who shall face the twin-born brothers by the mighty Bhima led,
And the vengeful chief Satyaki with his bow and arrows dread ?

Ancient Drupad wields his weapon peerless in the field of fight,
And his brave son, born of AGNI, owns an all-consuming might,

Abhimanyu, son of Arjun, whom the fair Subhadra bore,
And whose happy nuptials brought us from far Dwarka's sea-girt
shore,

Men on earth nor bright Immortals can the youthful hero face,
When with more than Arjun's prowess Abhimanyu leads the race !

Dhrita-rashtra's sons we conquer and Gandhara's wily son,
Vanquish Karna though world-honoured for his deeds of valour done,

Win the fierce-contested battle and redeem Yudhishthir's own,
Place the exile pious-hearted on his father's ancient throne !

And no sin Satyaki reckons slaughter of the mortal foe,
But to beg a grace of foemen were a mortal sin and woe,

Speed we then unto our duty, let our impious foemen yield,
Or the fiery son of Sini meets them on the battle-field ! "

IV

DRUPAD'S SPEECH

Fair Panchala's ancient monarch rose his secret thoughts to tell,
From his lips the words of wisdom with a graceful accent fell :

" Much I fear thou speakest truly, hard is Kuru's stubborn race,
Vain the hope, the effort futile, to beseech Duryodhan's grace !

Dhrita-rashtra pleadeth vainly, feeble is his fitful star,
Ancient Bhishma, righteous Drona, cannot stop this fatal war,

Archer Karna thirsts for battle, moved by jealousy and pride,
Deep Sakuni, false and wily, still supports Duryodhan's side !

Vain is Valadeva's counsel, vainly shall our envoy plead,
Half his empire proud Duryodhan yields not in his boundless greed,

In his pride he deems our mildness faint and feeble-hearted fear,
And our suit will fan his glory and his arrogance will cheer !

Therefore let our many heralds travel near and travel far,
Seek alliance of all monarchs in the great impending war,

Unto brave and noble chieftains, unto nations east and west,
North and south to warlike races speed our message and request !

Meanwhile peace and offered friendship we before Duryodhan place,
And my priest will seek Hastina, strive to win Duryodhan's grace,

If he renders Indra-prastha, peace will crown the happy land,
Or our troops will shake the empire from the east to western strand!"

Vainly were Panchala's Brahmans sent with messages of peace,
Vainly urged the Kuru elders that the fatal feud should cease,

Proud Duryodhan to his kinsmen would not yield their proper share,
Pandu's sons would not surrender, for they had the will to dare !

Fatal war and dire destruction did the mighty gods ordain,
Till the kings and arméd nations strewed the red and reeking plain,

Krishna in his righteous effort sought for wisdom from above,
Strove to stop the war of nations and to end the feud in love,

And to far Hastina's palace Krishna went to sue for peace,
Raised his voice against the slaughter, begged that strife and feud
should cease !

V

KRISHNA'S SPEECH AT HASTINA

Silent sat the listening chieftains in Hastina's council hall,
With the voice of rolling thunder Krishna spake unto them all:

" Listen, mighty Dhrita-rashtra, Kuru's great and ancient king,
Seek not war and death of kinsmen, word of peace and love I bring !

'Midst the wide earth's many nations Bharats in their worth excel,
Love and kindness, spotless virtue, in the Kuru-elders dwell,

Father of the noble nation, now retired from life's turmoil,
Ill beseems that sin or untruth should thy ancient bosom soil !

For thy sons in impious anger seek to do their kinsmen wrong,
And withhold the throne and kingdom which by right to them belong,

And a danger thus ariseth like the comet's baleful fire,
Slaughtered kinsmen, bleeding nations, soon shall feed its fatal ire !

Stretch thy hands, O Kuru monarch ! prove thy truth and holy grace,
Man of peace ! avert the slaughter and preserve thy ancient race,

Yet restrain thy fiery children, for thy mandates they obey,
I with sweet and soft persuasion Pandu's truthful sons will sway.

'Tis thy profit, Kuru monarch ! that the fatal feud should cease,
Brave Duryodhan, good Yudhishthir, rule in unmolested peace,

Pandu's sons are strong in valour, mighty in their arméd hand,
INDRA shall not shake thy empire when they guard the Kuru land !

Bhishma is thy kingdom's bulwark, doughty Drona rules the war,
Karna matchless with his arrows, Kripa peerless in his car,

Let Yudhishthir and stout Bhima by these noble warriors stand,
And let helmet-wearing Arjun guard the sacred Kuru land,

Who shall then contest thy prowess from the sea to farthest sea,
Ruler of a worldwide empire, king of kings and nations free ?

Sons and grandsons, friends and kinsmen, will surround thee in a ring,
And a race of loving heroes guard their ancient hero-king,

Dhrita-rashtra's lofty edicts will proclaim his boundless sway,
Nations work his righteous mandates and the kings his will obey !

If this concord be rejected and the lust of war prevail,
Soon within these ancient chambers will resound the sound of wail.

Grant thy children be victorious and the sons of Pandu slain,
Dear to thee are Pandu's children, and their death must cause thee
     pain !

But the Pandavs skilled in warfare are renowned both near and far,
And thy race and children's slaughter will methinks pollute this war,

Sons and grandsons, loving princes, thou shalt never see again,
Kinsmen brave and car-borne chieftains will bedeck the gory plain !

Ponder yet, O ancient monarch ! Rulers of each distant State,
Nations from the farthest regions gather thick to court their fate,

Father of a righteous nation ! Save the princes of the land,
On the armed and fated nations stretch, old man, thy saving hand !

Say the word, and at thy bidding leaders of each hostile race
Not the gory field of battle but the festive board will grace,

Robed in jewels, decked in garlands, they will quaff the ruddy wine,
Greet their foes in mutual kindness, bless thy holy name and thine !

Think, O man of many seasons ! When good Pandu left this throne,
And his helpless loving orphans thou didst cherish as thine own,

'Twas thy helping steadying fingers taught their infant steps to frame,
'Twas thy loving gentle accents taught their lips to lisp each name,

As thine own they grew and blossomed, dear to thee they yet remain,
Take them back unto thy bosom, be a father once again !

Unto thee, O Dhrita-rashtra ! Pandu's sons in homage bend,
And a loving peaceful message through my willing lips they send :

Tell our monarch, more than father, by his sacred stern command
We have lived in pathless jungle, wandered far from land to land,

True unto our plighted promise, for we ever felt and knew,
To his promise Dhrita-rashtra cannot, will not be untrue !

Years of anxious toil are over and of woe and bitterness,
Years of waiting and of watching, years of danger and distress.

Like a dark unending midnight hung on us this age forlorn,
Streaks of hope and dawning brightness usher now the radiant morn!

Be unto us as a father, loving not inspired by wrath,
Be unto us as a teacher, pointing us the righteous path,

If perchance astray we wander, thy strong arm shall lead aright,
If our feeble bosom fainteth, help us with a father's might !

This, O king ! the soft entreaty Pandu's sons to thee have made,
These are words the sons of Pandu unto Kuru's king have said,

Take their love, O gracious monarch ! Let thy closing days be fair,
Let Duryodhan keep his kingdom, let the Pandavs have their share.

Call to mind their noble suffering, for the tale is dark and long,
Of the outrage they have suffered, of the insult and the wrong,

Exiled into Varnavata, destined unto death by flame,
For the gods assist the righteous, they with added prowess came,

Exiled into Indra-prastha, by their toil and by their might
Cleared a forest, built a city, did the *rajasuya* rite,

Cheated of their realm and empire and of all they called their own,
In the jungle they have wandered and in Matsya lived unknown,

Once more quelling every evil they are stout of heart and hand,
Now redeem thy plighted promise and restore their throne and land !

Trust me, mighty Dhrita-rashtra ! trust me, lords who grace this hall,
Krishna pleads for peace and virtue, blessings unto you and all,

Slaughter not the arméd nations, slaughter not thy kith and kin,
Mark not, king, thy closing winters with the bloody stain of sin,

Let thy sons and Pandu's children stand beside thy ancient throne,
Cherish peace and cherish virtue, for thy days are almost done ! "

VI

BHISHMA'S SPEECH

From the monarch's ancient bosom sighs and sobs convulsive broke,
Bhishma wiped his manly eyelids and to proud Duryodhan spoke :

" Listen, prince, for righteous Krishna counsels love and holy peace,
Listen, youth, and may thy fortune with thy passing years increase !

Yield to Krishna's words of wisdom, for thy weal he nobly strives,
Yield and save thy friends and kinsmen, save thy cherished subjects'
    lives,

Foremost race in all this wide earth is Hastina's royal line,
Bring not on them dire destruction by a sinful act of thine !

Sons and fathers, friends and brothers, shall in mutual conflict die,
Kinsmen slain by dearest kinsmen shall upon the red field lie,

Hearken unto Krishna's counsel, unto wise Vidura's word,
Be thy mother's fond entreaty and thy father's mandate heard !

Tempt not wrath and fiery vengeance on thy old heroic race,
Tread not in the path of darkness, seek the path of light and grace,

Listen to thy king and father, he hath Kuru's empire graced,
Listen to thy queen and mother, she hath nursed thee on her breast ! ''

VII

DRONA'S SPEECH

Out spake Drona priest and warrior, and his words were few and high,
Clouded was Duryodhan's forehead, wrathful was Duryodhan's eye :

" Thou hast heard the holy counsel which the righteous Krishna said,
Ancient Bhishma's voice of warning thou hast in thy bosom weighed,

Peerless in their godlike wisdom are these chiefs in peace or strife,
Truest friends to thee, Duryodhan, pure and sinless in their life !

Take their counsel, and thy kinsmen fasten in the bonds of peace,
May the empire of the Kurus and their warlike fame increase,

List unto thy old preceptor ! Faithless is thy fitful star,
And they feed thy passions falsely, those who urge and counsel war !

Crownéd kings and arméd nations will contest for thee in vain,
Vainly brothers, sons, and kinsmen will for thee their lifeblood
  drain,

For the victor's crown and glory never, never can be thine,
Krishna conquers, and brave Arjun ! mark these deathless words of
  mine !

I have trained the youthful Arjun, seen him bend the warlike bow,
Marked him charge the hostile forces, marked him smite the scattered foe.

Fiery son of Jamadagni owned no greater loftier might,
Breathes on earth no mortal warrior conquers Arjun in the fight !

Krishna too, in war resistless, comes from Dwarka's distant shore,
And the bright-gods quake before him whom the fair Devaki
bore,

These are foes thou may'st not conquer, take an ancient warrior's
word,
Act thou as thy heart decideth, thou art Kuru's king and lord ! "

VIII

VIDURA'S SPEECH

Then in gentler voice Vidura sought his pensive mind to tell,
From his lips serene and softly words of woe and anguish fell :

" Not for thee I grieve, Duryodhan, slain by vengeance fierce and keen,
For thy father weeps my bosom and the aged Kuru queen !

Sons and grandsons, friends and kinsmen slaughtered in this fatal war,
Homeless, cheerless, on this wide earth they shall wander long and far,

Friendless, kinless, on this wide earth whither shall they turn and fly,
Like some birds bereft of plumage, they shall pine awhile and die,

Of their race and sad survivors they shall wander o'er the earth,
Curse the fatal day, Duryodhan, saw thy sad and woeful birth ! "

IX

DHRITA-RASHTRA'S SPEECH

Tear-drops filled his sightless eyeballs, anguish shook his agéd frame,
As the monarch soothed Duryodhan by each fond endearing name :

" Listen, dearest son, Duryodhan, shun this dark and fatal strife,
Cast not grief and death's black shadows on thy parents' closing life,

Krishna's heart is pure and spotless, true and wise the words he said,
We may win a worldwide empire with the noble Krishna's aid,

Seek the friendship of Yudhishthir loved of righteous gods above,
And unite the scattered Kurus by the lasting tie of love !

Now at full is tide of fortune, never may it come again,
Strive and win, or ever after all repentance may be vain.

Peace is righteous Krishna's counsel and he comes to offer peace,
Take the offered boon, Duryodhan! Let all strife and hatred cease !"

X

DURYODHAN'S SPEECH

Silent sat the proud Duryodhan wrathful in the council hall,
Spake to mighty-arméd Krishna and to Kuru warriors all :

" Ill becomes thee, Dwarka's chieftain, in the paths of sin to move,
Bear for me a secret hatred, for the Pandavs secret love,

And my father, wise Vidura, ancient Bhishma, Drona bold,
Join thee in this bitter hatred, turn on me their glances cold !

What great crime or darkening sorrow shadows o'er my bitter fate,
That ye chiefs and Kuru's monarch mark Duryodhan for your hate,

Speak, what nameless guilt or folly, secret sin to me unknown,
Turns from me your sweet affection, father's love that was my own ?

If Yudhishthir, fond of gambling, played a heedless reckless game,
Lost his empire and his freedom, was it then Duryodhan's blame,

And if freed from shame and bondage in his folly played again,
Lost again and went to exile, wherefore doth he now complain ?

Weak are they in friends and forces, feeble is their fitful star,
Wherefore then in pride and folly seek with us unequal war,

Shall we, who to mighty INDRA scarce will do the homage due,
Bow to homeless sons of Pandu and their comrades faint and few,

Bow to them while warlike Drona leads us as in days of old,
Bhishma greater than the bright-gods, archer Karna true and bold ?

If in dubious game of battle we should forfeit fame and life,
Heaven will ope its golden portals for the Kshatra slain in strife,

If unbending to our foemen we should press the gory plain,
Stingless is the bed of arrows, death for us will have no pain !

For the Kshatra knows no terror of his foeman in the field,
Breaks like hardened forest timber, bends not, knows not how to
    yield,

So the ancient sage Matanga of the warlike Kshatra said,
Save to priest and sage preceptor unto none he bends his head !

Indra-prastha which my father weakly to Yudhishthir gave,
Nevermore shall go unto him while I live and brothers brave,

Kuru's undivided kingdom Dhrita-rashtra rules alone,
Let us sheathe our swords in friendship and the monarch's empire
    own,

If in past in thoughtless folly once the realm was broke in twain,
Kuru-land is re-united, never shall be split again !

Take my message to my kinsmen, for Duryodhan's words are plain,
Portion of the Kuru empire sons of Pandu seek in vain,

Town nor village, mart nor hamlet, help us righteous gods in heaven,
Spot that needle's point can cover shall not unto them be given ! "

BOOK VIII

BHISHMA-BADHA

(*Fall of Bhishma*)

ALL negotiations for a peaceful partition of the Kuru kingdom having failed, both parties now prepared for a battle, perhaps the most sanguinary that was fought on the plains of India in the ancient times. It was a battle of nations, for all warlike races in Northern India took a share in it.

Duryodhan's army consisted of his own division, as well as the divisions of ten allied kings. Each allied power is said to have brought one *akshauhini* troops, and if we reduce this fabulous number to the moderate figure of ten thousand, including horse and foot, cars and elephants, Duryodhan's army including his own division was over a hundred thousand strong.

Yudhishthir had a smaller army, said to have been seven *akshauhinis* in number, which we may by a similar reduction reckon to be seventy thousand. His father-in-law the king of the Panchalas, and Arjun's relative the king of the Matsyas, were his principal allies. Krishna joined him as his friend and adviser, and as the charioteer of Arjun, but the Vrishnis as a nation had joined Duryodhan.

When the two armies were drawn up in array and faced each other, and Arjun saw his revered elders and dear friends and relations among his foes, he was unwilling to fight. It was on this occasion that Krishna explained to him the great principles of Duty in that memorable work called the *Bhagavat-gita* which has been translated into so many European languages. Belief in one Supreme Deity is the underlying thought of this work, and ever and anon, as Professor Garbe remarks, "does Krishna revert to the doctrine that for every man, no matter to what caste he may belong, the zealous performance of his duty and the discharge of his obligations is his most important work."

Duryodhan chose the grand old fighter Bhishma as the commander-in-chief of his army, and for ten days Bhishma held his own and inflicted serious loss on Yudhishthir's army. The principal incidents of these ten days, ending with the fall of Bhishma, are narrated in this Book.

This Book is an abridgment of Book vi. of the original text.

I

Pandavs Routed by Bhishma

Ushas with her crimson fingers oped the portals of the day,
Nations armed for mortal combat in the field of battle lay,

Beat of drum and blare of trumpet and the *sankha's* lofty sound,
By the answering cloud repeated, shook the hills and tented ground,

And the voice of sounding weapons which the warlike archers drew,
And the neigh of battle chargers as the arméd horsemen flew,

Mingled with the rolling thunder of each swiftly-speeding car,
And with pealing bells proclaiming mighty elephants of war !

Bhishma led the Kuru forces, strong as Death's resistless flail,
Human chiefs nor bright Immortals could against his might prevail,

Helmet-wearing, gallant Arjun came in pride and mighty wrath,
Held aloft his famed *Gandiva*, strove to cross the chieftain's path !

Abhimanyu son of Arjun, whom the fair Subhadra bore,
Drove against Kosala's monarch famed in arms and holy lore,

Hurling down Kosala's standard he the dubious combat won,
Barely escaped with life the monarch from the fiery Arjun's son !

With his fated foe Duryodhan, Bhima strove in deathful war,
And against the proud Duhsasan brave Nakula drove his car,

Sahadeva mighty bowman, then the fierce Durmukha sought,
And the righteous king Yudhishthir with the car-borne Salya fought,

Ancient feud and deathless hatred fired the Brahman warrior bold,
Drona with the proud Panchalas fought once more his feud of old !

Nations from the Eastern regions 'gainst the bold Virata pressed,
Kripa met the wild Kaikeyas hailing from the furthest West,

Drupad proud and peerless monarch with his cohorts onward bore
'Gainst the warlike Jayadratha chief of Sindhu's sounding shore,

Chedis and the valiant Matsyas, nations gathered from afar,
Bhojas and the fierce Kambojas mingled in the dubious war !

Through the day the battle lasted, and no mortal tongue can tell
What unnumbered chieftains perished and what countless soldiers fell.

And the son knew not his father, and the sire knew not his son,
Brother fought against his brother, strange the deeds of valour done !

Horses fell, and shafts of chariots shivered in resistless shock,
Hurled against the foreman's chariots speeding like the rolling rock,

Elephants by *mahuts* driven furiously each other tore,
Trumpeting with trunks uplifted on the serried soldiers bore !

Ceaseless plied the gallant troopers, with a stern unyielding might,
Pikes and axes, clubs and maces, swords and spears and lances bright,

Horsemen flew as forkéd lightning, heroes fought in shining mail,
Archers poured their feathered arrows like the bright and glistening
hail !

Bhishma leader of the Kurus, as declined the dreadful day,
Through the shattered Pandav legions forced his all-resistless way,

Onward went his palm-tree standard through the hostile ranks of war,
Matsyas, Kasis, nor Panchalas faced the mighty Bhishma's car !

But the fiery son of Arjun, filled with shame and bitter wrath,
Turned his car and tawny coursers to obstruct the chieftain's path,

Vainly fought the youthful warrior though his darts were pointed
well,
And dissevered from his chariot Bhishma's palm-tree standard fell,

Anger stirred the ancient Bhishma and he rose in all his might,
Abhimanyu pierced with arrows fell and fainted in the fight !

Then to save the son of Arjun, Matsya's gallant princes came,
Brave Uttara, noble Sweta, youthful warriors known to fame,

Ah ! too early fell the warriors in that sad and fatal strife,
Matsya's dames and dark-eyed maidens wept the princes' shortened
life !

Slain by cruel fate untimely fell two brothers young and good,
Dauntless still the youngest brother, proud and gallant Sankha stood,

But the helmet-wearing Arjun came to stop the victor's path,
And to save the fearless Sankha from the ancient Bhishma's wrath,

Drupad too, Panchala's monarch, swiftly rushed into the fray,
Strove to shield the broken Pandavs and to stop the victor's way.

But as fire consumes the forest, wrathful Bhishma slew the foe,
None could face his sounding chariot and his ever-circled bow,

And the fainting Pandav warriors marked the foe, resistless, bold,
Shook like unprotected cattle tethered in the blighting cold !

Onward came the mighty Bhishma and the slaughter fiercer grew,
From his bow like hissing serpents still the glistening arrows flew,

Onward came the ancient warrior and his path was strewn with dead,
And the broken Pandav forces, crushed and driven, scattered fled,

Friendly night and gathering darkness closed the slaughter of the day,
To their tents the sons of Pandu held their sad and weary way !

II

KURUS ROUTED BY ARJUN

Grieved at heart the good Yudhishthir wept the losses of the day,
Sought the aid of gallant Krishna for the morning's fresh array,

And when from the eastern mountains SURYA drove his fiery car,
Krishna and the helméd Arjun strove to turn the tide of war.

Bhishma's glorious palm-tree standard o'er the field of battle rose,
Arjun's monkey-standard glittered cleaving through the serried foes,

Devas from their cloud-borne chariots, and *Gandharvas* from the sky,
Gazed in mute and speechless wonder on the human chiefs from high!

While with dauntless valour Arjun still the mighty Bhishma sought,
Warlike prince of fair Panchala with the doughty Drona fought,

Ceaseless 'gainst the proud preceptor sent his darts like summer rain,
Baffled by the skill of Drona, Dhrista-dyumna strove in vain !

But the fiercer darts of Drona pierced the prince's shattered mail,
Hurtling on his battle chariot like an angry shower of hail,

And they rent in twain his bowstring and they cut his pond'rous mace,
Slew his steeds and chariot-driver, streaked with blood his godlike
face.

Dauntless still Panchala's hero, springing from his shattered car,
Like a hungry desert lion with his sabre rushed to war,

Dashed aside the darts of Drona with his broad and ample shield,
With his sabre brightly flaming fearless trod the reddened field !

In his fury and his rashness he had fallen on that day,
But the ever-watchful Bhima stopped the proud preceptor's way,

Proud Duryodhan marked with anger Bhima rushing in his car,
And he sent Kalinga's forces to the thickening ranks of war.

Onward came Kalinga's forces with the dark tornado's might,
Dusky chiefs, Nishada warriors, gloomy as the sable night,

Rose the shout of warring nations surging to the battle's fore,
Like the angry voice of tempest and the ocean's troubled roar,

And like darkly rolling breakers ranks of serried warriors flew,
Scarcely in the thickening darkness friends and kin from foemen knew !

Fell the young prince of Kalinga by the wrathful Bhima slain,
But against Kalinga's monarch baffled Bhima fought in vain,

Safely sat the eastern monarch on his *howda's* lofty seat,
Till upon the giant tusker Bhima sprang with agile feet,

Then he struck with fatal fury, brave Kalinga fell in twain,
Scattered fled his countless forces when they saw their leader slain !

Darkly rolled the tide of battle where Duryodhan's valiant son
Strove against the son of Arjun famed for deeds of valour done,

Proud Duryodhan marked the contest with a father's anxious heart,
Came to save his gallant Lakshman from brave Abhimanyu's dart,

And the helmet-wearing Arjun marked his son among his foes,
Wheeled from far his battle-chariot and in wrath terrific rose !

" Arjun ! " " Arjun ! " cried the Kurus, and in panic broke and fled,
Steed and tusker turned from battle, soldiers fell among the dead,

Godlike Krishna drove the coursers of resistless Arjun's car,
And the sound of Arjun's *sankha* rose above the cry of war,

And the voice of his *Gandiva* spread a terror far and near,
Crushed and broken, faint and frightened, fled the Kurus in their fear,

Onward still through scattered foemen conquering Arjun held his way,
Till the evening's gathering darkness closed the action of the day !

III

BHISHMA AND ARJUN MEET

Anxious was the proud Duryodhan when the golden morning came,
For before the car of Arjun fled each Kuru chief of fame,

Brave Duryodhan shook in anger and a tremor moved his frame,
As he spake to ancient Bhishma words of wrath in bitter shame :

" Bhishma ! dost thou lead the Kurus in this battle's crimson field,
Warlike Drona, doth he guard us like a broad and ample shield ?

Wherefore then before yon Arjun do the valiant Kurus fly,
Wherefore doth our leader linger when he hears the battle cry ?

Doth a secret love for Pandavs quell our leader's matchless might,
With a halting zeal for Kurus doth the noble Bhishma fight ?

Pardon, chief, if for the Pandavs doth thy partial heart incline,
Yield thy place, let faithful Karna lead my gallant Kuru line ! "

Anger flamed on Bhishma's forehead and the tear was in his eye,
And in accents few and trembling thus the warrior made reply :

" Vain our toil, unwise Duryodhan ! Nor can Bhishma warrior old,
Nor can Drona skilled in weapons, Karna archer proud and bold,

Wash the stain of deeds unholy and of wrongs and outraged laws,
Conquer with a load of cunning 'gainst a right and righteous cause,

Deaf to wisdom's voice, Duryodhan, deaf to parents and to kin,
Thou shalt perish in thy folly, in thy unrepented sin !

For the wrongs and insults offered unto good Yudhishthir's wife,
For the kingdom from him stolen, for the plots against his life,

For the dreadful oath of Bhima, for the holy counsel given,
Vainly given by saintly Krishna, thou art doomed by righteous
    Heaven !

Meanwhile since he leads thy forces, Bhishma still shall meet his foe,
Or to conquer or to perish to the battle's front I go."

Speaking thus, unto the battle ancient Bhishma held his way,
Sweeping all before his chariot as he swept them day by day,

And the army of Yudhishthir shook from end to farthest end,
Arjun nor the valiant Krishna could against the tide contend !

Cars were shattered, fled the coursers, elephants were pierced and slain,
Shafts of chariots, broken standards, lifeless soldiers strewed the
plain,

Coats of mail were left by warriors as they ran with streaming hair,
Soldiers fled like herds of cattle stricken by a sudden fear !

Krishna, Arjun's chariot-driver, and a chief of righteous fame,
Marked the broken Pandav forces, spake in grief and bitter shame :

" Arjun ! not in hour of battle hath it been they wont to fly,
Forward lay thy path of glory, or to conquer or to die !

If to-day with angry Bhishma, Arjun shuns the dubious fight,
Shame on Krishna ! if he joins thee in this sad inglorious flight,

Be it mine alone, O Arjun ! warrior's wonted work to know,
Krishna with his fiery discus smites the all-resistless foe ! "

Then he flung the reins to Arjun, left the steeds and sounding car,
Leaped upon the field of battle, rushed into the dreadful war,

" Shame ! " cried Arjun in his anger, "Krishna shall not wage the fight,
Nor shall Arjun like a recreant seek for safety in his flight ! "

And he dashed behind the warrior and on foot the chief pursued,
Caught him as the angry Krishna still his distant foeman viewed,

Stalwart Arjun lifted Krishna, as the storm lifts up a tree,
Placed him on his battle-chariot and he bent to him his knee :

" Pardon, Krishna, this compulsion, pardon this transgression bold,
But while Arjun lives, O chieftain ! weapon of thy wrath withhold !

By my warlike Abhimanyu, fair Subhadra's darling boy,
By my brothers, dearer, truer, than in hours of pride and joy,

By my troth I pledge thee, Krishna,—let thy angry discus sleep,—
Archer Arjun meets his foeman, and his plighted word will keep."

Forthwith rushed the fiery Arjun in his sounding battle-car,
And like waves before him parted serried ranks of hostile war,

Vainly hurled his lance Duryodhan 'gainst the valiant warrior's face,
Vainly Salya, king of Madra, threw with skill his pond'rous mace,

With disdain the godlike Arjun dashed the feeble darts aside,
Held aloft his famed *Gandiva* as he stood with haughty pride,

Beat of drum and blare of *sankha* and the thunder of his car,
And his weapon's fearful accents rose terrific near and far !

Came resistless Pandav forces, sweeping onward wave on wave,
Chedis, Matsyas, and Panchalas, chieftains true and warriors brave,

Onward too came forth the Kurus by the matchless Bhishma led,
Shouts arose and cry of anguish midst the dying and the dead,

But the evening closed in darkness and the night-fires fitful flared,
Fainting troops and bleeding chieftains to their various tents repaired !

IV

Duryodhan's Eight Brothers Slain

Dawned another day of battle ; Kurus knew that day too well,
Widowed queens of fair Hastina wept before the evening fell,

For as whirlwind of destruction Bhima swept in mighty wrath,
Broke the serried line of tuskers vainly sent to cross his path,

Smote Duryodhan with his arrows, three terrific darts and five,
Smote proud Salya; from the battle scarce they bore the chiefs alive!

Then Duryodhan's fourteen brothers rushed into the dreadful fray,
Fatal was the luckless moment, inauspicious was the day,

Licked his mouth the vengeful Bhima, and he shook his bow and lance,
As the lion lolls his red tongue when he see his prey advance,

Short and fierce the furious combat ; six pale princes turned and fled,
Eight of proud Duryodhan's brothers fell and slumbered with the dead !

V

Satyaki's Sons Slain

Morning with her fiery radiance oped the portals of the day,
Shone once more on Kuru warriors, Pandav chiefs in dread array,

Bhima and the gallant Arjun led once more the van of war,
But the proud preceptor Drona faced them in his sounding car !

Still with gallant son of Arjun, Lakshman strove with bow and shield,
Vainly strove ; his faithful henchman bore him bleeding from the field,

Lakshman son of proud Duryodhan, Abhimanyu Arjun's son,
Doomed to die in youth and glory 'neath the same revolving sun !

Sad the day for Vrishni warriors ! Brave Satyaki's sons of might
'Gainst the cruel Bhuri-sravas strove in unrelenting fight,

Ten brave brothers, pride of Vrishni, fell upon that fatal day,
Slain by mighty Bhuri-sravas on the battle's red field lay !

VI

Bhima's Danger and Rescue

Dawned another day of slaughter ; heedless Bhima forced his way
Through Duryodhan's serried legions, where dark death and danger lay,

And a hundred foemen gathered and unequal was the strife,
Bhima strove with furious valour, for his forfeit was his life !

Fair Panchala's watchful monarch saw the danger from afar,
Forced his way where bleeding Bhima fought beside his shattered car,

And he helped the fainting warrior, placed him on his chariot-seat,
But the Kurus darkly gathered, surging round as waters meet !

Arjun's son and twelve brave chieftains dashed into the dubious fray,
Rescued Bhima and proud Drupad from the Kurus' grim array,

Surging still the Kuru forces onward came with ceaseless might,
Drona smote the scattered Pandavs till the darksome hours of night !

VII

Pandavs Routed by Bhishma

Morning came and angry Arjun rushed into the dreadful war,
Krishna drove his milk-white coursers, onward flew his sounding car,

And before his monkey banner quailed the faint and frightened foes,
Till like star on billowy ocean Bhishma's palm-tree banner rose !

Vainly then the good Yudhishthir, stalwart Bhima, Arjun brave,
Strove with useless toil and valour shattered ranks of war to save,

Vainly too the Pandav brothers on the peerless Bhishma fell,
Gods in sky nor earthly warriors Bhishma's matchless might could
    quell !

Fell Yudhishthir's lofty standard, shook his chariot battle-tost,
Fell his proud and fiery coursers, and the dreadful day was lost,

Sahadeva and Nakula vainly strove with all their might,
Till their broken scattered forces rested in the shades of night !

VIII

Iravat Slain

Morning saw the turn of battle ; Bhishma's charioteer was slain,
And his coursers uncontrolléd flew across the reddened plain,

Ill it fared with Kuru forces when their leader went astray,
And their foremost chiefs and warriors with the dead and dying lay.

But Gandhara's mounted princes rode across the battle-ground,—
For its steeds and matchless chargers is Gandhara's realm renowned,

And to smite the young Iravat fierce Gandhara's princes swore,—
Brave Iravat son of Arjun, whom a Naga princess bore !

Mounted on their milk-white chargers proudly did the princes sweep,
Like the sea-birds skimming gaily o'er the bosom of the deep,

Five of stout Gandhara's princes in that fatal combat fell,
And a sixth in fear and faintness fled the woeful tale to tell !

Short, alas, Iravat's triumph, transient was the victor's joy,
Alumbusha dark and dreadful came against the gallant boy,

Fierce and fateful was the combat, mournful is the tale to tell,
Like a lotus rudely severed gallant son of Arjun fell !

Arjun heard the tale of sorrow and his heart was filled with grief,
And he spake a father's anguish in his accents few and brief :

" Wherefore, Krishna, for a kingdom mingle in this fatal fray,
Kinsmen killed and comrades slaughtered,—dear, alas, the price
    we pay !

Woe unto Hastina's empire built upon our children's grave,
Dearer than the throne of monarchs was Iravat young and brave,

Young in years and rich in beauty, with thy mother's winsome eye,
Art thou slain, my gallant warrior, and thy father was not nigh ?

But thy young blood calls for vengeance ! noble Krishna, drive the car,
Let them feel the father's prowess, those who slew the son in war ! "

And he dashed the rising tear-drop and his words were few and brief,
Broken ranks and slaughtered chieftains spoke an angry father's grief,

Bhima too revenged Iravat, and as onward still he flew,
Brothers of the proud Duryodhan in that fatal combat slew,

Still advanced the fatal carnage till the darksome close of day,
When the wounded and the weary with the dead and lying lay !

IX

Pandavs Routed by Bhishma

Fell the thickening shades of darkness on the red and ghastly plain,
Torches by the white tents flickered, red fires showed the countless
slain,

With a bosom sorrow-laden proud Duryodhan drew his breath,
Wept the issue of the battle and his warlike brother's death.

Spent with grief and silent sorrow slow the Kuru monarch went
Where arose in dewy starlight Bhishma's proud and snowy tent,

And with tears and soft entreaty thus the sad Duryodhan spoke,
And his mournful bitter accents oft by heaving sighs were broke :

"Bhishma ! on thy matchless prowess Kuru's hopes and fates depend,
Gods nor men with warlike Bhishma can in field of war contend,

Brave in war are sons of Pandu, but they face not Bhishma's might,
In their fierce and deathless hatred slay my brothers in the fight !

Mind thy pledge, O chief of Kurus, save Hastina's royal race,
On the ancient king my father grant thy never-failing grace,

If within thy noble bosom,—pardon cruel words I say,—
Secret love for sons of Pandu holds a soft and partial sway,

If thy inner heart's affection unto Pandu's sons incline,
Grant that Karna lead my forces 'gainst the foeman's hostile line ! "

Bhishma's heart was full of sadness and his eyelids dropped a tear,
Soft and mournful were his accents and his vision true and clear :

" Vain, Duryodhan, is this contest, and thy mighty host is vain,
Why with blood of friendly nations drench this red and reeking plain?

They must win who, strong in virtue, fight for virtue's stainless laws,
Doubly armed the stalwart warrior who is armed in righteous cause,

Think, Duryodhan, when *Gandharvas* took thee captive and a slave,
Did not Arjun rend thy fetters, Arjun righteous chief and brave,

When in Matsya's fields of pasture captured we Virata's kine,
Did not Arjun in his valour beat thy countless force and mine ?

Krishna now hath come to Arjun, Krishna drives his battle-car,
Gods nor men can face these heroes in the field of righteous war,

Ruin frowns on thee, Duryodhan, and upon thy impious State,
In thy pride and in thy folly thou hast courted cruel fate,

Bhishma still will do his duty, and his end it is not far,
Then may other chieftains follow,—fatal is this Kuru war ! "

Dawned a day of mighty slaughter and of dread and deathful war,
Ancient Bhishma in his anger drove once more his sounding car,

Morn to noon and noon to evening none could face the victor's wrath,
Broke and shattered, faint and frightened, Pandavs fled before his
     path,

Still amidst the dead and dying moved his proud resistless car,
Till the gathering night and darkness closed the horrors of the war !

X

Fall of Bhishma

Good Yudhishthir gazed with sorrow on the dark and ghastly plain,
Shed his tears on chiefs and warriors by the matchless Bhishma slain:

" Vain this unavailing battle, vain this woeful loss of life,
'Gainst the death-compelling Bhishma hopeless in this arduous strife!

As a lordly tusker tramples on a marsh of feeble reeds,
As a forest conflagration on the parchéd woodland feeds,

Bhishma tramples on my forces in his mighty battle-car,
God nor mortal chief can face him in the gory field of war !

Vain our toil and vain the valour of our kinsmen loved and lost,
Vainly fight my faithful brothers by a luckless fortune crost,

Nations pour their lifeblood vainly, ceaseless wakes the sound of woe,
Krishna, stop this cruel carnage, unto woods once more we go ! "

Sad they held a midnight council and the chiefs in silence met,
And they went to ancient Bhishma, love and mercy to entreat,

Bhishma loved the sons of Pandu with a father's loving heart,
But from troth unto Duryodhan righteous Bhishma would not part !

" Sons of Pandu ! " said the chieftain, " Prince Duryodhan is my lord,
Bhishma is no faithless servant nor will break his plighted word,

Valiant are ye, noble princes, but the chief is yet unborn,
While I lead the course of battle, who the tide of war can turn !

Listen more.   With vanquished foeman, or who falls or takes to fight,
Casts his weapons, craves for mercy, ancient Bhishma doth not fight,

Bhishma doth not fight a rival who submits, fatigued and worn,
Bhishma doth not fight the wounded, doth not fight a woman born!"

Back unto their tents the Pandavs turn with Krishna deep and wise,
He unto the anxious Arjun thus in solemn whisper cries :

" Arjun, there is hope of triumph ! Hath not truthful Bhishma sworn
He will fight no wounded warrior, he will fight no woman born ?

Female child was brave Sikhandin, Drupad's youngest son of pride,
Gods have turned him to a warrior, placed him by Yudhishthir's side,

Place him in the van of battle, mighty Bhishma leaves the strife,
Then with ease we fight and conquer, and the forfeit is his life ! "

" Shame ! " exclaimed the angry Arjun, " not in secret heroes fight,
Not behind a child or woman screen their valour and their might,

Krishna, loth is archer Arjun to pursue this hateful strife,
Trick against the sinless Bhishma, fraud upon his spotless life !

Listen, good and noble Krishna ; as a child I climbed his knee,
As a boy I called him father, hung upon him lovingly,

Perish conquest dearly purchased by a mean deceitful strife,
Perish crown and jewelled sceptre won with Bhishma's saintly life ! "

Gravely answered noble Krishna : " Bhishma falls by close of day,
Victim to the cause of virtue, he himself hath showed the way,

Dear or hated be the foeman, Arjun, thou shalt fight and slay,
Wherefore else the blood of nations hast thou poured from day to
    day ? "

Morning dawned, and mighty Arjun, Abhimanyu young and bold,
Drupad monarch of Panchala, and Virata stern and old,

Brave Yudhishthir and his brothers clad in arms and shining mail,
Rushed to war where Bhishma's standard gleamed and glittered in
    the gale !

Proud Duryodhan marked their onset and its fatal purpose knew,
And his bravest men and chieftains 'gainst the fiery Pandavs threw,

With Kamboja's stalwart monarch and with Drona's mighty son,
With the valiant bowman Kripa stemmed the battle still unwon !

And his younger, fierce Duhsasan, thirsting for the deathful war,
'Gainst the helmet-wearing Arjun drew his mighty battle-car,

As the high and rugged mountain meets the angry ocean's sway,
Proud Duhsasan warred with Arjun in his wild and onward way,

And as myriad white-winged sea-birds swoop upon the darksome
    wave,
Clouds of darts and glistening lances drank the red blood of the
    brave !

Other warlike Kuru chieftains came, the bravest and the best,
Drona's self and Bhagadatta monarch of the farthest East,

Car-borne Salya mighty warrior, king of Madra's distant land,
Princes from Avanti's regions, chiefs from Malwa's rocky strand,

Jayadratha matchless fighter, king of Sindhu's sounding shore,
Chitrasena and Vikarna, countless chiefs and warriors more !

And they faced the fiery Pandavs peerless in their warlike might,
Long and dreadful raged the combat, darkly closed the dubious fight,

Dust arose like clouds of summer, glistening darts like lightning
played,
Darksome grew the sky with arrows, thicker grew the gloomy shade,

Cars went down and mailéd horsemen, soldiers fell in dread array,
Elephants with white tusks broken and with mangled bodies lay !

Arjun and the stalwart Bhima piercing through their countless foes,
Side by side impelled their chariots where the palm-tree standard
rose,

Where the peerless ancient Bhishma on that dark and fatal day,
Warring with the banded nations still resistless held his way !

On he came, his palm-tree standard still the front of battle knew,
And like sun from dark clouds parting Bhishma burst on Arjun's
view,

And his eyes brave Arjun shaded at the awe-inspiring sight,
Half he wished to turn for shelter from that chief of godlike might !

But bold Krishna drove his chariot, whispered low his fatal plan,
Arjun placed the young Sikhandin in the deathful battle's van,

Bhishma viewed the Pandav forces with a calm unmoving face,
Saw not Arjun's fair *Gandiva*, saw not Bhima's mighty mace,

Smiled to see the young Sikhandin rushing to the battle's fore,
Like the foam upon the billow when the mighty storm-winds roar !

Bhishma thought of word he plighted and of oath that he had sworn,
Dropped his arms before the warrior who a female child was born,

And the standard which no warrior ever saw in base retreat,
Idly stood upon the chariot, threw its shade on Bhishma's seat,

And the flagstaff fell dissevered on the crushed and broken car,
As from azure sky of midnight falls the meteor's flaming star !

Not Sikhandin's feeble arrows did the palm-tree standard fell,
Not Sikhandin's feeble lances did the peerless Bhishma quell,

True to oath and unresisting, Bhishma turned his face away,
Turned and fell ; the sun declining marked the closing of the day !

Ended thus the fatal battle, truce came with the close of day,
Kurus and the silent Pandavs went where Bhishma dying lay,

Arjun wept as for a father weeps a sad and sorrowing son,
Good Yudhishthir cursed the morning Kuru-kshetra's war begun,

Stood Duryodhan and his brothers mantled in the gloom of grief,
Foes like loving brothers sorrowed round the great the dying chief !

Arjun's keen and pointed arrows made the hero's dying bed,
And in soft and gentle accents to Duryodhan thus he said :

" List unto my words, Duryodhan, uttered with my latest breath,
List to Bhishma's dying counsel and revere the voice of death,

End this dread and deathful battle if thy stony heart can grieve,
Save the chieftains doomed to slaughter, bid the fated nations live,

Grant his kingdom to Yudhishthir righteous man beloved ot Heaven,
Keep thy own Hastina's regions, be the hapless past forgiven ! "

Vain, alas, the voice of Bhishma like the voice of angel spoke,
Hatred dearer than his lifeblood in the proud Duryodhan woke !

Darker grew the gloomy midnight and the princes went their way,
On his bed of pointed arrows Bhishma lone and dying lay,

Karna, though he loved not Bhishma whilst the chieftain lived in
        fame,
Gently to the dying Bhishma in the midnight darkness came !

Bhishma heard the tread of Karna and he oped his glazing eye,
Spake in love and spake in sadness and his bosom heaved a sigh :

" Pride and envy, noble Karna, filled our warlike hearts with strife,
Discord ends with breath departing, envy sinks with fleeting life !

More I have to tell thee, Karna, but my parting breath may fail,
Feeble are my dying accents and my parchéd lips are pale,

Arjun beats not noble Karna in the deeds of valour done,
Nor excels in birth and lineage, Karna, thou art Pritha's son !

Pritha bore thee, still unwedded, and the Sun inspired thy birth,
God-born man ! No mightier archer treads this broad and spacious
        earth,

Pritha cast thee in her sorrow, hid thee with a maiden's shame,
And a driver, not thy father, nursed thee, chief of warlike fame,

Arjun is thy brother, Karna, end this sad fraternal war,
Seek not lifeblood of thy brother nor against him drive thy car ! "

Vain, alas, the voice of Bhishma like the voice of angel spoke,
Hatred dearer than his lifeblood in the vengeful Karna woke !

BOOK IX
DRONA-BADHA
(*Fall of Drona*)

ON the fall of Bhishma the Brahman chief Drona, preceptor of
the Kuru and Pandav princes, was appointed the leader of
the Kuru forces. For five days Drona held his own against the
Pandavs, and some of the incidents of these days, like the fall
of Abhimanyu and the vengeance of Arjun, are among the most
stirring passages in the Epic. The description of the different standards of the Pandav and the Kuru warriors is also interesting. At
last Drona slew his ancient foe the king of the Panchalas, and
was then slain by his son the prince of the Panchalas.

The Book is an abridgment of Book vii. of the original text.

I

SINGLE COMBAT BETWEEN BHIMA AND SALYA

Morning ushered in the battle ; Pandav warriors heard with dread
Drona priest and proud preceptor now the Kuru forces led,

And the foe-compelling Drona pledged his troth and solemn word,
He would take Yudhishthir captive to Hastina's haughty lord !

But the ever faithful Arjun to his virtuous elder bowed,
And in clear and manful accents spake his warlike thoughts aloud :

" Sacred is our great preceptor, sacred is *acharya's* life,
Arjun may not slay his teacher even in this mortal strife !

Saving this, command, O monarch, Arjun's bow and warlike sword,
For thy safety, honoured elder, Arjun stakes his plighted word,

Matchless in the art of battle is our teacher fierce and dread,
But he comes not to Yudhishthir save o'er blood of Arjun shed ! "

Morning witnessed doughty Drona foremost in the battle's tide,
But Yudhishthir's warlike chieftains compassed him on every side,

Foremost of the youthful chieftains came resistless Arjun's son,—
Father's blood and milk of mothers fired his deeds of valour done !

As the lion of the jungle drags the ox into his lair,
Abhimanyu from his chariot dragged Paurava by the hair,

Jayadratha king of Sindhu marked the faint and captive chief,
Leaping from his car of battle wrathful came to his relief,

Abhimanyu left his captive, turned upon the mightier foe,
And with sword and hardened buckler gave and parried many a blow !

Rank to rank from both the forces cry of admiration rose,
Streaming men poured forth in wonder, watched the combat fierce
    and close,

Piercing Abhimanyu's buckler Jayadratha sent his stroke,
But the turned and twisted sword-blade snapping in the midway
    broke !

Weaponless the king of Sindhu ran into his sheltering car,
Salya came unto his rescue from a battle-field afar,

Dauntless, on the new assailant Arjun's son his weapon drew,
Interposing 'twixt the fighters Bhima's self on Salya flew !

Stoutest wrestlers in the armies, fiercest fighters with the mace,
Bhima and the stalwart Salya stood as rivals face to face,

Hempen fastening bound their maces and the wire of twisted gold,
Whirling bright in circling flashes, shook their staff the warriors
    bold !

Oft they struck, and sparks of red fire issued from the seasoned wood,
And like hornéd bulls infuriate Madra's king and Bhima stood,

Closer still they came like tigers closing with their reddened paws,
Or like tuskers with their red tusks, eagles with their rending claws !

Loud as INDRA's peals of thunder still their blows were echoed round
Rank to rank the startled soldiers heard the oft-repeated sound,

But as strikes in vain the lightning on the solid mountain-rock,
Bhima nor the fearless Salya fell or moved beneath the shock !

Closer drew the watchful heroes and their clubs were wielded well,
Till by many blows belaboured both the fainting fighters fell,

Like a drunkard dazed and reeling Bhima rose his staff to wield,
Senseless Salya, heavy-breathing, henchman carried from the field,

Writhing like a wounded serpent, lifted from the field of war,
He was carried by his soldiers to the shelter of his car !

Drona still with matchless prowess strove to keep his plighted word,
Sought to take Yudhishthir captive to Duryodhan, Kuru's lord,

Vainly then the twin-born brothers came to cross the conqueror's
    path,
Matsya's lord, Panchala's monarch, vainly faced him in his wrath,

Rank to rank the cry resounded circling o'er the battle-field,
" Drona takes Yudhishthir captive with his bow and sword and
    shield ! "

Arjun heard the dreadful message and in haste and fury came,
Strove to save his king and elder and redeem his loyal fame,

Speeding with his milk-white coursers dashed into the thick of war,
Blew his shrill and dreaded *sankha*, drove his sounding battle-car,

Fiercer, darker grew the battle, when above the reddened plain,
Evening drew her peaceful mantle o'er the living and the slain !

II

STANDARDS OF THE PANDAVS

Morning came ; still round Yudhishthir Drona led the gathering war,
Arjun fought the Sam-saptakas in the battle-field afar,

But the prince of fair Panchala marked his father's ancient foe,
And against the doughty Drona, Dhrishta-dyumna bent his bow !

But as darksome cloudy masses angry gusts of storm divide,
Through the scattered fainting foemen Drona drove his car in pride,

Steeds went down and riven chariots, young Panchala turned and
    fled,
Onward drove resistless Drona o'er the dying and the dead !

One more prince of fair Panchala 'gainst the mighty Drona came,
Ancient feud ran in the red blood of Panchala's chiefs of fame,

Fated youth ! with reckless valour still he fought his father's foe,
Fought and fell ; relentless Drona laid the brave Satyajit low !

Surging still like ocean's billows other Pandav warriors came,
To protect their virtuous monarch and redeem their ancient fame,

Came in various battle-chariots drawn by steeds of every hue,
Various were the chieftains' standards which the warring nations
    knew !

Bhima drove his stalwart horses tinted like the dappled deer,
Grey and pigeon-coloured coursers bore Panchala's prince and peer,

Horses bred in famed Kamboja, dark and grey of deepest hue,
Brave Nakula's sumptuous chariot in the deathful battle drew,

Piebald horses trained to battle did young Sahadeva rein,
Ivory-white Yudhishthir's coursers with their flowing ebon mane,

And by him with gold umbrella valiant monarch Drupad came,
Horses of a bright bay-colour carried Matsya's king of fame.

Varied as their varied courses gallantly their standards rose,
With their wondrous strange devices, terror of their arméd foes,

Water-jar on tawny deerskin, such was Drona's sign of war,—
Drona as a tender infant rested in a water-jar,

Golden moon with stars surrounding was Yudhishthir's sign of yore,
Silver lion was the standard tiger-waisted Bhima bore,

Brave Nakula's sign was red deer with its back of burnished gold,
Silver swan with bells resounding Sahadeva's onset told,

Golden peacock rich-emblazoned was young Abhimanyu's joy,
Vulture shone on Ghatotkacha, Bhima's proud and gallant boy.

Now Duryodhan marked the foemen heaving like the rising tide,
And he faced the wrathful Bhima towering in his tameless pride.

Short the war ; for proud Duryodhan wounded from the battle fled,
And his warriors from fair Anga rested with the countless dead !

Wild with anger Bhagadatta, monarch of the farthest East,
With his still unconquered forces on the valiant Bhima pressed,

Came from far the wrathful Arjun and the battle's front he sought,
Where by eastern foes surrounded still the stalwart Bhima fought !

Fated monarch from the mighty Brahma-putra's sounding shore,
Land of rising sun will hail him and his noble peers no more,

For his tusker pierced by arrows trumpeted his dying wail,
Like a red and flaming meteor gallant Bhagadatta fell !

Then with rising wrath and anguish Karna's noble bosom bled,—
Karna who had stayed from battle while his rival Bhishma led,

Ancient hate and jealous anger clouded Karna's warlike heart,
And while Bhishma led, all idly slumbered Karna's bow and dart,

Now he marked with warrior's anguish all his comrades fled afar,
And his foeman Arjun sweeping o'er the red field of the war !

Hatred like a tongue of red fire shot from Karna's flaming eye,
And he sprang to meet his foeman or to conquer or to die,

Fierce and dubious was the battle, answering clouds gave back the
din,
Karna met his dearest foeman and, alas, his nearest kin !

Bhima and Panchala's warriors unto Arjun's rescue came,
Proud Duryodhan came to Karna, and fair Sindhu's king of fame,

Fiercely raged the gory combat, when the night its shadows threw,
Wounded men and blood-stained chieftains to their nightly tents
withdrew !

III

ABHIMANYU'S DEATH

Fatal was the blood-red morning purpling o'er the angry east,
Fatal day for Abhimanyu, bravest warrior and the best,

Countless were the gallant chieftains like the sands beside the sea,
None with braver bosom battled, none with hands more stout and
free !

Brief, alas, thy radiant summers, fair Subhadra's gallant boy,
Loved of Matsya's soft-eyed princess and her young heart's pride
and joy,

Brief, alas, thy sunlit winters, light of war too early quenched,
Peerless son of peerless Arjun, in the blood of foemen drenched !

Drona on that fatal morning ranged his dreadful battle-line
In a circle darkly spreading where the chiefs with chiefs combine,

And the Pandavs looked despairing on the battle's dread array,
Vainly strove to force a passage, vainly sought their onward way !

Abhimanyu, young and fiery, dashed alone into the war,
Reckless through the shattered forces all resistless drove his car,

Elephants and crashing standards, neighing steeds and warriors slain
Fell before the furious hero as he made a ghastly lane !

Proud Duryodhan rushed to battle, strove to stop the turning tide,
And his stoutest truest warriors fought by proud Duryodhan's side,

Onward still went Abhimanyu, Kurus strove and fought in vain,
Backward reeled and fell Duryodhan and his bravest chiefs were
slain !

Next came Salya car-borne monarch 'gainst the young resistless foe,
Urged his fiery battle-coursers, stretched his death-compelling bow,

Onward still went Abhimanyu, Salya strove and fought in vain,
And his warriors took him bleeding from the reddened battle-plain !

Next Duhsasan darkly lowering thundered with his bended bow,
Abhimanyu smiled to see him, kinsman and the dearest foe,

" Art thou he," said Abhimanyu, " known for cruel word and deed,
Impious in thy heart and purpose, base and ruthless in thy greed ?

Didst thou with the false Sakuni win a realm by low device,
Win his kingdom from Yudhishthir by ignoble trick of dice,

Didst thou in the council chamber with your insults foul and keen
By her flowing raven tresses drag Yudhishthir's stainless queen,

Didst thou speak to warlike Bhima as thy serf and bounden slave,
Wrong my father righteous Arjun, peerless prince and warrior brave?

Welcome ! I have sought thee often, wished to cross thy tainted path,
Welcome ! Dearest of all victims to my nursed and cherished wrath,

Reap the meed of sin and insult, draw on earth thy latest breath,
For I owe to Queen Draupadi, impious prince, thy speedy death ! "

Like a snake upon an ant-hill, on Duhsasan's wicked heart
Fell with hissing wrath and fury Abhimanyu's fiery dart,

From the loss of blood Duhsasan fainted on his battle-car,
Kuru chieftains bore him senseless from the blood-stained scene of
    war !

Next in gleaming arms accoutred came Duryodhan's gallant son,
Proud and warlike as his father, famed for deeds of valour done,

Young in years and rich in valour, for alas ! he fought too well,
And before his weeping father proud and gallant Lakshman fell !

Onward still went Abhimanyu midst the dying and the dead,
Shook from rank to rank the Kurus and their shattered army fled,

Then the impious Jayadratha, king of Sindhu's sounding shore,
Came forth in unrighteous concert with six car-borne warriors more,

Darkly closed the fatal circle with the gulfing surge's moan,
Dauntless with the seven brave chieftains Abhimanyu fought alone !

Fell, alas, his peacock standard and his car was broke in twain,
Bow and sabre rent and shattered and his faithful driver slain,

Heedless yet of death and danger, misty with the loss of blood,
Abhimanyu wiped his forehead, gazed where dark his foemen stood !

Then with wild despairing valour, flickering flame and closing life,
Mace in hand the heedless warrior rushed to end the mortal strife,

Rushed upon his startled foemen, Abhimanyu fought and fell,
And his deeds to distant ages bards and wand'ring minstrels tell !

Like a tusker of the forest by surrounding hunters slain,
Like a wood-consuming wildfire quenched upon the distant plain,

Like a mountain-shaking tempest spent in force and hushed and still,
Like the red resplendent day-god setting on the western hill,

Like the moon serene and beauteous quenched in eclipse dark and
    pale,
Lifeless slumbered Abhimanyu when the softened starlight fell !

Done the day of death and slaughter, darkening shadows close around,
Wearied warriors seek for shelter on the vast and tented ground,

Soldiers' camp-fires brightly blazing, tent-lights shining from afar,
Cast their fitful gleam and radiance on the carnage of the war !

Arjun from a field at distance, where upon that day he fought,
With the ever faithful Krishna now his nightly shelter sought,

" Wherefore, Krishna," uttered Arjun, " evil omens strike my eye,
Thoughts of sadness fill my bosom, wake the long-forgotten sigh,

Wherefore voice of evening bugle speaks not on the battle-field,
Merry conch nor sounding trumpet music to the warriors yield ?

Harp is hushed within the dark tents and the voice of warlike song,
Bards beside the evening camp-fire tales of war do not prolong,

Good Yudhishthir's tent is voiceless and my brothers look so pale,
Abhimanyu comes not joyous Krishna and his sire to hail,

Abhimanyu's love and greeting bless like blessings from above,
Fair Subhadra's joy and treasure, Arjun's pride and hope and love ! "

Softly and with many tear-drops did the sad Yudhishthir tell,
How in dreadful field of battle gallant Abhimanyu fell,

How the impious Jayadratha fell on Arjun's youthful son,—
He with six proud Kuru chieftains,—Abhimanyu all alone,

How the young prince reft of weapon and deprived of steel and car,
Fell as falls a Kshatra warrior fighting on the field of war !

Arjun heard ; the father's bosom felt the cruel cureless wound,
" Brave and gallant boy ! " he uttered as he sank upon the
    ground,

Moments passed of voiceless sorrow and of speechless bitter tear,
Sobs within his mailéd bosom smote the weeping listener's ear !

Moments passed ; with rising anger quivered Arjun's iron frame,
Abhimanyu's cruel murder smote the father's heart to flame,

" Didst thou say that Sindhu's monarch on my Abhimanyu bore,—
He alone,—and Jayadratha leagued with six marauders more,

Didst thou say the impious Kurus stooped unto this deed of shame,
Outrage on the laws of honour, stain upon a warrior's fame ?

Father's curse and warrior's hatred sting them to their dying breath,
For they feared my boy in battle, hunted him to cruel death,

Hear my vow, benign Yudhishthir, hear me, Krishna righteous lord,
Arjun's hand shall slay the slayer, Arjun plights his solemn word !

May I never reach the bright sky where the righteous fathers dwell,
May I with the darkest sinners live within the deepest hell,—

With the men who slay their fathers, shed their loving mothers'
   blood,
Stain the sacred bed of *gurus*, steal their gold and holy food,

Cherish envy, cheat their kinsmen, speak the low and dastard lie,—
If, ere comes to-morrow's sunset, Jayadratha doth not die,

Jayadratha dies to-morrow, victim to my vengeful ire,
Arjun else shall yield his weapons, perish on the flaming pyre ! "

Softer tear-drops wept the mother, joyless was Subhadra's life,—
Krishna's fair and honoured sister, Arjun's dear and lovéd wife :

" Dost thou lie on field of battle smeared with dust and foeman's gore,
Child of light and love and sweetness whom thy hapless mother bore,

Soft thine eye as budding lotus, sweet and gentle was thy face,
Are those soft eyes closed in slumber, faded in that peerless grace,

And thy limbs so young and tender, on the bare earth do they lie,
Where the hungry jackal prowleth and the vulture flutters nigh,

Gold and jewels graced thy bosom, gems bedecked thy lofty crest,
Doth the crimson mark of sabre decorate that manly breast ?

Rend Subhadra's stony bosom with a mother's cureless grief,
Let her follow Abhimanyu and in death obtain relief,

Earth to me is void and cheerless, joyless in my hearth and home,
Dreary without Abhimanyu is this weary world to roam !

And oh ! cheerless is that young heart, Abhimanyu's princess-wife,
What can sad Subhadra offer to her joyless sunless life,

Close our life in equal darkness, for our day on earth is done,
For our love and light and treasure, Abhimanyu, he is gone ! "

Long bewailed the anguished mother, fair Draupadi tore her hair,
Matsya's princess early widowed shed her young heart's blood in tear!

IV

Standards of the Kurus : Arjun's Revenge

Morning from the face of battle night's depending curtain drew,
Long and shrill his sounding *sankha* then the wrathful Arjun blew,

Kurus knew the vow of Arjun, heard the *sankha's* deathful blare,
As it rose above the red field, thrilled the startled morning air,

" Speed, my Krishna," out spake Arjun, as he held aloft his bow,
" For to-day my task is dreadful, cruel is my mighty vow ! "

Fiery coursers urged by Krishna flew with lightning's rapid course,
Dashing through the hostile warriors and the serried Kuru force,

Brave Durmarsan faced the hero but he strove and fought in vain,
Onward thundered Arjun's chariot o'er the dying and the slain,

Fierce Duhsasan with his tuskers rushed into the line of war,
But the tuskers broke in panic, onward still went Arjun's car !

Drona then, the proud preceptor, Arjun's furious progress stayed,
Tear-drops filled the eye of Arjun as these gentle words he said :

" Pardon, father, if thy pupil shuns to-day thy offered war,
'Gainst his Abhimanyu's slayer Arjun speeds his battle-car,

Not against my great *acharya* is my wrathful bow-string drawn,
Not against a lovéd father fights a loving duteous son !

Heavy on this bleeding bosom sits the darkening load of woe,
And an injured father's vengeance seeks the slaughtered hero's foe,

Pardon then if sorrowing Arjun seeks a far and distant way,
Mighty is the vow of Arjun, cruel is his task to-day ! "

Passing by the doughty Drona onward sped the fiery car,
Through the broken line of warriors, through the shattered ranks
    of war,

Angas and the brave Kalingas vainly crossed his wrathful way,
Proud Avantis from the regions where fair Chambal's waters stray,

Famed Avanti's fated princes vainly led their highland force,
Fell beneath the wrath of Arjun, stayed nor stopped his onward
    course,

Onward still with speed of lightning thundered Arjun's battle-car,
To the spot where Jayadratha stood behind the ranks of war !

Now the sun from highest zenith red and fiery radiance lent,
Long and weary was the passage, Arjun's foaming steeds were spent,

" Arjun ! " said the faithful Krishna, " arduous is thy cruel quest,
But thy foaming coursers falter and they need a moment's rest,"

" Be it so," brave Arjun answered, " from our chariot we alight,
Rest awhile the weary horses, Krishna, I will watch the fight ! "

Speaking thus the arméd Arjun lightly leaped upon the lea,
Stood on guard with bow and arrow by the green and shady tree,

Krishna groomed the jaded horses, faint and feeble, red with gore,
With a healing hand he tended wounds the bleeding coursers bore,

Watered them beside a river by the zephyrs soft caressed,
Gave unto them welcome fodder, gave unto them needful rest,

Thus refreshed, the noble coursers Krishna harnessed to the car,
And the gleaming fiery Arjun rushed once more to fatal war !

Came on him the Kuru warriors, darksome wave succeeding wave,
Standards decked with strange devices, streaming banners rich and
    brave.

Foremost was the glorious standard of preceptor Drona's son,
Lion's tail in golden brilliance on his battle-chariot shone,

Elephant's rope was Karna's ensign made of rich and burnished gold,
And a bull bedecked the standard of the bowman Kripa bold,

Peacock made of precious metal, decked with jewels rich and rare,
Vrishasena's noble standard shone aloft serene and fair,

Ploughshare of a golden lustre shining like the radiant flame,
Spoke the car of mighty Salya, Madra's king of warlike fame,

Far and guarded well by chieftains shone the dazzling silver-boar,
Ensign proud of Jayadratha brought from Sindhu's sounding shore,

On the car of Somadatta shone a stake of sacrifice,
Silver-boar and golden parrots, these were Salwa's proud device,

Last and brightest of the standards, on the prince Duryodhan's car,
Lordly elephant in jewels proudly shone above the war !

Nine heroic Kuru chieftains, bravest warriors and the best,
Leagued they came to grapple Arjun and on faithful Krishna pressed,

Arjun swept like sweeping whirlwind all resistless in his force,
Sought no foe and waged no combat, held his ever onward course,

For he sighted Jayadratha midst the circling chiefs of war,
'Gainst that warrior, grim and silent, Arjun drove his furious car !

Now the day-god rolled his chariot on the western clouds aflame,
Karna's self and five great chieftains round brave Jayadratha came,

Vainly strove the valiant Arjun struggling 'gainst the Kuru line,
Charged upon the peerless Karna as he marked the day's decline,

Krishna then a prayer whispered ; came a friendly sable cloud,
Veiled the red sun's dazzling brilliance in a dark and inky shroud !

Karna deemed the closing darkness now proclaimed the close of strife,
Failing in his plighted promise Arjun must surrender life,

And his comrade chiefs rejoicing slackened in their furious fight,
Jayadratha hailed with gladness thickening shades of welcome night!

In that sad and fatal error did the Kuru chiefs combine,
Arjun quick as bolt of lightning broke their all unguarded line,

Like an onward sweeping wildfire shooting forth its lolling tongue,
On the startled Jayadratha, Arjun in his fury flung !

Short the strife ; as angry falcon swoops upon its helpless prey,
Arjun sped his vengeful arrow and his foeman lifeless lay,

Friendly winds removed the dark cloud from the reddening western
        hill,
And the sun in crimson lustre cast its fiery radiance still !

Ere the evening's mantling darkness fell o'er distant hill and plain,
Proud Duryodhan's many brothers were by vengeful Bhima slain,

And Duryodhan stung by sorrow waged the still unceasing fight,
In the thick and gathering darkness torches lit the gloom of night !

Karna furious in his anger for his Jayadratha slain,
And for brothers of Duryodhan sleeping lifeless on the plain,

'Gainst the gallant son of Bhima drove his deep resounding car,
And in gloom and midnight darkness waked the echoes of the war !

Bhima's son brave Ghatotkacha twice the steeds of Karna slew,
Twice the humbled steedless Karna from the dubious battle flew,

Came again the fiery Karna, vengeance flamed within his heart,
Like the midnight's lurid lightning sped his fell and fatal dart,

Woeful was the hour of darkness, luckless was the starry sway,
Bhima's son in youth and valour lifeless on the red field lay !

Then was closed the midnight battle, silent shone the starry light,
Bhima knew nor rest nor slumber through the long and woeful night !

V

Fall of Drona

Ere the crimson morning glittered proud Duryodhan sad at heart,
To the leader of the Kurus did his sorrows thus impart :

" Sadly speeds the contest, Drona, on the battle's gory plain,
Kuru chiefs are thinned and fallen and my brothers mostly slain,

Can it be, O best of Brahmans, peerless in the art of war,
Can it be that we shall falter while thou speed'st the battle-car ?

Pandu's sons are but thy pupils, Arjun meets thee not in fight,
None can face the great *acharya* in his wrath and warlike might,

Wherefore then in every battle are the Kuru chieftains slain,
Wherefore lie my warlike brothers lifeless on the ghastly plain ?

Is it that the fates of battle 'gainst the Kuru house combine,
Is it that thy heart's affection unto Pandu's sons incline ?

If thy secret love and mercy still the sons of Pandu claim,
Yield thy place to gallant Karna, Anga's prince of warlike fame ! "

Answered Drona brief and wrathful : " Fair Gandhari's royal son,
Reapest thou the gory harvest of thy sinful actions done,

Cast no blame in youth's presumption on a warrior's fleecy hair,
Faithful unto death is Drona to his promise plighted fair !

Ask thyself, O prince Duryodhan, bound by battle's sacred laws,
Wherefore fightest not with Arjun for thy house and for thy cause,

Ask the dark and deep Sakuni, where is now his low device,
Wherefore wields he not his weapon as he wields the loaded dice,

Ask the chief who proudly boasted, archer Arjun he would slay,
Helméd Arjun sways the battle, whither now doth Karna stay ?

Know the truth ; the gallant Arjun hath no peer on earth below,
And no warrior breathes, Duryodhan, who can face thy helméd foe,

Drona knows his sacred duty, and 'tis willed by Heaven on high,
Arjun or preceptor Drona shall in this day's battle die ! "

Now the Sun in crimson splendour rolled his car of glistening gold,
Sent his shafts of purple radiance on the plain and mountain bold,

And from elephant and charger, from each bravely bannered car,
Lighted mailéd kings and chieftains and the leaders of the war,

Faced the sun with hands conjoinéd and the sacred *mantra* told,—
Hymns by ancient *rishis* chanted, sanctified by bards of old !

Worship done, each silent warrior mounted on his car or steed,
Onward to the deathful contest did his gallant forces lead,

Ill it fared with Pandav forces, doughty Drona took the field,
Peer was none midst living warriors of the Brahman trained and
  skilled,

Arjun, faithful to his promise, his preceptor would not fight,
King nor chief nor other archer dared to face his peerless might.

But old feud like potent poison fires the warrior's heart with strife,
Sire to son still unforgotten leaps the hate from death to life,

Wrathful princes of Panchala by their deathless hatred stung,
Saw their ancient foe in Drona and on him for vengeance sprung !

Darkly thought the ancient warrior of the old relentless feud,
Fiercely like a jungle-tiger fell upon the hostile brood,

Royal Drupad's valiant grandsons in their youth untimely slain,
Victims of a deathless discord, pressed the gory battle-plain !

Drupad pale with grief and anger marked his gallant grandsons dead,
And his army crushed and routed and his bravest chieftains fled,

Filled with unforgotten hatred and with father's grief and pride,
Rushed the king, and bold Virata charged by doughty Drupad's
  side !

Rose a cry of nameless terror o'er the red and ghastly plain,
Noble Drupad, brave Virata, lay among the countless slain,

Burning tears the proud Draupadi wept for noble father killed,
Maid and matron with their wailing fair Panchala's empire filled,

Matsya's joyless widowed princess, for her fate was early crost,
Wept with added tears and anguish for her father loved and lost !

Waged the war with fearful slaughter, Drona onward urged his way,
Fate alone and battle's chances changed the fortunes of the day,

Aswa-thaman son of Drona was a chief of peerless fame,
And an elephant of battle bore that chieftain's warlike name,

And that proud and lordly tusker Bhima in his prowess slew,
Rank to rank from friend to foeman then a garbled message flew :

" Aswa-thaman son of Drona is by mighty Bhima slain,"
Drona heard that fatal message, bent his anguished head in pain !

" Speak Yudhishthir, soul of virtue ! " thus the proud preceptor
 cried,
" Thou in truth hast never faltered and thy lips have never lied,

Speak of valiant Aswa-thaman, Drona's hope and pride and joy,
Hath he fallen in this battle, is he slain, my gallant boy,

Feeble are the hands of Drona and his prowess quenched and gone,
Fleecy are his ancient tresses and his earthly task is done ! "

Said Yudhishthir thus in answer : " Tusker Aswa-thaman's dead,"
Drona heard but half the accents, feebly drooped his sinking head,

Then the prince of fair Panchala swiftly drove across the plain,
Marked his father's cruel slayer, marked his noble father slain !

Dhrista-dyumna bent his weapon and his shaft was pointed well,
And the priest and proud preceptor, peerless Drona lifeless fell,

And the fatal day was ended, Kurus fled in abject fear,
Arjun for his ancient teacher dropped a silent filial tear !

BOOK X

KARNA-BADHA

(*Fall of Karna*)

KARNA was chosen as the leader of the Kuru forces after the death of Drona, and held his own for two days. The great contest between Karna and Arjun, long expected and long deferred, came on at last. It is the crowning incident of the Indian Epic, as the contest between Hector and Achilles is the crowning incident of the Iliad. With a truer artistic skill than that of Homer, the Indian poet represents Karna as equal to Arjun in strength and skill, and his defeat is only due to an accident.

After the death of Karna, Salya led the Kuru troops on the eighteenth and last day of the war, and fell. A midnight slaughter in the Pandav camp, perpetrated by the vengeful son of Drona, concludes the war. Duryodhan, left wounded by Bhima, heard of the slaughter and died happy.

Books viii., ix., and x. of the original have been abridged in this Book.

I

KARNA AND ARJUN MEET

Sights of red and ghastly carnage day disclosed upon the plain,
Mighty chiefs and countless warriors round the warlike Drona slain,

Sad Duryodhan gazed in sorrow and the tear was in his eye,
Till his glances fell on Karna and his warlike heart beat high !

" Karna ! " so exclaimed Duryodhan, " hero of resistless might,
Thou alone canst serve the Kuru in this dread and dubious fight,

Step forth, Kuru's chief and leader, mount thy sounding battle-car,
Lead the still unconquered Kurus to the trophies of the war !

Matchless was the ancient Bhishma in this famed and warlike land,
But a weakness for Yudhishthir palsied Bhishma's slaying hand,

Matchless too was doughty Drona in the warrior's skill and art,
Kindness for his pupil Arjun lurked within the teacher's heart !

Greater than the ancient grandsire, greater than the Brahman old,
Fiercer in thy deathless hatred, stronger in thy prowess bold,

Peerless Karna, lead us onward to a brighter happier fate,
For thy arm is nerved to action by an unforgotten hate !

Lead us as the martial SKANDA led the conquering gods of old,
Smite the foe as angry INDRA smote the Danavs fierce and bold,

As before the light of morning flies the baleful gloom of night,
Pandavs and the proud Panchalas fly before thy conquering might !"

Priests with hymns and chanted *mantra* and with every sacred rite
Hailed him Leader of the Kurus, chieftain of unconquered might,

Earthen jars they placed around him with the sacred water full,
Elephant's tusk they laid beside him and the horn of mighty bull,

Gem and jewel, corn and produce, by the arméd hero laid,
Silken cloth of finest lustre o'er his crownéd head they spread,

Brahmans poured the holy water, bards his lofty praises sung,
Kshatras, Vaisyas, purer Sudras hailed him Leader bold and strong !

" Vanquish warlike sons of Pritha !" thus the holy Brahmans blessed,
Gold and garments, food and cattle, joyous Karna on them pressed,

And the holy rite concluded, Karna ranged his men in war,
To the dreaded front of battle drove his swift and conquering car !

Morn to noon and noon to evening raged the battle on the plain,
Countless warriors fought and perished, car-borne chiefs were pierced
      and slain,

Helméd Arjun, crownéd Karna, met at last by will of fate,
Life-long was their mutual anger, deathless was their mutual hate !

And the firm earth shook and trembled 'neath the furious rush of
      war,
And the echoing welkin answered shouts that nations heard afar,

And the thickening cloud of arrows filled the firmament on high,
Darker, deeper, dread and deadlier, grew the angry face of sky,

Till the evening's sable garment mantled o'er the battle-field,
And the angry rivals parted, neither chief could win or yield !

II

FALL OF KARNA

At the break of morning Karna unto Prince Duryodhan went,
Thus in slow and measured accents to his inner thoughts gave vent :

" Morning dawns, O Kuru's monarch ! mighty Arjun shall be slain,
Or fulfilling warrior's duty Karna dyes the gory plain !

Long through life within our bosoms ever burnt the mutual hate,
Oft we met and often parted, rescued by the will of fate,

But yon sun with crimson lustre sees us meet to part no more,
Gallant Arjun's course this evening or proud Karna's shall be o'er,

Room is none for Arjun's glory and for archer Karna's fame,
One must sink and one must sparkle with a brighter richer flame !

List yet more ; in wealth of arrows and in wondrous strength of bow,
Arjun scarcely me surpasseth, scarcely I excel my foe,

In the light skill of the archer and in sight and truth of aim,
Arjun beats not, scarcely rivals, Karna's proud and peerless fame !

If his wondrous bow *Gandiva* is the gift of gods in heaven,
Karna's bow the famed *Vijaya* is by Par'su-Rama given,

Ay, the son of Jamadagni, kings of earth who proudly slayed,
On the youthful arms of Karna his destructive weapon laid !

Yet I own, O king of Kuru ! Arjun doth his foe excel,—
Matchless are his fiery coursers, peerless Krishna leads them well,

Krishna holds the reins for Arjun, Krishna speeds his battle-car,
Drives the lightning-wingéd coursers o'er the startled field of war,

Sweeps in pride his sounding chariot till it almost seems to fly,
Arjun lords it o'er the battle like the comet in the sky !

Grant me, monarch, mighty Salya drive my swift and warlike steed,
And against the car-borne Arjun, Karna's fiery chariot lead,

Salya too is skilled, like Krishna, with the steed and battle-car,
Equal thus I meet my foeman in this last and fatal war ! ''

Spake Duryodhan ; warlike Salya mounted Karna's sounding car,
Karna sought for mighty Arjun in the serried ranks of war :

" Hundred milch-kine Karna offers, costly garment, yellow gold,
Unto him who in this battle points to me my foeman bold,

Cars and steeds and fertile acres, peaceful hamlets rich and fair,
Dark-eyed damsels lotus-bosomed, crowned with glossy raven hair,

These are his who points out Arjun hiding from this fatal war,
Arjun's snowy steeds and banner and his swift and thund'ring car ! ''

Karna spake, but long and loudly laughed the king of Madra's land,
As he reined the fiery coursers with his strong and skilful hand,

" Of rewards and gifts," he uttered, " little need is there, I ween,
Arjun is not wont to tarry from the battle's glorious scene,

Soon will Arjun's snowy coursers shake the battle's startled field,
Helméd Arjun like a comet gleam with bow and sword and shield !

As the forest-ranging tiger springs upon his fated prey,
As the hornéd bull infuriate doth the weakling cattle slay,

As the fierce and lordly lion smites the timid jungle-deer,
Arjun soon shall smite thee, Karna, for he knows nor dread nor fear,

Save thee then, O mighty archer ! while I drive my sounding car,
Pandu's son hath met no equal in the valiant art of war ! ''

Darkly frowned the angry Karna, Salya held the loosened rein,
Dashing through the hostile forces then the warrior sped amain,

Through the serried ranks of battle Karna drove in furious mood,
Facing him in royal splendour good Yudhishthir fearless stood !

Surging ranks of brave Nishadas closed between and fought in vain,
Proud Panchalas stout and faithful vainly strove among the slain,

Onward came the fiery Karna like the ocean's heaving swell,
With the sweeping wrath of tempest on the good Yudhishthir fell !

Wrathful then the son of Pandu marked his noblest chieftains dead,
And in words of scornful anger thus to archer Karna said :

" Hast thou, Karna, vowed the slaughter of my younger Arjun brave,
Wilt thou do Duryodhan's mandate, proud Duryodhan's willing
slave,

Unfulfilled thy vow remaineth, for the righteous gods ordain,
By Yudhishthir's hand thou fallest, go and slumber with the slain ! "

Fiercely drew his bow Yudhishthir, fiercely was the arrow driven,
Rocky cliff or solid mountain might the shaft have pierced and riven,

Lightning-like it came on Karna, struck and pierced him on the left,
And the warrior fell and fainted as of life and sense bereft !

Soon he rose ; the cloud of anger darkened o'er his livid face,
And he drew his godlike weapon with a more than godlike grace,

Arrows keen and dark as midnight gleaming in their lightning flight,
Struck Yudhishthir's royal armour with a fierce resistless might !

Clanking fell the shattered armour from his person fair and pale,
As from sun's meridian splendour clouds are drifted by the gale,

Armourless but bright and radiant brave Yudhishthir waged the
fight,
Bright as sky with stars bespangled on a clear and cloudless night,

And he threw his pointed lances like the summer's bursting flood,
Once again Yudhishthir's weapons drank his fiery foeman's blood !

Pale with anguish, wrathful Karna fiercely turned the tide of war,
Cut Yudhishthir's royal standard, crushed his sumptuous battle-car,

And he urged his gallant coursers till his chariot bounding flew,
And with more than godlike prowess then his famed *Vijaya* drew,

Faint Yudhishthir sorely bleeding waged no more the fatal fight,
Carless, steedless, void of armour, sought his safety in his flight !

" Speed, thou timid man of penance ! " thus insulting Karna said,
" Famed for virtue not for valour ! blood of thine I will not shed,

Speed and chant thy wonted *mantra*, do the rites that sages know,
Bid the helméd warrior Arjun come and meet his warlike foe ! "

To his tent retired Yudhishthir in his wrath and in his shame,
Spake to Arjun who from battle to his angry elder came :

" Hast thou yet, O tardy Arjun, base insulting Karna slain,
Karna dealing dire destruction on this battle's reddened plain ?

Like his teacher Par'su-Rama dyes in purple blood his course,
Like a snake of deathful poison Karna guards the Kuru force,

Karna smote my chariot-driver and my standard rent in twain,
Shattered car and lifeless horses strew the red inglorious plain,

Scarce with life in speechless anguish from the battle-field I fled,
Scorn of foes and shame of kinsmen ! Warrior's fame and honour
dead !

Ten long years and three Yudhishthir joy nor peace nor rest hath
seen,
And while Karna lives and glories all our insults still are green,

Hast thou, Arjun, slain that chieftain as in swelling pride he stood,
Hast thou wiped our wrongs and insults in that chariot-driver's
blood ? "

" At a distance," Krishna answered, " fiery Arjun fought his way,
Now he seeks the archer Karna and he vows his death to-day."

Anger lit Yudhishthir's forehead and a tremor shook his frame,
As he spake to silent Arjun words of insult and of shame :

" Wherefore like a painted warrior doth the helméd Arjun stand,
Wherefore useless lies *Gandiva* in his weak and nerveless hand,

Wherefore hangs yon mighty sabre from his belt of silk and gold,
Wherefore doth the peerless Krishna drive his coursers fleet and
bold,

If afar from war's arena timid Arjun seeks to hide,
If he shuns the mighty Karna battling in unconquered pride ?

Arjun ! yield thy famed *Gandiva* unto worthier hands than thine,
On some braver, truer warrior let thy mighty standard shine,

Yield thy helmet and thy armour, yield thy gleaming sword and
shield,
Hide thee from this deathful battle, matchless Karna rules the
field ! "

Sparkled Arjun's eye in anger with a red and livid flame,
And the tempest of his passion shook his more than mortal frame,

Heedless, on the sword-hilt Arjun placed his swift and trembling
hand,
Heedless, with a warrior's instinct drew the dark and glistening
brand !

Sacred blood of king and elder would have stained his trenchant steel,
But the wise and noble Krishna strove the fatal feud to heal:

" Not before thy elder, Arjun, but in yonder purple field,
'Gainst thy rival and thy foeman use thy warlike sword and shield,

Render honour to thy elder, quench thy hasty impious wrath,
Render faith to holy *sastra*, leave not virtue's sacred path,

Bow before thy virtuous elder as before the gods in heaven,
Sheathe thy sword and quell thy passion, be thy hasty sin forgiven !"

Duteous Arjun silent listened and obeyed the mandate high,
Tears of manly sorrow trickled from his soft and altered eye,

Dear in joy and dear in suffering, calm his righteous elder stood,
Dear in Indra-prastha's mansions, dearer in the jungle wood !

Arjun sheathed his flashing sabre, joined his hands and hung his head,
Fixed his eye on good Yudhishthir and in humble accents said:

" Pardon, great and saintly monarch, vassal's disrespectful word,
Pardon, elder, if a younger heedless drew his sinful sword,

But thy hest to yield my weapon stung my soul to bitter strife,
Dearer is the bow *Gandiva* unto Arjun than his life,

Pardon if the blood of anger mantled o'er this rugged brow,
Pardon if I drew my sabre 'gainst my duty and my vow,

For that hasty act repenting Arjun bows thy heart to move,
Grant me, holy king and elder, monarch's grace and brother's love !"

From Yudhishthir's altered eyelids gentle tears of sorrow start,
And he lifts his younger brother to his ever-loving heart:

" Arjun, I have wronged thee brother, and no fault or sin is thine,
Hasty words of thoughtless anger 'scaped these sinful lips of mine,

Bitter was my shame and anguish when from Karna's car I fled,
Redder than my bleeding bosom warrior's fame and honour bled,

Hasty words I uttered, Arjun, by my pain and anguish driven,
Wipe them with a brother's kindness, be thy elder's sin forgiven ! "

Stronger by his elder's blessing Arjun mounts the battle-car,
Krishna drives the milk-white coursers to the thickening ranks of war.

Onward came the fiery Karna with his chiefs and arméd men,
Salya urged his flying coursers with the whip and loosened rein,

Often met and often parted, life-long rivals in their fame,
Not to part again the heroes, each before the other came,

Not to part until a chieftain by the other chief was slain,
Arjun dead or lifeless Karna pressed the Kuru-kshetra plain !

Long they strove, but neither archer could his gallant foeman beat,
Though like surging ocean billows did the angry warriors meet,

Arjun's arrows fell on Karna like the summer's angry flood,
Karna's shafts like hissing serpents drank the valiant Arjun's blood,

Fierce and quick from his *Gandiva* angry accents Arjun woke,
Till the bow-string strained and heated was by sudden impulse broke!

" Hold," cried Arjun to his rival, " mind the honoured rules of war,
Warriors strike not helpless foemen thus disabled on the car,

Hold, brave Karna, until Arjun mends his over-strainéd bow,
Arjun then will crave for mercy nor from god nor mortal foe ! "

Vain he spake, for wild with anger heedless Karna fiercely lowered,
Thick and fast on bowless Arjun countless arrows darkly showered,

Like the cobra dark and hissing Karna's gleaming lightning dart,
Struck the helpless archer Arjun on his broad and bleeding heart !

Furious like a wounded tiger quivering in the darksome wood,
With his mended warlike weapon now the angry Arjun stood,

Blazing with a mighty radiance like a flame in summer night,
Fierce he fell on archer Karna with his more than mortal might !

Little recked the dauntless Karna if his foe in anger rose,
Karna feared not face of mortal, dreaded not immortal foes,

Nor with all his wrath and valour Arjun conquered him in war,
Till within the soft earth sinking stuck the wheel of Karna's car !

Stood unmoved the tilted chariot, vainly wrathful Salya strove,
Urging still the struggling coursers Karna's heavy car to move,

Vainly too the gallant Karna leaped upon the humid soil,
Sought to lift the sunken axle with a hard unwonted toil,

" Hold," he cried to noble Arjun, " wage no false and impious war
On a foeman, helpless, carless,—thou upon thy lofty car."

Loudly laughed the helméd Arjun, answer nor rejoinder gave,
Unto Karna pleading virtue Krishna answered calm and grave :

" Didst thou seek the path of virtue, mighty Karna, archer bold,
When Sakuni robbed Yudhishthir of his empire and his gold,

Didst thou tread the path of honour on Yudhishthir's fatal fall,
Heaping insults on Draupadi in Hastina's council hall ?

Didst thou then fulfil thy duty when, Yudhishthir's exile crost,
Krishna asked in right and justice for Yudhishthir's empire lost,

Didst thou fight a holy battle when with six marauders skilled,
Karna hunted Abhimanyu and the youthful hero killed ?

Speak not then of rules of honour, blackened in your sins you die,
Death is come in shape of Arjun, Karna's fatal hour is nigh ! "

Stung to fury and to madness, faint but frantic Karna fought,
Reckless, ruthless, and relentless, valiant Arjun's life he sought,

Sent his last resistless arrow on his foeman's mighty chest,
Arjun felt a shock of thunder on his broad and mailéd breast !

Fainting fell the bleeding Arjun, darkness dimmed his manly eye,
Pale and breathless watched his warriors, anxious watched the gods
     in sky,

Then it passed, and helméd Arjun rose like newly lighted fire,
Abhimanyu's sad remembrance kindled fresh a father's ire !

And he drew his bow *Gandiva*, aimed his dart with stifled breath,
Vengeance for his murdered hero winged the fatal dart of death,

Like the fiery bolt of lightning Arjun's lurid arrow sped,
Like a rock by thunder riven Karna fell among the dead !

III

FALL OF SALYA

Darkly closed the shades of midnight, Karna still and lifeless lay,
Ghast and pale o'er slaughtered thousands fell the morning's sickly
ray,

Bowman brave and proud preceptor Kripa to Duryodhan said,
Tear bedimmed the warrior's eyelids and his manly bosom bled :

" Leaderless are Kuru's forces by a dire misfortune crost,
Like the moonless shades of midnight in their utter darkness lost,

Like a summer-dried river, weary waste of arid sand,
Lost its pride of fresh'ning waters sweeping o'er the grateful land !

As a spark of fire consumeth summer's parched and sapless wood,
Kuru's lordless, lifeless forces shall be angry Arjun's food,

Bhima too shall seek fulfilment of the dreadful vow he made,
Brave Satyaki wreak his vengeance for his sons untimely slayed !

Bid this battle cease, Duryodhan, pale and fitful is thy star,
Blood enough of friendly nations soaks this crimson field of war,

Bid them live,—the few survivors of a vast and countless host,
Let thy few remaining brothers live,—for many are the lost,

Kindly heart hath good Yudhishthir, still he seeks for rightful peace,
Render back his ancient kingdom, bid this war of kinsmen cease ! "

" Kripa," so Duryodhan answered, " in this sad and fatal strife,
Ever foremost of our warriors, ever careless of thy life,

Ever in the council chamber thou hast words of wisdom said,
Needless war and dire destruction by thy peaceful counsel stayed,

Every word thou speakest, Kripa, is a word of truth and weight,
Nathless thy advice for concord, wise preceptor, comes too late !

Hope not that the good Yudhishthir will again our friendship own.
Cheated once by deep Sakuni of his kingdom and his throne,

Rugged Bhima will not palter, fatal is the vow he made,
Vengeful Arjun will not pardon gallant Abhimanyu dead !

Fair Draupadi doth her penance, so our ancient matrons say,
In our blood to wash her insult and her proud insulters slay,

Fair Subhadra morn and evening weeps her dear departed son,
Feeds Draupadi's deathless anger for the hero dead and gone,

Deeply in their bosoms rankle wrongs and insults we have given,
Blood alone can wash it, Kripa, such the cruel will of Heaven !

And the hour for peace is over, for our best sleep on the plain,
Brothers, kinsmen, friends, and elders slumber with the countless
    slain,

Shall Duryodhan like a recreant now avoid the deathful strife,
After all his bravest warriors have in war surrendered life,

Shall he, sending them to slaughter, now survive and learn to flee,
Shall he, ruler over monarchs, learn to bend the servile knee ?

Proud Duryodhan sues no favour even with his dying breath,
Unsubdued and still unconquered, changeless even unto death,

Salya valiant king of Madra leads our arméd hosts to-day,
Or to perish or to conquer, gallant Kripa, lead the way ! "

Meanwhile round the brave Yudhishthir calmly stood the Pandav
    force,
As the final day of battle now began its fatal course,

" Brothers, kinsmen, hero-warriors," so the good Yudhishthir said,
" Ye have done your share in battle, witness countless foemen dead

Sad Yudhishthir is your eldest, let him end this fatal strife,
Slay the last of Kuru chieftains or surrender throne and life !

Bold Satyaki ever faithful with his arms protects my right,
Drupad's son with watchful valour guards my left with wonted might,

In the front doth Bhima battle, careful Arjun guards the rear,
I will lead the battle's centre which shall know nor flight nor fear ! "

Truly on that fatal morning brave Yudhishthir kept his word,
Long and fiercely waged the combat with fair Madra's valiant lord,

Thick and fast the arrows whistled and the lances pointed well,
Till with crashing sound of thunder Salya's mighty standard fell !

Rescued by the son of Drona, Salya rushed again to war,
Slew the noble milk-white coursers of Yudhishthir's royal car,

And as springs the hungry lion on the spotted jungle-deer,
Salya rushed upon Yudhishthir reckless and unknown to fear !

Brave Yudhishthir marked him coming and he hurled his fatal dart,
Like the fatal curse of Brahman sank the weapon in his heart,

Blood suffused his eye and nostril, quivered still his feeble hand,
Like a cliff by thunder riven Salya fell and shook the land !

Ended was the fatal battle, for the *Mlechcha* king was slain,
Pierced by angry Sahadeva false Sakuni pressed the plain,

All the brothers of Duryodhan tiger-waisted Bhima slew,
Proud Duryodhan pale and panting from the field of battle flew !

IV

NIGHT OF SLAUGHTER : DURYODHAN'S DEATH

Far from battle's toil and slaughter, by a dark and limpid lake,
Sad and slow and faint Duryodhan did his humble shelter take,

But the valiant sons of Pandu with the hunter's watchful care,
Thither tracked their fallen foeman like a wild beast in its lair !

" Gods be witness," said Duryodhan, flaming in his shame and wrath,
" Boy to manhood ever hating we have crossed each other's path,

Now we meet to part no longer, proud Duryodhan fights you all,
Perish he, or sons of Pandu, may this evening see your fall ! "

Bhima answered : " For the insults long endured but not forgiven,
Me alone you fight, Duryodhan, witness righteous gods in heaven,

Call to mind the dark destruction planned of old in fiendish ire,
In the halls of Varnavata to consume us in the fire,

Call to mind the scheme deceitful, deep Sakuni's dark device,
Cheating us of fame and empire by the trick of loaded dice,

Call to mind that coward insult and the outrage foul and keen,
Flung on Drupad's saintly daughter and our noble spotless queen,

Call to mind the stainless Bhishma for thy sins and folly slain,
Lifeless proud preceptor Drona, Karna lifeless on the plain,

Perish in thy sins, Duryodhan, perish too thy hated name,
And thy dark life crime-polluted ends, Duryodhan, in thy shame ! "

Like two bulls that fight in fury blind with wounds and oozing blood,
Like two wild and warring tuskers shaking all the echoing wood,

Like the thunder-wielding INDRA, YAMA monarch of the dead,
Dauntless Bhima and Duryodhan fiercely strove and fought and
    bled !

Sparks of fire shot from their maces and their faces ran with blood,
Neither won and neither yielded, matched in strength the rivals
    stood,

Till his vow remembered Bhima, and he raised his weapon high,
With a foul attack but fatal broke Duryodhan's shattered knee !

Through the sky a voice resounded as the great Duryodhan fell,
And the earth the voice re-echoed o'er her distant hill and dale,

Beasts and birds in consternation flew o'er land and azure sky,
Men below and heavenly *Siddhas* trembled at the fatal cry !

Darkness fell upon the battle, proud Duryodhan dying lay,
But the slaughter of the combat closed not with the closing day,

Ancient feud and hatred linger after battle's sweeping flood,
And the father's deathless anger courseth in the children's blood,

Drona slept and gallant Drupad, for their earthly task was done,
Vengeance fired the son of Drona 'gainst the royal Drupad's son !

Sable shadows of the midnight fell o'er battle's silent plain,
Faintly shone the fitful planets on the dying and the slain,

And the vengeful son of Drona fired by omens dark and dread,
Stole into the tents of foemen with a soft and noiseless tread !

Dhrista-dyumna and Sikhandin, princes of Panchala's land,
Fell beneath the proud avenger Aswa-thaman's reeking hand,

Ay, where Drupad's sleeping grandsons, fair Draupadi's children lay,
Stole the cruel arm of vengeance, smothered them ere dawn of day !

Done the ghastly work of slaughter, Aswa-thaman bent his way
Where beside the limpid waters lone Duryodhan dying lay,

And Duryodhan blessed the hero with his feeble fleeting breath,
Joy of vengeance cheered his bosom and he died a happy death !

BOOK XI

SRADDHA

(*Funeral Rites*)

THE death of Duryodhan concludes the war, and it is followed by
the lament of women and the funerals of the deceased warriors.
The passages translated in this Book form Section x., portions of
Sections xvi., xvii., and xxvi., and the whole of Section xxvii.
of Book xi. of the original text.

I

KURU WOMEN VISIT THE BATTLE-FIELD

Spake the ancient Dhrita-rashtra, father of a hundred sons,
Sonless now and sorrow-stricken, dark his ebbing life-tide runs :

" Gods fulfil my life's last wishes ! Henchmen, yoke my royal car,
Dhrita-rashtra meets his princes in the silent field of war,

Speed unto the Queen Gandhari, to the dames of Kuru's house,
To each dear departed warrior wends his fair and faithful spouse ! "

Queen Gandhari sorrow-laden with the ancient Pritha came,
And each weeping widowed princess and each wailing childless dame,

And they saw the hoary monarch, father of a perished race,
Fresh and loud awoke their sorrow, welling tears suffused their face,

Good Vidura ever gentle whispered comfort unto all,
Placed the dames within their chariots, left Hastina's palace hall !

Loud the wail of woe and sorrow rose from every Kuru house,
Children wept beside their mothers for each widowed royal spouse,

Veiléd dwellers of the palace, scarce the gods their face had seen,
Heedless now through mart and city sped each widowed childless
    queen,

From their royal brow and bosom gem and jewel cast aside,
Loose their robes and loose their tresses, quenched their haughty
    queenly pride !

So when falls the antlered monarch, struck by woe and sudden fear
Issuing from their snowy mountains listless stray the dappled deer,

So when smit by sudden panic, milk-white mares that scour the plain,
Wildly toss their flowing tresses, shake their soft and glossy mane !

Clinging to her weeping sister wept each dame in cureless pain,
For the lord the son or father in the deathful battle slain,

Wept and smote her throbbing bosom and in bitter anguish wailed,
Till her senses reeled in sorrow, till her woman's reason failed !

Veiléd queens and bashful maidens, erst they shunned the public eye,
Blush nor shame suffused their faces as they passed the city by,

Gentle-bosomed, kindly hearted, erst they wiped each other's tear,
Now by common sorrow laden knew no sister's words of cheer !

With this troop of wailing women, deep in woe, disconsolate,
Slow the monarch of the Kurus passed Hastina's outer gate,

Men from stall and loom and anvil, men of every guild and trade,
Left the city with the monarch, through the open country strayed,

And a universal sorrow filled the air and answering sky,
As when ends the mortal's *Yuga* and the end of world is nigh !

II

GANDHARI'S LAMENT FOR THE SLAIN

Stainless Queen and stainless woman, ever righteous ever good,
Stately in her mighty sorrow on the field Gandhari stood !

Strewn with skulls and clotted tresses, darkened by the stream of gore,
With the limbs of countless warriors is the red field covered o'er,

Elephants and steeds of battle, car-borne chiefs untimely slain,
Headless trunks and heads dissevered fill the red and ghastly plain,

And the long-drawn howl of jackals o'er the scene of carnage rings,
And the vulture and the raven flap their dark and loathsome wings.

Feasting on the blood of warriors foul *Pisachas* fill the air,
Viewless forms of hungry *Rakshas* limb from limb the corpses tear !

Through this scene of death and carnage was the ancient monarch led,
Kuru dames with faltering footsteps stepped amidst the countless
    dead,

And a piercing wail of anguish burst upon the echoing plain,
As they saw their sons or fathers, brothers, lords, amidst the slain,

As they saw the wolves of jungle feed upon the destined prey,
Darksome wanderers of the midnight prowling in the light of day !

Shriek of pain and wail of anguish o'er the ghastly field resound,
And their feeble footsteps falter and they sink upon the ground,

Sense and life desert the mourners as they faint in common grief.
Death-like swoon succeeding sorrow yields a moment's short relief !

Then a mighty sigh of anguish from Gandhari's bosom broke,
Gazing on her anguished daughters unto Krishna thus she spoke :

" Mark my unconsoléd daughters, widowed queens of Kuru's house,
Wailing for their dear departed, like the osprey for her spouse !

How each cold and fading feature wakes in them a woman's love,
How amidst the lifeless warriors still with restless steps they rove,

Mothers hug their slaughtered children all unconscious in their sleep,
Widows bend upon their husbands and in ceaseless sorrow weep,

Mighty Bhishma, hath he fallen, quenched is archer Karna's pride,
Doth the monarch of Panchala sleep by foeman Drona's side ?

Shining mail and costly jewels, royal bangles strew the plain,
Golden garlands rich and burnished deck the chiefs untimely slain,

Lances hurled by stalwart fighters, clubs of mighty wrestlers killed,
Swords and bows of ample measure, quivers still with arrows filled !

Mark the unforgotten heroes, jungle prowlers 'mid them stray,
On their brow and mailéd bosoms heedless perch the birds of prey,

Mark the great unconquered heroes famed on earth from west to east,
Kankas perch upon their foreheads, hungry wolves upon them feast !

Mark the kings, on softest cushion scarce the needed rest they found,
Now they lie in peaceful slumber on the hard and reddened ground,

Mark the youths who morn and evening listed to the minstrel's song,
In their ear the loathsome jackal doth his doleful wail prolong !

See the chieftains with their maces and their swords of trusty steel,
Still they grasp their tried weapons,—do they still the life-pulse
    feel ? "

III

Gandhari's Lament for Duryodhan

Thus to Krishna, Queen Gandhari strove her woeful thoughts to tell,
When, alas, her wandering vision on her son Duryodhan fell,

Sudden anguish smote her bosom and her senses seemed to stray,
Like a tree by tempest shaken senseless on the earth she lay !

Once again she waked in sorrow, once again she cast her eye
Where her son in blood empurpled slept beneath the open sky,

And she clasped her dear Duryodhan, held him close unto her breast,
Sobs convulsive shook her bosom as the lifeless form she prest,

And her tears like rains of summer fell and washed his noble head,
Decked with garlands still untarnished, graced with *nishkas* bright
    and red !

" ' Mother ! ' said my dear Duryodhan when he went unto the war,
' Wish me joy and wish me triumph as I mount the battle-car,'

' Son ! ' I said to dear Duryodhan, ' Heaven avert a cruel fate,
Yato dharma stato jayah ! Triumph doth on Virtue wait ! '

But he set his heart on battle, by his valour wiped his sins,
Now he dwells in realms celestial which the faithful warrior wins,

And I weep not for Duryodhan, like a prince he fought and fell,
But my sorrow-stricken husband, who can his misfortunes tell !

Ay ! my son was brave and princely, all resistless in the war,
Now he sleeps the sleep of warriors, sunk in gloom his glorious star,

Ay ! my son 'mid crownéd monarchs held the first and foremost way,
Now he rests upon the red earth, quenched his bright effulgent ray,

Ay ! my son the best of heroes, he hath won the warrior's sky,
Kshatras nobly conquer, Krishna, when in war they nobly die !

Hark the loathsome cry of jackals, how the wolves their vigils keep,
Maidens rich in song and beauty erst were wont to watch his sleep,

Hark the foul and blood-beaked vultures flap their wings upon the
  dead,
Maidens waved their feathery *pankhas* round Duryodhan's royal bed,

Peerless bowman ! mighty monarch ! nations still his hests obeyed,
As a lion slays a tiger, Bhima hath Duryodhan slayed !

Thirteen years o'er Kuru's empire proud Duryodhan held his sway,
Ruled Hastina's ancient city where fair Ganga's waters stray,

I have seen his regal splendour with these ancient eyes of mine,
Elephants and battle-chariots, steeds of war and herds of kine,

Kuru owns another master and Duryodhan's day is fled,
And I live to be a witness ! Krishna, O that I were dead !

Mark Duryodhan's noble widow, mother proud of Lakshman bold,
Queenly in her youth and beauty, like an altar of bright gold,

Torn from husband's sweet embraces, from her son's entwining arms,
Doomed to life-long woe and anguish in her youth and in her charms,

Rend my hard and stony bosom crushed beneath this cruel pain,
Should Gandhari live to witness noble son and grandson slain ?

Mark again Duryodhan's widow, how she hugs his gory head,
How with gentle hands and tender softly holds him on his bed,

How from dear departed husband turns she to her dearer son,
And the tear-drops of the mother choke the widow's bitter groan,

Like the fibre of the lotus tender-golden is her frame,
O my lotus ! O my daughter ! Bharat's pride and Kuru's fame !

If the truth resides in *Vedas*, brave Duryodhan dwells above,
Wherefore linger we in sadness severed from his cherished love,

If the truth resides in *Sastra*, dwells in sky my hero son,
Wherefore linger we in sorrow since their earthly task is done ? "

IV

FUNERAL RITE

Victor of a deathful battle, sad Yudhishthir viewed the plain,
Friends and kinsmen, kings and chieftains, countless troops untimely
    slain,

And he spake to wise Sudharman pious priest of Kuru's race,
Unto Sanjay, unto Dhaumya, to Vidura full of grace,

Spake unto the brave Yuyutsu, Kuru's last surviving chief,
Spake to faithful Indrasena and to warriors sunk in grief :

" Pious rites are due to foemen and to friends and kinsmen slain,
None shall lack a fitting funeral, none shall perish on the plain."

Wise Vidura and his comrades sped on sacred duty bound,
Sandalwood and scented aloes, fragrant oil and perfumes found,

Silken robes of costly splendour, fabrics by the artist wove,
Dry wood from the thorny jungle, perfume from the scented grove,

Shattered cars and splintered lances, hewed and ready for the fire,
Piled and ranged in perfect order into many a funeral pyre.

Kings and princes, noble warriors, were in rank and order laid,
And with streams of fragrant *ghrita* were the rich libations made,

Blazed the fire with wondrous radiance by the rich libations fed,
Sanctifying and consuming mortal remnants of the dead.

Brave Duryodhan and his brothers, Salya of the mighty car,
Bhurisravas king of nations, Jayadratha famed in war,

Abhimanyu son of Arjun, Lakshman proud Duryodhan's son,
Somadatta and the Srinjays famed for deeds of valour done,

Matsya's monarch proud Virata, Drupad fair Panchala's king,
And his sons, Panchala's princes, whose great deeds the minstrels sing,

Cultured monarch of Kosala and Gandhara's wily lord,
Karna proud and peerless archer, matchless with his flaming sword,

Bhagadatta eastern monarch all resistless in his car,
Ghatotkacha son of Bhima, Alambusha famed in war,

And a hundred other monarchs all received the pious rite,
Till the radiance of the fire-light chased the shadows of the night !

Pitri-medha due to fathers was performed with pious care,
Hymns and wails and lamentations mingled in the midnight air,

Sacred songs of *rik* and *saman* rose with women's piercing wail,
And the creatures of the wide earth heard the sound subdued and pale,

Smokeless and with radiant lustre shone each red and lighted pyre,
Like the planets of the bright sky throbbing with celestial fire !

Men in nations, countless, nameless, from each court and camp afar,
From the east and west collected, fell in Kuru-Kshetra's war,

Thousand fires for them were lighted, they received the pious rite,
Such was good Yudhishthir's mandate, such was wise Vidura's might,

All the dead were burned to ashes and the sacred rite was o'er,
Dhrita-rashtra and Yudhishthir slowly walked to Ganga's shore !

V

OBLATION TO KARNA

Sacred Ganga, ample-bosomed, sweeps along in regal pride,
Rolling down her limpid waters through high banks on either side,

Childless dames and weeping widows thither in their anguish came,
Due and holy rites to render to departed chiefs of fame,

Casting forth their jewelled girdles, gems and scarfs belaced with gold,
Gave oblations of the water unto warriors true and bold,

Unto fathers, unto husbands, unto sons in battle slayed,
Offerings of the sacred water sorrowing wives and mothers made.

And so great the host of mourners wending to perform the rite,
That their footsteps made a pathway in the sad and sacred site,

And the shelving banks of Ganga, peopled by the sorrowing train,
Wide-expanding, vast and sealike, formed a scene of woe and pain !

But a wave of keener sorrow swept o'er Pritha's heaving breast,
As unto her weeping children thus her secret she expressed :

" *He, my sons, the peerless bowman, mighty in his battle-car,*
Who by will of fate untimely was by Arjun slain in war,

He whom as the son of Radha, chariot-driver ye have thought,
But who shone with SURYA'S *lustre as his countless foes he fought,*

He who faced your stoutest warriors and in battle never failed,
Bravely led the Kuru forces and in danger never quailed,

He who knew no peer in prowess, owned in war no haughtier name,
Yielded life but not his honour and by death hath conquered fame,

He in truth who never faltered, never left his vow undone,
Offer unto him oblation, Karna was my eldest son !

Karna was your honoured elder and the Sun inspired his birth,
Karna in his rings and armour Sun-like trod the spacious earth ! "

Pritha spake ; the Pandav brothers groaned in penitence and pain,
And they wept in woe and anguish for the brother they had slain,

Hissing forth his sigh of anguish like a crushed and wounded snake,
Sad Yudhishthir to his mother thus his inward feelings spake :

" Didst thou, mother, bear the hero fathomless like ocean dread,
Whose unfailing glistening arrows like its countless billows sped,

Didst thou bear that peerless archer all-resistless in his car,
Sweeping with the roar of ocean through the shattered ranks of war ?

Didst thou hide the mighty warrior, mortal man of heavenly birth,
Crushing 'neath his arm of valour all his foemen on the earth,

Didst thou hide the birth and lineage of that chief of deathful ire,
As a man in folds of garments seeks to hide the flaming fire ?

Arjun wielder of *Gandiva* was for us no truer stay
Than was Karna for the Kurus in the battle's dread array,

Monarchs matched not Karna's glory nor his deeds of valour done,
Midst the mighty car-borne warriors mightiest warrior Karna shone !

Woe to us ! our eldest brother we have in the battle slain,
And our nearest dearest elder fell upon the gory plain,

Not the death of Abhimanyu from the fair Subhadra torn,
Not the slaughter of the princes by the proud Draupadi borne,

Not the fall of friends and kinsmen and Panchala's mighty host,
Like thy death afflicts my bosom, noble Karna loved and lost !

Monarch's empire, victor's glory, all the treasures earth can yield,
Righteous bliss and heavenly gladness, harvest of the heavenly field,

All that wish can shape and utter, all that nourish hope and pride,
All were ours, O noble Karna, hadst thou rested by our side,

And this carnage of the Kurus these sad eyes had never seen,
Peace had graced our blessed empire, happy would the earth have
    been ! "

Long bewailed the sad Yudhishthir for his elder loved and dead,
And oblation of the water to the noble Karna made,

And the royal dames of Kuru viewed the sight with freshening pain,
Wept to see the good Yudhishthir offering to his brother slain,

And the widowed queen of Karna with the women of his house
Gave oblations to her hero, wept her loved and slaughtered spouse !

Done the rites to the departed, done oblations to the dead,
Slowly then the sad survivors on the river's margin spread,

Far along the shore and sandbank of the sacred sealike stream
Maid and matron lave their bodies 'neath the morning's holy beam,

And ablutions done, the Kurus slow and sad and cheerless part,
Wend their way to far Hastina with a void and vacant heart.

BOOK XII

ASWA-MEDHA

(*Sacrifice of the Horse*)

THE real Epic ends with the war and the funerals of the deceased warriors. Much of what follows in the original Sanscrit poem is either episodical or comparatively recent interpolation. The great and venerable warrior Bhishma, still lying on his death-bed, discourses for the instruction of the newly crowned Yudhishthir on various subjects like the Duties of Kings, the Duties of the Four Castes, and the Four Stages of Life. He repeats the discourses of other saints, of Bhrigu and Bharadwaja, of Manu and Brihaspati, of Vyasa and Suka, of Yajnavalkya and Janaka, of Narada and Narayana. He explains *Sankhya* philosophy and *Yoga* philosophy, and lays down the laws of Marriage, the laws of Succession, the rules of Gifts, and the rules of Funeral Rites. He preaches the cult of Krishna, and narrates endless legends, tales, traditions, and myths about sages and saints, gods and mortal kings. All this is told in two Books containing about twenty-two thousand couplets, and forming nearly one-fourth of the entire Sanscrit Epic !

The reason of adding all this episodical and comparatively recent matter to the ancient Epic is not far to seek. The Epic became more popular with the nation at large than dry codes of law and philosophy, and generations of Brahmanical writers laboured therefore to insert in the Epic itself their rules of caste and moral conduct, their laws and philosophy. There is no more venerable character in the Epic than Bhishma, and these rules and laws have therefore been supposed to come from his lips on the solemn occasion of his death. As a storehouse of Hindu laws and traditions and moral rules these episodes are invaluable ; but they form no part of the real Epic, they are not a portion of the leading story of the Epic, and we pass them by.

Bhishma dies and is cremated ; but the endless exposition of laws, legends, and moral rules is not yet over. Krishna himself takes up the task in a new Book, and, as he has done once before in the *Bhagavat-gita*, he now once more explains to Arjun in the *Anu-gita* the great truths about Soul and Emancipation, Creation and the Wheel of Life, True Knowledge and Rites and Penance. The adventures of the sage Utanka, whom Krishna meets, then take up a good many pages. All this forms no part of the real Epic, and we pass it by.

Yudhishthir has in the meantime been crowned king of the Kurus at Hastinapura, and a posthumous child of Abhimanyu is named Parikshit, and is destined to succeed to the throne of the Kurus. But Yudhishthir's mind is still troubled with the thoughts of the carnage of the war, of which he considers himself guilty, and the great saint Vyasa advises the performance of the *aswamedha*, or the Sacrifice of the Horse, for the expiation of the sin.

The Sacrifice of the Horse was an ancient Hindu custom practised by kings exercising suzerain powers over surrounding kings. A horse was let free, and was allowed to wander from place to place, accompanied by the king's guard. If any neighbouring king ventured to detain the animal, it was a signal for war. If no king ventured to restrain the wanderer, it was considered a tacit mark of submission to the owner of the animal. And when the horse returned from its peregrinations, it was sacrificed with great pomp and splendour at a feast to which all neighbouring kings were invited.

Yudhishthir allowed the sacrificial horse to wander at will, and Arjun accompanied it. Wherever the horse was stopped, Arjun fought and conquered, and thus proclaimed the supremacy of Yudhishthir over all neighbouring potentates. After various wars and adventures in various regions, Arjun at last returned victorious with the steed to Hastinapura, and the sacrifice commenced.

The description of the sacrifice is somewhat artificial, and concerns itself with rites and ceremonious details and gifts to Brahmans, and altogether bears unmistakable evidence of the interpolating hand of later priestly writers. Nevertheless we cannot exclude from this translation of the leading incidents of the Epic the last great and crowning act of Yudhishthir, now anointed monarch of Kuruland.

The portion translated in this Book forms Sections lxxxv. and parts of Sections lxxxviii. and lxxxix. of Book xiv. of the original text.

I

The Gathering

Victor of a hundred battles, Arjun bent his homeward way,
Following still the sacred charger free to wander as it may,

Strolling minstrels to Yudhishthir spake of the returning steed,
Spake of Arjun wending homeward with the victor's crown of meed,

And they sang of Arjun's triumphs in Gandhara's distant vale,
On the banks of Brahmaputra and in Sindhu's rocky dale.

Twelfth day came of *Magha's* bright moon and auspicious was the star,
Nigher came the victor Arjun from his conquests near and far,

Good Yudhishthir called his brothers, faithful twins and Bhima true,
Spake to them in gentle accents, and his words were grave and few :

" Bhima ! Now returneth Arjun with the steed from many a fray,
So they tell me, noble brother, who have met him on the way,

And the time of *aswa-medha* day by day is drawing nigh,
Magha's full moon is approaching, and the winter passeth by,

Let the Brahmans versed in Vedas choose the sacrificial site,
For the feast of many nations, for the *aswa-medha* rite."

Bhima heard of Arjun's coming,—hero with the curly hair,—
And to do Yudhishthir's mandate did with gladsome heart repair,

Brahmans versed in sacrifices, cunning architects of fame,
Builders of each various altar with the son of Pritha came,

And upon a level greensward measured forth the sacred site,
Laid it out with halls and pathways for the sacrificial rite.

Mansions graced with gem and jewel round the bright arena shone,
Palaces of golden lustre glinted in the morning sun,

Gilt and blazoned with devices lofty columns stood around,
Graceful arches gold-surmounted spanned the consecrated ground,

Gay pavilions rose in beauty round the sacrificial site,
For the queens of crownéd monarchs wending to the holy rite,

Humbler dwellings rose for Brahmans, priests of learning and of fame,
Come to view Yudhishthir's *yajna* and to bless Yudhishthir's name.

Messengers with kindly greetings went to monarchs far-renowned,
Asked them to Hastina's city, to the consecrated ground,

And to please the great Yudhishthir came each king and chieftain bold,
With their slaves and dark-eye damsels, arms and horses, gems and
  gold,

Came and found a royal welcome in pavilions rich and high,
And the sealike voice of nations smote the echoing vault of sky !

With his greetings did Yudhishthir, for each chief and king of men,
Cooling drinks and sumptuous viands, beds of regal pride ordain,

Stables filled with corn and barley and with milk and luscious cane
Greeted tall and warlike tuskers and the steeds with flowing mane.

Munis from their hermitages to the sacred *yajna* came,
Rishis from the grove and forest lisping BRAHMA's holy name,

Famed *Acharyas* versed in Vedas to the city held their way,
Brahmacharins with grass-girdle, chanting sweet the *saman* lay,

Welcomed Kuru's pious monarch, saint and sage and man of grace,
And with gentle condescension showed each priest his fitting place.

Skilled mechanics, cunning artists, raised the structures for the rite,
And with every needful object graced the sacrificial site,

Every duty thus completed, joyful Yudhishthir's mind,
And he blessed his faithful brothers with an elder's blessings kind.

II

THE FEASTING

Men in nations are assembled, hymns are sung by saint and sage,
And in learnéd disputations keen disputants oft engage,

And the concourse of the monarchs view the splendour of the rite,
Like the glorious sky of INDRA is the sacrificial site !

Bright festoons and flaming streamers are on golden arches hung,
Groups of men and gay-dressed women form a bright and joyous
  throng,

Jars of cool and sparkling waters, vessels rich with gold inlaid,
Costly cups and golden vases are in order due arrayed.

Sacrificial stakes of timber with their golden fastenings graced,
Consecrated by the *mantra* are in sumptuous order placed,

Countless creatures of the wide earth, fishes from the lake and flood,
Buffaloes and bulls from pasture, beasts of prey from jungle wood,

Birds and every egg-born creature, insects that from moisture spring,
Denizens of cave and mountain for the sacrifice they bring.

Noble chiefs and mighty monarchs gaze in wonder on the site,
Filled with every living object, corn and cattle for the rite,

Curd and cake and sweet confection are for feasting Brahmans spread,
And a hundred thousand people are with sumptuous viands fed !

With the accents of the rain-cloud drum and trumpet raise their voice,
Speak Yudhishthir's noble bounty, bid the sons of men rejoice,

Day by day the holy *yajna* grows in splendour and in joy,
Rice in hillocks feeds all comers, maid and matron, man and boy,

Lakes of curd and lakes of butter speak Yudhishthir's bounteous feast,
Nations of the Jambu-dwipa share it, greatest and the least !

For a hundred diverse races from a hundred regions came,
Ate of good Yudhishthir's bounty, sang of good Yudhishthir's fame,

And a thousand proud attendants, gay with earrings, garland-graced,
Carried food unto the feeders and the sweet confections placed,

Viands fit for crownéd monarchs were unto the Brahmans given,
Drinks of rich and cooling fragrance like the nectar-drink of heaven !

III

Sacrifice of Animals

Victor of a hundred battles, Arjun came with conquering steed,
Vyasa herald of the Vedas bade the holy rite proceed :

" For the day is come, Yudhishthir, let the sacrifice be done,
Let the priests repeat the *mantra* golden as the morning sun !

Threefold bounteous be thy presents and a threefold merit gain,
For thy wealth of gold is ample, be thy gifts like summer's rain,

May the threefold rich performance purify the darkening stain,
Blood of warriors and of kinsmen slaughtered on the gory plain,

May the *yajna's* pure ablution wash thee of the cruel sin,
And the meed of sacrificers may the good Yudhishthir win ! "

Vyasa spake ; and good Yudhishthir took the *diksha* of the rite,
And commenced the *aswa-medha* gladdening every living wight,

Round the altar's holy lustre moved the priests with sacred awe,
Swerved not from the rule of duty, failed not in the sacred law.

Done the rite of pure *pravargya* with the pious hymn and lay,
To the task of *abhishava* priests and Brahmans led the way,

And the holy Soma-drinkers pressed the sacred Soma plant,
And performed the pure *savana* with the solemn *saman* chant.

Bounty waits on squalid hunger, gifts dispel the suppliant's fear,
Gold revives the poor and lowly, mercy wipes the mourner's tear,

Tender care relieves the stricken by the gracious king's command,
Charity with loving sweetness spreads her smile o'er all the land !

Day by day the *aswa-medha* doth with sacred rites proceed,
Day by day on royal bounty poor and grateful myriads feed,

And adept in six Vedangas, strict in vow and rich in lore,
Sage preceptors, holy teachers, grew in virtue ever more !

Six good stakes of *vilwa* timber, six of hard *khadira* wood,
Six of seasoned *sarvavarnin*, on the place of *yajna* stood,

Two were made of *devadaru*, pine that on Himalay grows,
One was made of wood of *slesha*, which the sacrificer knows,

Other stakes of golden lustre quaint with curious carving done,
Draped in silk and gold-brocaded like the constellations shone !

And the consecrated altar built and raised of bricks of gold,
Shone in splendour like the altar Daksha built in days of old,

Eighteen cubits square the structure, four deep layers of brick in
    height,
With a spacious winged triangle like an eagle in its flight !

Beasts whose flesh is pure and wholesome, dwellers of the lake or sky,
Priests assigned each varied offering to each heavenly power on high,

Bulls of various breed and colour, steeds of mettle true and tried,
Other creatures, full three hundred, to the many stakes were tied.

Deva-rishis viewed the feasting, sweet *Gandharvas* woke the song,
Apsaras like gleams of sunlight on the greensward tripped along,

Kinnaras and *Kim-purushas* mingled in the holy rite,
Siddhas of austerest penance stood around the sacred site,

Vyasa's great and gifted pupils who the holy hymns compiled,
Helped the royal *aswa-medha*, on the royal *yajna* smiled !

From the bright ethereal mansions heavenly minstrel Narad came,
Chitra-sena woke the music, singer of celestial fame,

Cheered by more than mortal music priests their holy task begun,
And Yudhishthir's fame and virtue with a brighter lustre shone !

VI

SACRIFICE OF THE HORSE

Birds and beasts were immolated for the sacrificial food,
Then before the sacred charger priests in rank and order stood,

And by rules of Veda guided slew the horse of noble breed,
Placed Draupadi, *Queen of yajna*, by the slain and lifeless steed,

Hymns and gifts and deep devotion sanctified the noble Queen,
Woman's true and stainless virtue, woman's worth and wisdom
    keen !

Priests adept in sacred duty cooked the steed with pious rite,
And the steam of welcome fragrance sanctified the sacred site,

Good Yudhishthir and his brothers, by the rules by *rishis* spoke,
Piously inhaled the fragrance and the sin-destroying smoke !

Severed limbs and sacred fragments of the courser duly dressed,
Priests upon the blazing altar as a pious offering placed,

Vyasa herald of the Vedas raised his voice in holy song,
Blessed Hastina's righteous monarch and the many-nationed
    throng !

V

GIFTS

Unto Brahmans gave Yudhishthir countless *nishkas* of bright gold,
Unto sage and saintly Vyasa all his realm and wealth untold,

But the bard and ancient *rishi* who the holy Vedas spake,
Rendered back the monarch's present, earthly gift he might not take!

" Thine is Kuru's ancient empire, rule the nations of the earth,
Gods have destined thee as monarch from the moment of thy birth,

Gold and wealth and costly present let the priests and Brahmans
    hoard,
Be it thine to rule thy subjects as their father and their lord !

Krishna too in gentle accents to the doubting monarch said :
" Vyasa speaketh word of wisdom and his mandate be obeyed ! "

From the *rishi* good Yudhishthir then received the Kuru-land,
With a threefold gift of riches gladdened all the priestly band,

Pious priests and grateful nations to their distant regions went,
And his share of presents Vyasa to the ancient Pritha sent.

Fame and virtue Kuru's monarch by the *aswa-medha* wins,
And the rite of pure ablution cleanses all Yudhishthir's sins,

And he stands amid his brothers, brightly beaming, pure and high,
Even as INDRA stands encircled by the dwellers of the sky,

And the concourse of the monarchs grace Yudhishthir's regal might,
As the stars and radiant planets grace the stillness of the night !

Gems and jewels in his bounty, gold and garments rich and rare,
Gave Yudhishthir to each monarch, slaves and damsels passing fair,

Loving gifts to dear relations gave the king of righteous fame,
And the grateful parting monarchs blessed Yudhishthir's hallowed
    name.

Last of all with many tear-drops Krishna mounts his lofty car,
Faithful still in joy or sorrow, faithful still in peace or war,

Arjun's comrade, Bhima's helper, good Yudhishthir's friend of yore,
Krishna leaves Hastina's mansions for the sea-girt Dwarka's shore !

CONCLUSION

THE real Epic ends with the war and with the funerals of the deceased warriors, as we have stated before, and Yudhishthir's Horse-Sacrifice is rather a crowning ornament than a part of the solid edifice. What follows the sacrifice is in no sense a part of the real Epic; it consists merely of concluding personal narratives of the heroes who have figured in the poem.

Dhrita-rashtra retires into a forest with his queen Gandhari, and Pritha, the mother of the Pandav brothers, accompanies them. In the solitude of the forest the old Dhrita-rashtra sees as in a vision the spirits of all the slain warriors, his sons and grandsons and kinsmen, clad and armed as they were in battle. The spirits disappear in the morning at the bidding of Vyasa, who had called them up. At last Dhrita-rashtra and Gandhari and Pritha are burnt to death in a forest conflagration, death by fire being considered holy.

Krishna at Dwarka meets with strange and tragic adventures. The Vrishnis and the Andhakas become irreligious and addicted to drinking, and fall a prey to internal dissensions. Valadeva and Krishna die shortly after, and the city of the Yadavas is swallowed up by the ocean.

Then follow the two concluding Books of the Epic, the *Great Journey* and the *Ascent to Heaven*, so beautifully rendered into English by Sir Edwin Arnold. On hearing of the death of their friend Krishna, the Pandav brothers place Prakshit, the grandson of Arjun, on the throne, and retire to the Himalayas. Draupadi drops down dead on the way, then Sahadeva, then Nakula, then Arjun, and then Bhima. Yudhishthir alone proceeds to heaven in person in a celestial car.

There Yudhishthir undergoes some trial, bathes in the celestial Ganges, and rises with a celestial body. He then meets Krishna, now in his heavenly form, blazing in splendour and glory. He meets his brothers whom he had lost on earth, but who are now Immortals in the sky, clad in heavenly forms. INDRA himself appears before Yudhishthir, and introduces him to others who were dear to him on earth, and are dear to him in heaven. Thus speaks INDRA to Yudhishthir:

" This is She the fair Immortal ! Her no human mother bore,
Sprung from altar as Draupadi human shape for thee she wore,

By the Wielder of the Trident she was waked to form and life,
Born in royal Drupad's mansion, righteous man, to be thy wife,

These are bright aërial beings, went for thee to lower earth,
Borne by Drupad's stainless daughter as thy children took their
    birth !

This is monarch Dhrita-rashtra who doth o'er *Gandharvas* reign,
This is peerless archer Karna, erst on earth by Arjun slain,

Like the Sun in ruddy splendour, for the Sun inspired his birth,
As the son of chariot-driver he was known upon the earth !

'Midst the *Sadhyas* and the *Maruts*, 'midst Immortals pure and bright,
Seek thy friends the faithful Vrishnis matchless in their warlike might.

Seek and find the brave Satyaki who upheld thy cause so well,
Seek the Bhojas and Andhakas who in Kuru-kshetra fell !

This is gallant Abhimanyu whom the fair Subhadra bore,
Still unconquered in the battle, slain by fraud in yonder shore,

Abhimanyu son of Arjun, wielding Arjun's peerless might,
With the Lord of Night he ranges, beauteous as the Lord of Night !

This, Yudhishthir, is thy father, by thy mother joined in heaven,
Oft he comes into my mansions in his flowery chariot driven.

This is Bhishma stainless warrior, by the *Vasus* is his place,
By the god of heavenly wisdom teacher Drona sits in grace !

These and other mighty warriors in the earthly battle slain,
By their valour and their virtue walk the bright ethereal plain,

They have cast their mortal bodies, crossed the radiant gate of heaven,
For to win celestial mansions unto mortals it is given,

Let them strive by kindly action, gentle speech, endurance long,—
Brighter life and holier future unto sons of men belong ! "

EPILOGUE TO THE *MAHA-BHARATA*

BY THE TRANSLATOR

ANCIENT India, like ancient Greece, boasts of two great Epics. The *Ramayana*, describing the adventures of a prince, banished from his country and wandering for long years in the wilderness of Southern India, has something in common with the Odyssey. The *Maha-bharata*, based on the legends and traditions of a great historical war in which all the warlike races of Northern India took a share, is the Iliad of India.

The great war which is the subject of the *Maha-bharata* is believed to have been fought in the thirteenth or fourteenth century before Christ. For generations and centuries after the war its main incidents must have been sung by bards and minstrels in the courts of Northern India. The war thus became the centre of a cycle of legends, songs, and poems in ancient India, even as Charlemagne and Arthur became the centres of legends in mediæval Europe. And then, probably under the direction of some enlightened king, the vast mass of legends and poetry, accumulated during centuries, was cast in a narrative form and formed the Epic of the Great Bharata nation, and therefore called the *Maha-bharata*. The real facts of the war had been obliterated by age, legendary heroes had become the principal actors, and, as is invariably the case in India, the thread of a high moral purpose, of the triumph of virtue and the subjugation of vice, was woven into the fabric of the great Epic.

We should have been thankful if this Epic, as it was thus originally put together some centuries before the Christian era, had been preserved to us. But this was not to be. The Epic became so popular that it went on growing with the growth of centuries. Every generation of poets had something to add; every distant nation in Northern India was anxious to interpolate some account of its deeds in the old record of the international war; every preacher of a new creed desired to have in the old Epic some sanction for the new truths he inculcated. Passages from legal and moral codes were incorporated in the work which appealed to the nation much more effectively than dry codes; and rules about the different castes and about the different stages of the human life were included for the same purpose. All the floating mass of tales, traditions, legends, and myths, for which ancient India was famous, found a shelter under the expanding wings of this wonderful Epic ; and as Krishna-worship became the prevailing religion of India after the decay of Buddhism, the old Epic caught the complexion of the times, and Krishna-cult is its dominating religious idea in its present shape.   It is thus that the work went on growing for a thousand years after it was first compiled and put together in the form of an Epic ; until the crystal rill of the Epic itself was all but lost in an unending morass of religious and didactic episodes, legends, tales, and traditions.

When the mischief had been done, and the Epic had nearly assumed its present proportions, a few centuries after Christ according to the late Dr. Bühler, an attempt was made to prevent the further expansion of the work.   The contents of the Epic were described in some prefatory verses, and the number of couplets in each Book was stated.   The total number of couplets, according to this metrical preface, is about eighty-five thousand.   But the limit so fixed has been exceeded in still later centuries ; further additions and inter-polations have been made ; and the Epic as printed and published in Calcutta in this century contains over ninety thousand couplets, excluding the Supplement about the Race of Hari.

The modern reader will now understand the reason why this great Epic—the greatest work of imagination that Asia has pro-duced—has never yet been put before the European reader in a read-able form.   A poem of ninety thousand couplets, about seven times the size of the Iliad and the Odyssey put together, is more than what the average reader can stand ; and the heterogeneous nature of its contents does not add to the interest of the work.   If the religious works of Hooker and Jeremy Taylor, the philosophy of Hobbes and Locke, the commentaries of Blackstone and the ballads of Percy, together with the tractarian writings of Newman, Keble, and Pusey, were all thrown into blank verse and incorporated with the *Paradise Lost*, the reader would scarcely be much to blame if he failed to appreciate that delectable compound.   A complete translation of the *Maha-bharata* therefore into English verse is neither possible nor desirable, but portions of it have now and then been placed before English readers by distinguished writers.   Dean Milman's graceful rendering of the story of Nala and Damayanti is still read and appreciated by a select circle of readers ; and Sir Edwin Arnold's beautiful translation of the concluding books of the Epic is familiar to a larger circle of Englishmen.   A complete translation of the

Epic into English prose has also been published in India, and is useful to Sanscrit scholars for the purpose of reference.

But although the old Epic had thus been spoilt by unlimited expansion, yet nevertheless the leading incidents and characters of the real Epic are still discernible, uninjured by the mass of foreign substance in which they are embedded—even like those immortal marble figures which have been recovered from the ruins of an ancient world, and now beautify the museums of modern Europe. For years past I have thought that it was perhaps not impossible to exhume this buried Epic from the superincumbent mass of episodical matter, and to restore it to the modern world. For years past I have felt a longing to undertake this work, but the task was by no means an easy one. Leaving out all episodical matter, the leading narrative of the Epic forms about one-fourth of the work ; and a complete translation even of this leading story would be unreadable, both from its length and its prolixness. On the other hand, to condense the story into shorter limits would be, not to make a translation, but virtually to write a new poem ; and that was not what I desired to undertake, nor what I was competent to perform.

There seemed to me only one way out of this difficulty. The main incidents of the Epic are narrated in the original work in passages which are neither diffuse nor unduly prolix, and which are interspersed in the leading narrative of the Epic, at that narrative itself is interspersed in the midst of more lengthy episodes. The more carefully I examined the arrangement, the more clearly it appeared to me that these main incidents of the Epic would bear a full and unabridged translation into English verse ; and that these translations, linked together by short connecting notes, would virtually present the entire story of the Epic to the modern reader in a form and within limits which might be acceptable. It would be, no doubt, a condensed version of the original Epic, but the condensation would be effected, not by the translator telling a short story in his own language, but by linking together those passages of the original which describe the main and striking incidents, and thus telling the main story as told in the original work. The advantage of this arrangement is that, in the passages presented to the reader, it is the poet who speaks to him, not the translator. Though vast portions of the original are skipped over, those which are presented are the portions which narrate the main incidents of the Epic, and they describe those incidents as told by the poet himself.

This is the plan I have generally adopted in the present work.

Except in the three books which describe the actual war (Books viii., ix., and x.), the other nine books of this translation are complete translations of selected passages of the original work. I have not attempted to condense these passages nor to expand them; I have endeavoured to put them before the English reader as they have been told by the poet in Sanscrit. Occasionally, but rarely, a few redundant couplets have been left out, or a long list of proper names or obscure allusions has been shortened; and in one place only, at the beginning of the Fifth Book, I have added twelve couplets of my own to explain the circumstances under which the story of Savitri is told. Generally, therefore, the translation may be accepted as an unabridged, though necessarily a free translation of the passages describing the main incidents of the Epic.

From this method I have been compelled to depart, much against my wish, in the three books describing the actual war. No translation of an Epic relating to a great war can be acceptable which does not narrate the main events of the war. The war of the *Maha-bharata* was a series of eighteen battles, fought on eighteen consecutive days, and I felt it necessary to present the reader with an account of each day's work. In order to do so, I have been compelled to condense, and not merely to translate selected passages. For the transactions of the war, unlike the other incidents of the Epic, have been narrated in the original with almost inconceivable prolixity and endless repetition; and the process of condensation in these three books has therefore been severe and thorough. But, nevertheless, even in these books I have endeavoured to preserve the character and the spirit of the original. Not only are the incidents narrated in the same order as in the original, but they are told in the style of the poet as far as possible. Even the similes and metaphors and figures of speech are all or mostly adopted from the original;. the translator has not ventured either to adopt his own distinct style of narration, or to improve on the style of the original with his own decorations.

Such is the scheme I have adopted in presenting an Epic of ninety thousand Sanscrit couplets in about two thousand English couplets.

The excellent and deservedly popular prose translation of the Odyssey of Homer by Messrs. Butcher and Lang often led me to think that perhaps a prose translation of these selected passages from the *Maha-bharata* might be more acceptable to the modern reader. But a more serious consideration of the question dispelled that idea. Homer has an interest for the European reader which the *Maha-*

bharata cannot lay claim to ; as the father of European poetry he has a claim on the veneration of modern Europe which an Indian poet can never pretend to. To thousands of European readers Homer is familiar in the original, to hundreds of thousands he is known in various translations in various modern languages. What Homer actually wrote, a numerous class of students in Europe wish to know ; and a literal prose translation therefore is welcome, after the great Epic has been so often translated in verse. The case is very different with the *Maha-bharata*, practically unknown to European readers. And the translators of Homer themselves gracefully acknowledge, " We have tried to transfer, not all the truth about the poem, but the historical truth into English. In this process Homer must lose at least half his charm, his bright and equable speed, the musical current of that narrative, which, like the river of Egypt, flows from an undiscoverable source, and mirrors the temples and the palaces of unforgotten gods and kings. Without the music of verse, only a half truth about Homer can be told."

Another earnest worker of the present day, who is endeavouring to interpret to modern Englishmen the thoughts and sentiments and poetry of their Anglo-Saxon ancestors, has emphatically declared that " of all possible translations of poetry, a merely prose translation is the most inaccurate." " Prose," says Mr. Stopford Brooke, further on, " no more represents poetry than architecture does music. Translations of poetry are never much good, but at least they should always endeavour to have the musical movement of poetry, and to obey the laws of the verse they translate. "

This appears to me to be a very sound maxim. And one of my greatest difficulties in the task I have undertaken has been to try and preserve something of the " musical movement " of the sonorous Sanscrit poetry in the English translation. Much of the Sanscrit Epic is written in the well-known *Sloka* metre of sixteen syllables in each line, and I endeavoured to choose some English metre which is familiar to the English ear, and which would reproduce to some extent the rhythm, the majesty, and the long and measured sweep of the Sanscrit verse. It was necessary to adopt such a metre in order to transfer something of the truth about the *Maha-bharata* into English, for without such reproduction or imitation of the musical movement of the original very much less than a half truth is told. My kind friend Mr. Edmund Russell, impelled by that enthusiasm for Indian poetry and Indian art which is a part of him, rendered me valuable help and assistance in this matter, and I gratefully acknowledge the benefit I have derived from his advice and suggestions. After considerable trouble and anxiety, and after rendering several books in different English metres, I felt convinced that the one finally adopted was a nearer approach to the Sanscrit *Sloka* than any other familiar English metre known to me.

I have recited a verse in this English metre and a *Sloka* in presence of listeners who have a better ear for music than myself, and they have marked the close resemblance. I quote a few lines from the Sanscrit showing varieties of the *Sloka* metre, and comparing them with the scheme of the English metre selected.

Esha Kuntisutah sriman | esha madhyama Pandavah
Esha putro Mahendrasya | Kurunam esha rakshita
—*Maha-bharata*, i. 5357.

Yet I doubt not through the ages | one increasing purpose runs
And the thoughts of men are widened | with the process of the suns
—*Locksley Hall.*

Malancha samupadaya | kanchanim samalamkritam
Avatirna tato rangam | Draupadi Bharatarshabha
—*Maha-bharata*, i. 6974.

Visions of the days departed | shadowy phantoms filled my brain;
Those who live in history only | seemed to walk the earth again
—*Belfry of Bruges.*

Asuryam iva suryena | nirvatam iva vayuna
Bhasitam hladitanchaiva | Krishnenedam sado hi nah
—*Maha-bharata*, ii. 1334.

Quaint old town of toil and traffic | quaint old town of art and song,

Memories haunt thy pointed gables, | like the rooks that round thee
throng.
—*Nuremberg.*

Ha Pando ha maharaja | kvasi kim samupekshase

Putran vivasyatah sadhun | aribhir dyutanirjitan
—*Maha-bharata,* ii. 2610.

In her ear he whispers gaily, | If my heart by signs can tell,

Maiden I have watched thee daily, | And I think thou lov'st me well
—*Lord of Burleigh.*

It would be too much to assume that even with the help of this
similarity in metres, I have been able to transfer into my English
that sweep and majesty of verse which is the charm of Sanscrit, and
which often sustains and elevates the simplest narration and the
plainest ideas. Without the support of those sustaining wings, my
poor narration must often plod through the dust ; and I can only
ask for the indulgence of the reader, which every translator of
poetry from a foreign language can with reason ask, if the story as
told in the translation is sometimes but a plain, simple, and homely
narrative. For any artistic decoration I have neither the inclination nor the necessary qualification. The crisp and ornate style,
the quaint expression, the chiselled word, the new-coined phrase,
in which modern English poetry is rich, would scarcely suit the
translation of an old Epic whose predominating characteristic is
its simple and easy flow of narrative. Indeed, the *Maha-bharata*
would lose that unadorned simplicity which is its first and foremost
feature if the translator ventured to decorate it with the art of the
modern day, even if he had been qualified to do so.

For if there is one characteristic feature which distinguishes the
Maha-bharata (as well as the other Indian Epic, the *Ramayana*)
from all later Sanscrit literature, it is the grand simplicity of its
narrative, which contrasts with the artificial graces of later Sanscrit
poetry. The poetry of Kalidasa, for instance, is ornate and beautiful,

and almost scintillates with similes in every verse ; the poetry of the *Maha-bharata* is plain and unpolished, and scarcely stoops to a simile or a figure of speech unless the simile comes naturally to the poet. The great deeds of godlike kings sometimes suggest to the poet the mighty deeds of gods ; the rushing of warriors suggests the rushing of angry elephants in the echoing jungle ; the flight of whistling arrows suggests the flight of sea-birds ; the sound and movement of surging crowds suggest the heaving of billows ; the erect attitude of a warrior suggests a tall cliff ; the beauty of a maiden suggests the soft beauty of the blue lotus. When such comparisons come naturally to the poet, he accepts them and notes them down, but he never seems to go in quest of them, he is never anxious to beautify and decorate. He seems to trust entirely to his grand narrative, to his heroic characters, to his stirring incidents, to hold millions of listeners in perpetual thrall. The majestic and sonorous Sanscrit metre is at his command, and even this he uses carelessly, and with frequent slips, known as *arsha* to later grammarians. The poet certainly seeks for no art to decorate his tale, he trusts to the lofty chronicle of bygone heroes to enchain the listening mankind.

And what heroes ! In the delineation of character the *Maha-bharata* is far above anything which we find in later Sanscrit poetry. Indeed, with much that is fresh and sweet and lovely in later Sanscrit poetry, there is little or no portraiture of character. All heroes are cast much in the same heroic mould ; all love-sick heroines suffer in silence and burn with fever, all fools are shrewd and impudent by turns, all knaves are heartless and cruel and suffer in the end. There is not much to distinguish between one warrior and another, between one tender woman and her sister. In the *Maha-bharata* we find just the reverse ; each hero has a distinct individuality, a character of his own, clearly discernible from that of other heroes. No work of the imagination that could be named, always excepting the Iliad, is so rich and so true as the *Maha-bharata* in the portraiture of the human character,—not in torment and suffering as in Dante, not under overwhelming passions as in Shakespeare,—but human character in its calm dignity of strength and repose, like those immortal figures in marble which the ancients turned out, and which modern sculptors have vainly sought to reproduce. The old Kuru monarch Dhrita-rashtra, sightless and feeble, but majestic in his ancient grandeur ; the noble grandsire Bhishma, " death's subduer " and unconquerable in war ; the doughty Drona,

venerable priest and vengeful warrior ; and the proud and peerless
archer Karna—have each a distinct character of his own which cannot be mistaken for a moment. The good and royal Yudhishthir,
(I omit the final *a* in some long names which occur frequently),
the " tiger-waisted " Bhima, and the " helmet-wearing " Arjun
are the Agamemnon, the Ajax, and the Achilles of the Indian
Epic. The proud and unyielding Duryodhan, and the fierce and
fiery Duhsasan stand out foremost among the wrathful sons of the
feeble old Kuru monarch. And Krishna possesses a character
higher than that of Ulysses ; unmatched in human wisdom, ever
striving for righteousness and peace, he is thorough and unrelenting in war when war has begun. And the women of the Indian
Epic possess characters as marked as those of the men. The
stately and majestic queen Gandhari, the loving and doting mother
Pritha, the proud and scornful Draupadi nursing her wrath till
her wrongs are fearfully revenged, and the bright and brilliant and
sunny Subhadra,—these are distinct images pencilled by the hand
of a true master in the realm of creative imagination.

And if the characters of the *Maha-bharata* impress themselves
on the reader, the incidents of the Epic are no less striking. Every
scene on the shifting stage is a perfect and impressive picture.
The tournament of the princes in which Arjun and Karna—the
Achilles and Hector of the Indian Epic—first met and each marked
the other for his foe ; the gorgeous bridal of Draupadi ; the equally
gorgeous coronation of Yudhishthir and the death of the proud
and boisterous Sisupala ; the fatal game of dice and the scornful
wrath of Draupadi against her insulters ; the calm beauty of the
forest life of the Pandavs ; the cattle-lifting in Matsyaland in which
the gallant Arjun threw off his disguise and stood forth as warrior
and conqueror ; and the Homeric speeches of the warriors in the
council of war on the eve of the great contest,—each scene of this
venerable old Epic impresses itself on the mind of the hushed and
astonished reader. Then follows the war of eighteen days. The
first few days are more or less uneventful, and have been condensed
in this translation often into a few couplets ; but the interest of the
reader increases as he approaches the final battle and fall of the
grand old fighter Bhishma. Then follows the stirring story of
the death of Arjun's gallant boy, and Arjun's fierce revenge, and
the death of the priest and warrior, doughty Drona. Last comes
the crowning event of the Epic, the final contest between Arjun
and Karna, the heroes of the Epic, and the war ends in a midnight

slaughter and the death of Duryodhan. The rest of the story is told in this translation in two books describing the funerals of the deceased warriors, and Yudhishthir's horse-sacrifice.

"The poems of Homer," says Mr. Gladstone, "differ from all other known poetry in this, that they constitute in themselves an encyclopædia of life and knowledge ; at a time when knowledge, indeed, such as lies beyond the bounds of actual experience, was extremely limited, and when life was singularly fresh, vivid, and expansive." This remark applies with even greater force to the *Maha-bharata ;* it is an encyclopædia of the life and knowledge of Ancient India. And it discloses to us an ancient and forgotten world, a proud and noble civilisation which has passed away. Northern India was then parcelled among warlike races living side by side under their warlike kings, speaking the same language, performing the same religious rites and ceremonies, rejoicing in a common literature, rivalling each other in their schools of philosophy and learning as in the arts of peace and civilisation, and forming a confederation of Hindu nations unknown to and unknowing the outside world. What this confederation of nations has done for the cause of human knowledge and human civilisation is a matter of history. Their inquiries into the hidden truths of religion, embalmed in the ancient *Upanishads*, have never been excelled within the last three thousand years. Their inquiries into philosophy, preserved in the *Sankhya* and the *Vedanta* systems, were the first systems of true philosophy which the world produced. And their great works of imagination, the *Maha-bharata* and the *Ramayana*, will be placed without hesitation by the side of Homer by critics who survey the world's literatures from a lofty standpoint, and judge impartially of the wares turned out by the hand of man in all parts of the globe. It is scarcely necessary to add that the discoveries of the ancient Hindus in science, and specially in mathematics, are the heritage of the modern world ; and that the lofty religion of Buddha, proclaimed in India five centuries before Christ, is now the religion of a third of the human race.

For the rest, the people of modern India know how to appreciate their ancient heritage. It is not an exaggeration to state that the two hundred millions of Hindus of the present day cherish in their hearts the story of their ancient Epics. The Hindu scarcely lives, man or woman, high or low, educated or ignorant, whose earliest recollections do not cling round the story and the characters of the great Epics. The almost illiterate oil-manufacturer or confectioner of Bengal spells out some modern translation of the *Maha-bharata* to while away his leisure hour. The tall and stalwart peasantry of the North-West know of the five Pandav brothers, and of their friend the righteous Krishna. The people of Bombay and Madras cherish with equal ardour the story of the righteous war. And even the traditions and tales interspersed in the Epic, and which spoil the work as an Epic, have themselves a charm and an attraction ; and the morals inculcated in these tales sink into the hearts of a naturally religious people, and form the basis of their moral education. Mothers in India know no better theme for imparting wisdom and instruction to their daughters, and elderly men know no richer storehouse for narrating tales to children, than these stories preserved in the Epics. No work in Europe, not Homer in Greece or Virgil in Italy, not Shakespeare or Milton in English-speaking lands, is the *national* property of the nations to the same extent as the Epics of India are of the Hindus. No single work except the Bible has such influence in affording moral instruction in Christian lands as the *Maha-bharata* and the *Ramayana* in India. They have been the cherished heritage of the Hindus for three thousand years ; they are to the present day interwoven with the thoughts and beliefs and moral ideas of a nation numbering two hundred millions.

ROMESH DUTT.

GLOSSARY

ABHISHAVA, a religious rite.

ABHISHEKA, sacred ablution.

ACHARYA, preceptor.

AGNIHOTRA, a sacrifice to the fire performed with a daily offering of milk morning and evening.

AGRAYANA, an autumn harvest festival performed with offering of new grain.

AJYA, a form of sacrificial offering.

APRAMATTA, without pride or passion.

APSARA, celestial nymph.

ARGHYA, an offering due to an honoured guest.

ARYA, an honourable person, an Aryan.

ASOKA, name of a flower, orange and scarlet.

ASRAMA, hermitage.

ASURA, demon, enemies of gods.

ASWAKARNA, a flower.

ASWAMEDHA, a horse-sacrifice.

BAIDURYA, lapis-lazuli.

BHINDIPALA, a weapon of war.

BRAHMACHARIN, one who has taken vows and lives an austere life.

CHAITYA, a shrine or temple.

CHAKRAVAKA, a ruddy goose, the male and female being regarded as a pattern of conjugal love.

CHAMPAKA, a tree with yellow blossom ; also the flower of the tree.

CHANDAN, sandal-tree ; also the fragrant sandal paste.

CHOWRI (properly CHAMARI), the yak, the tail of which is used as a fan.

DAKSHINA, gifts made at sacrifices.

DASAPUTRA, son of a slave.

DEVA, gods.

DEVADARU (lit. heavenly tree), the Himalayan pine.

DEVA-KANYA, celestial maid.

DEVA-RISHI, celestial saint.

DHARMA-RAJA, monarch by reason of piety and virtue.

DIKSHA, initiation into a sacred rite.

DUNDUBHI, drum.

GANDHARVA, celestial musician.

GANDIVA, Arjun's bow.

GAURI, a goddess, wife of Siva.

GHRITA or GHEE, clarified butter.

GRAHA, the being of darkness who is supposed to seize the sun and the moon at eclipse ; a planet with malignant influence.

GURU, preceptor.

HANSA, swan or goose.

HOMA, a sacrificial rite or offering.

HOWDA, the seat on an elephant.

IDA, a form of sacrificial offering.

KANKA, a bird of prey.

KARMA, act which brings its fruit in life or in after life.

KARNIKARA, a tree ; also its flower.

KARTIKA, October–November.

KAUTUKA, wedding investiture with the nuptial chord.

KETAKA, a strong-scented plant.

KHADIRA, a tree, a kind of acacia.

KIMPURUSHA, a class of imaginary beings.

KINNARA, a fabulous being with the body of a man and the face of a horse, the counterpart of the Greek Centaur.

KINSUKA, a flower.

KOKIL, an Indian bird answering to the English cuckoo, and prized for its sweet note.

KUSA, grass strewn round the altar at sacrifice.

LODHRA, a tree.

MAGHA, a winter month.

MAHAMATRA, a royal officer.

MAHUA (properly MADHUKA), a tree, Bassia latifolia.

MAHUT or MAHAMATRA, elephant driver.

MANTRA, hymn, incantation.

MAYA, illusion.

MLECHCHA, outer barbarian. All who were not Hindus were designated by this name.

MRIDANGA, a kind of drum.

MUNI, saint, anchorite.

NAGA, snake ; a being of the lower or snake world ; also a tribe in Eastern India.

NISHADA, an aboriginal race.

NISHKA, a coin, often used as ornament.

NULLA, a rivulet or rill.

NYAGRODHA, the banyan or Indian fig-tree.

PALASA, a tree bearing large red blossoms with no scent.

PANKHA (from Sanscrit paksha, wing), a fan.

PATAHA, a kind of drum.

PISHACHA, ghost or goblin.

PITRI-MEDHA, sacrifice and offering due to departed ancestors.

PRAVARGYA, a religious rite.

PRIYANGU, a fragrant ointment.

PUNNAGA, a flower tree.

PURANA, ancient and sacred chronicles.

PURUSHA, the soul.

RAHU, the being of darkness who is supposed to seize the sun and the moon at eclipses.

RAJASUYA, an imperial sacrifice.

RAKSHA, a class of fabulous beings represented as demons and night-rangers, and wearing various shapes at will. The inhabitants of Ceylon, with whom the hero of the Epic fought, are represented as Rakshas.

RIK, hymn recited at sacrifice.

RISHI, saint or anchorite.

SABDA-BEDHI, an archer who shoots an invisible game by hearing the sound it makes.

SAKTI, javelin.

SALA, a tall forest tree.

SAMADHI, austere religious practice.

SAMAN, hymn chanted at sacrifice.

SAMI, a dark leafy tree.

SANKHA, conch-shell used as a sounding instrument in wars and in festivities.

SAPTA-PARNA, a plant with a seven-branched leaf.

SARASA, the Indian crane.

SARVAVARNIN, an Indian tree.

SASTRA, sacred scriptures.

SATAGHNI, a weapon of war, supposed to kill a hundred men at one discharge.

SAVANA, a religious rite.

SAVITRI, a hymn ; also the goddess of the hymn.

SIDDHA, holy celestial beings.

SLESHA, an Indian tree.

SRAVANA, July–August.

SRI, the goddess of beauty and wealth, wife of Vishnu.

SUPARNA, celestial bird.

SWARGA, heaven.

SWASTI, a word uttered to dispel evil.

SWAYAMVARA, a form of bridal, the bride selecting her husband from among suitors.

TALA, a species of palm-tree bearing a large round fruit ; also the fruit of the tree.

TAMALA, a graceful leafy tree.

TIRTHA, holy rites at the crossing of rivers.

TRIRATRA, a three nights' penance and fast.

USIRA, a kind of hard wood.

VANARA, monkey. The hill tribes of Southern India, who formed an alliance with the hero of the Epic, are represented as Vanaras.

VEDA, the most ancient and holiest scriptures of the Hindus.

VIJAYA, Karna's bow.

VILWA, a tree bearing an edible fruit.

VINA, the lyre.

YAJNA, sacrifice.

YATO DHARMA STATO JAYAH, where there is virtue there is victory.

YOJANA, a measure of distance equal to about nine English miles.

YUGA, the period of the world's existence.